PUBLIC EXPENDITURE, MANAGEMENT AND CONTROL

Public Expenditure, Management and Control

The Development of the Public Expenditure Survey Committee (PESC)

SIR RICHARD CLARKE

edited by Sir Alec Cairncross

First published 1978 by
THE MACMILLAN PRESS LTD
London and Basingstoke
Associated companies in Delhi
Dublin Hong Kong Johannesburg Lagos
Melbourne New York Singapore Tokyo

British Library Cataloguing in Publication Data

Clarke, *Sir* Richard, b. 1910
Public expenditure, management and control
  1. Great Britain. Treasury – History
  2. Great Britain – Appropriations and
expenditures
  I. Title II. Cairncross, *Sir* Alec
336.3'9'0941   HJ7766

ISBN 978-1-349-03740-7   ISBN 978-1-349-03738-4 (eBook)
DOI 10.1007/978-1-349-03738-4

Contents

Foreword by Sir Alec Cairncross   vii

Personal Introduction   xix

Acknowledgment   xxiii

1 The Background to Plowden   1

2 Long-Term Operations: 1955–59   7

3 The Plowden Report   25

4 The Initial Operations: 1960–62   41

5 The First PESC Report: 1960–61   50

6 PESC in Reflation: 1962–63   61

7 The Impact of NEDC   70

8 PESC in 1963–64   78

9 State of Play: Summer 1964   86

10 Stamp Memorial Lecture   102

11 PESC and the 1964–66 Labour Government   110

12 Public Sector Control at the Top   138

13 PESC: Past and Future   147

Appendix A Mr Gladstone's Budget Speech, 1860   165

Appendix B The Management of the Public Sector of the
   National Economy   168

Appendix C An extract from Treasury Evidence to the
(Robbins) Committee on Higher Education, 1962   191

Index   198

Foreword by Sir Alec Cairncross

For most of his working life Sir Richard Clarke (known to most of his friends as Otto) was a civil servant, but his career did not begin or end in the civil service. He was the son of a schoolmaster and schoolmistress, educated at Christ's Hospital and the University of Cambridge, where he graduated in mathematics in 1931 as a Wrangler. He stayed on for a fourth year, studying economics, before looking for employment and had the satisfaction of rounding off his studies by winning in 1932 the Frances Wood Memorial Prize awarded by the Royal Statistical Society. The essay on steel prices with which he won the prize was a striking early example of his talent for simple exposition of complex data.

By this time the slump was at its worst and it was only after applying for forty jobs (including one at the Bank of England) that he was taken on by the British Electrical and Allied Manufacturers Association. After a short spell with them he joined the staff of the *Financial News*, remaining there for the next six years up to the outbreak of war in 1939. During that time he devised what was later to become the *Financial Times* Index of Ordinary Share prices and wrote his first book, *The Socialisation of Iron and Steel*, published under the pseudonym 'Ingot' by Gollancz in 1936 and issued to all Left Book Club subscribers. At one time he wrote the Lex column; and he also developed an interest in quantitive economic history of which one illustration is a survey of the growth of the British railway system over the past hundred years, which he contributed to a special issue of the *Financial News*. After war broke out he published in January 1940 his second book, *The Economic Effort of War*, and a pamphlet for the Ministries of Information and Economic Warfare, *Britain's Blockade*, which he was amused to find still on sale (in Dutch) at Djakarta airport in 1950.

Otto was proud of his journalistic training, which not only made him extraordinarily fast and lucid in drafting documents but brought home to him the importance of coming quickly to the point. He was apt later to deride his colleagues for their proneness to 'testify', i.e., deliver themselves of views that were not brought to bear on the issue to be decided, and he always gave thought to the purpose to be served by whatever he wrote. Conscious of his gift for developing arguments with great force and persuasiveness, he liked to undertake the drafting of major documents himself and no one else could have done so with such fluency and skill.

His career as a civil servant began in the Ministry of Information from which he moved successively to the Ministries of Economic Warfare, Supply and Production, spending one year of great importance for his own education in the Combined Production and Resources Board in Washington. Vivid memories from this period were of his visits to Ottawa at the request of the Treasury in July 1944 and again in October 1944 to assist Keynes and others in Canadian war finance negotiations. It was in the autumn of 1944 that the Treasury asked the Ministry of Production for his transfer to them to be Assistant Secretary in charge of a Division called 'Export-Import'. For a few months he served both Departments and in March 1945 joined the Treasury *de facto*.

At the end of the war he was faced with the major decision of his career: whether to stay in the civil service. He decided to remain and continued to serve in the Overseas Finance Division of the Treasury, being promoted to an Undersecretaryship in 1947. He held a key post since he was the chairman of the Programmes Committee which wrestled throughout the early post-war period with the problem of balancing limited earnings of foreign exchange against almost unlimited requirements for imports. Within a short time he was one of the most familiar, yet commanding, personalities in Whitehall.

It was during this period that he wrote in 1947 the first *Economic Survey*, an exposition of indicative planning before the phrase had been invented. He also took a leading part in drafting the later, more ambitious, 'plan' for 1948 - 52 that was submitted to OEEC as evidence of the way in which Marshall Aid would support economic recovery in the United Kingdom.

Although I saw something of him during the early post-war years, I was not able to take the measures of his abilities until one weekend in January 1950 when he arrived in Paris from London with a draft in his pocket of the key opening chapter of the Second Report of the OEEC. It had been prepared at top speed, almost overnight, while I had made negligible progress over a much longer period with a parallel draft of my own, and it was admirably adapted to its purpose. It was, of course, accepted with enthusiasm and published without amendment.

This was only one of the many documents he drafted in the days of the Marshall Plan when he played a major role as the 'rear link' in Whitehall in the activities connected with the setting up of the OEEC, the economic and financial aspects of NATO and the later negotiations for a European Free Trade Area. In 1952 he was one of the three main protagonists – *Rowan, Bolton* and *Otto* Clarke – who gave the name of Robot to a project for making the pound convertible at a floating rate of exchange while blocking simultaneously a large part of the sterling holdings of countries outside the dollar area. It was his intention to set down his reflections on these events and the part that he had played in them in the book on external economic policy with which he was occupied in the months before his death.

Otto's long association with the public expenditure side of the Treasury began in 1953 when he became head of the Social Services Division – a rather surprising break with his previous interests and duties (although he had, it is true, contributed to a volume on *Social Security Housekeeping*, edited by Professor W. A. Robson and published a paper on 'The Beveridge Report and After' in 1943). Two years later he was promoted to be what would now be called Deputy Secretary in charge of the Home and Overseas Planning Staff. At the beginning of 1960 he became responsible for public expenditure under Sir Thomas Padmore, whom he succeeded as Second Secretary in November 1962 after a reorganisation of the Treasury of which he was one of the main architects. These moves and his subsequent departure to the Ministry of Aviation where he became Permanent Secretary in March 1966 are described briefly in his 'Personal Introduction'.

His last civil service appointment was as successor to Sir Maurice Dean at the head of the new Ministry of Technology. This gave fresh scope to his administrative abilities. It was no mean task to give shape to a rapidly developing super-Ministry and use it to bring together the resources of the State in an effort to resolve the complex problems of major British industries. But Otto revelled in it. Few other assignments so successfully united his gifts or appealed to so many of his interests.

When he retired from the civil service he was offered many business appointments and as Lord Kearton has put it:

> He made a catholic choice: embracing engineering, textiles, leisure, science, culture and entertainment, and merchant banking. . . . As a member of a board in private industry, Otto was superb. Always well briefed and well read, his questions were penetrating and illuminating. His comments were invariably pithy, and could be devastating. His independence was absolute. His counsel was wise and far-seeing.

In addition to his business interests he involved himself in many public duties. For example, he was a member of the Council of the Manchester Business School and of the Council of Industry for Management Education, Chairman of the International Panel of the British Standards Institution and a Vice President of the Royal Institution.

During those years he found time to write extensively on the machinery of government and other matters. He published a series of lectures at the Civil Service College on *New Trends in Government* (HMSO, 1971), a lengthy analysis of the prospects for incomes policy, *Incomes Policy in Phase IV* (Manchester Business School, June 1973), an account of the problems of creating the new Ministry of Technology, *Mintech in Retrospect* (*Omega*, Vol. 1, No. 1 and No. 2, 1973), and a development of his views on tax policy, 'The Long-term Planning of Taxation' (in *Taxation Policy*, ed. B. Crick and W. A. Robson, Pelican edition 1973).[1]

In a tribute at the memorial service Lord Douglas Allen, then Head of the Civil Service, described Otto as:

a big man, physically, intellectually and spiritually. He was inevitably a
controversial character. He lived with and on argument. Controversial
too, because he was bold, imaginative and ruthless. Although personally
warm-hearted and generous in his approach to people, he was ruthless in
the pursuit of effective solutions, ruthless in the demolition of soft advice,
soft decisions, soft colleagues and soft Ministers.

He had a sharp and subtle intellect. But he was a simplifier, not a
complicator. He used his restless intellectual and analytical strengths to
isolate the heart of an issue; and then harnessed his energy, personality
and power to reduce and solve it.

Others who knew him in the Treasury recall that they found him a little
less 'ruthless', though no less formidable, after his marriage in 1950 to
Brenda Skinner. His happy family life contributed greatly to the humour,
warmth and understanding that qualified a somewhat combative manner.

My own contacts with him were always happy. He showed a touching
anxiety to profit from any advice I could give him. But he was not an easy
man to argue with and he put so much passion into everything he did that
it was tempting to give up and succumb to his assertiveness. If crossed, he
would talk in a fast excited stutter, ending with a pursing of the lips and a
disapproving sideways glare through his spectacles.

It is easier, however, to remember his chuckles than his frowns. His
temperament was resilient, his ideas always well-considered and his
natural bent constructive. He had a fertile and original mind which he
devoted to getting things done and still more towards devising a framework
which would ensure that things would get done in a certain way. When his
ideas were adopted he was still on the look-out for weaknesses in them that
he could remedy; his approach to administration was essentially
experimental.

It would be impossible in this short foreword to do full justice to the man
and his career. Let it suffice that he was one of the most admired and
influential figures in Whitehall of his generation and that one who served
under him, Peter Jay, has saluted him publicly as 'the greatest of all the
civil servants'.

Six months before his death in June 1975 he completed the present volume
and I have edited it for publication at the request of Lady Clarke. It was
drafted with his customary speed when he was already aware that he had
not long to live, and in the time remaining to him he pushed on with
another manuscript on the handling of balance of payments policy in the
years after 1945.

On public expenditure, as on the balance of payments, he could write
with first-hand experience. For thirteen out of his twenty-one years in the
Treasury he was responsible, in one official capacity or another, for the
control of public expenditure. He was the recognisable driving force
behind the creation of PESC (the Public Expenditure Survey Committee),

and the system of control that went with PESC. No doubt the recommendations that led to PESC were those of the Plowden Report of 1961. But as one of Otto's successors at the Treasury, Sir Samuel Goldman, has told us:

It is an open secret that the principal ideas and analysis which made the Plowden Report so seminal a document came from the mind of Sir Richard Clarke, then Third Secretary in charge of public expenditure at the Treasury. It was his imagination and insight that produced the first comprehensive picture of the public sector and laid down the main lines on which it should be measured and analysed. (Lecture on 26 March 1973 at the Civil Service College).

It is therefore fitting that he should have this memorial to his labours, constructed by himself from the recollections and reflections that he sought to perpetuate. It is not altogether in the form he would have wished. He had no opportunity of revising the manuscript before his death or of bringing it up to date in the light of all the controversies over public expenditure since it was completed. He had also hoped to be able to include excerpts from a number of official papers, including the version of the Plowden Report actually submitted to the Chancellor, the first PESC Report of 1960 - 61, a memorandum of his own written in July 1964 on the basic problems of the next five years, and a summary, item by item, of the sequence of minutes that he wrote over a period of twelve months as Second Secretary in charge of public expenditure in the Treasury. It has been necessary to omit all of these in order to comply with the Official Secrets Act. A number of other changes have been made in the text for the same reason.

None of these omissions or alterations, however, interrupts or distorts the flow of the argument. The book stands as an authoritative record of the development of PESC by one uniquely qualified to write it as a skilled journalist, an experienced administrator, and the architect and inventor of the new system.

The history of PESC is traced in detail from its origins in the late 1950s through its evolution in the 1960s down to the author's departure from the Treasury in 1966. Later events are referred to only in passing; and although in the final chapter the whole period after 1961 is passed in review and the lessons of experience are summed up in characteristic style, the book should be read as an exposition of the system of expenditure control as it took shape in the 1960s, not as a commentary on the state of the art in the more inflationary world of the seventies.

Not that Otto failed to see how the system was threatened by inflation. He suggested (para. 433) that the most critical problem for PESC was likely to be that of survival in inflationary conditions. And so it has proved. Cash limits - an adjustment to those conditions not easily reconciled with PESC - were just beyond the horizon when he died. But he was already foreshadowing an alternative adjustment, the use of manpower limits, that was more consistent with the principles underlying PESC (para. 434 et seq.). Unfortunately, ceilings on employment are not a very attractive alternative if inflation is accompanied by a high level of unemployment: any more than cash limits are likely to hold if inflation goes beyond the rate implicit in them.

There are two places in the book where Otto was conscious of some inconsistency. The first relates to the need to strengthen the hand of the Chancellor by establishing collective Ministerial responsibility for public expenditure. Of the conclusions reached by the Plowden Committee this was the one to which they attached most importance. It is a conclusion fully endorsed by Otto, who dwells at some length on the strength of the forces making for a progressive expansion in public expenditure, the absence of any significant body of opinion opposing this and the danger of leaving it to the Chancellor alone to withstand the pressure in 'a process of piecemeal decisions with no central review by Ministers collectively' (para. 67). At one point he expresses pessimism about the effectiveness of a Ministerial Committee, or any other change in the machinery of government, as a remedy for the situation, and looks instead to a firm and public alliance between the Chancellor and the Prime Minister (para. 401). Earlier, he is more hopeful of building up Ministerial backing for the Chancellor without, however, withdrawing his insistence on the need for Prime Ministers to make public expenditure one of their major pre-occupations (para. 76). He recommends a review of the big expenditure issues by a standing committee of senior Ministers before submission to the Cabinet. But it was never his view, nor was it that of the Plowden Committee, that such a committee should be made up of non-spending Ministers as has been suggested by Heclo and Wildavsky.[2]

The Chancellor would seem to be in a somewhat stronger position now than in the period when PESC was coming into being. There are at least some striking differences in the climate of opinion about public expenditure and a greater measure of public and intellectual approval for containing it and keeping it under firm control. Indeed, there might even be a danger of excessive caution in public spending and exaggeration of the demands that it makes on the economy. It remains true, however, that the Chancellor must depend heavily on the consistent interest and support of the Prime Minister.

What scope there is for a Ministerial Committee on public expenditure is less clear and has been subject in the past to the accident of personalities and the pressure of events. There have been attempts to engage the interest of Ministers in PAR as well as PESC and these are likely to continue. But non-spending Ministers rarely show any sustained appetite for the examination in depth of departmental programmes while spending Ministers prefer to go straight to the Cabinet if the usual bilateral deal with the Chancellor on major items cannot be concluded. In the last resort the Cabinet has to find more time for issues that lie at the root of its economic strategy; and if it does not do so of design repeated crises force it to do so in the end.

If one looks back on the development of PESC in the 1960s what stands out is the antithesis between the promise of stability in public expenditure plans as they moved forward along a carefully surveyed route and the wobbles and excesses that marked the route actually taken. The aspirations of officials were overborne by the expansionist mood of Ministers, which allowed public expenditure to increase in real terms by over 9 per cent in 1967 – 68. It is not at all obvious that this would have been avoided by any combination of central reviews and Ministerial Committees. What mattered was the absence of Ministerial will to contain public expenditure. This became very apparent when Roy Jenkins came on the scene after devaluation and the celebrated 30-hour Cabinets of January 1968 cut the planned rate of growth so drastically that in 1969 – 70 the actual increase fell to 1 per cent. That indeed was the heyday of PESC, although it was at the opposite pole to Otto's dream of steady, well-regulated expansion. It demonstrated conclusively how powerfully the PESC system could be used to control expenditure in the hands of a determined Chancellor who could count on having his way in Cabinet.

The second example of hesitation in pronouncing on the working of PESC arrangements arises over the time-horizon appropriate to a 'forward look'. At para. 129 Otto plumps for a universal four-year programme in place of one covering five years with individual 'forward looks' for programmes with longer time-scales. But at para. 411, while still insisting that a universal five-year period has been proved wrong, he proposes to substitute a three-year PESC operation combined with individual programmes stretching over seven or eight years for blocks of expenditure needing longer periods.

He rests this proposal partly on the tendency in the 1960s to move to the third year as the 'crucial one' – a tendency interrupted by the post-devaluation operation in January 1968 which set down programmes for the first two years only. The first annual White Paper issued in 1969 gave programmes for each of the first three years and 'provisional allocations' for the next two. Thereafter all annual White Papers have given programmes for each of the five years but have emphasised that the further one looks ahead the more uncertain the figures must be.

The argument for the proposal turns on something rather more fundamental than the difference between five years and four or even three. The issue is essentially one of stability in the face of uncertainty. The Plowden Committee called for 'the greatest practicable stability of decisions on public expenditure when taken' and Otto was himself no admirer of stop-go. But when the economy fluctuates cyclically one has to face the consequences of these fluctuations. It is necessary on the one hand to look beyond the immediate cyclical situation to a trend position in which the economy can be expected to be back in balance; and this in itself points to a period substantially longer than that covered by short-term forecasts–indeed the period just beyond that horizon is often the most difficult to assess. It is also necessary to review and revise spending commitments in the light of fluctuations in the resources immediately available and in prospective future resources. To make these commitments immune from revision and leave public spending untouched would be to concentrate cuts automatically on the private sector where there may be an equally valid case for planning in long-run terms.

Again, what if the fluctuations are such as to involve a continuing loss of potential output or to throw doubt on the underlying trend in GNP and make it impossible to say with confidence when and at what level a dip in economic activity will end? For example, a rise in commodity prices which reduces the real income of the country by 5 per cent through a change in the terms of trade inflicts an immediate loss, to which some adjustment must be made, and a longer-term loss the magnitude of which cannot readily be assessed. There are no good grounds for exempting public expenditure from the consequences, either in the short term or in the long, of so drastic a change in available resources. This is true both of short-term spending commitments and of long-term spending commitments; all cuts have to be judged in terms of alternatives, ranked according to their relative undesirability. Hence the time-period of any projection of total spending commitments does not imply immunity from revision of commitments within that period. On the one hand it should be short enough to allow the balance between resources and commitments to be foreseen with some hope of success; on the other hand it should be long enough to make it possible to visualise the terminal year as normal in the sense that the economy as a whole can be assumed to be in balance at an acceptable pressure of demand.

If the path over the years ahead is plotted in detail, how far can it stretch before the figures for commitments are lost in a haze of uncertainty? No doubt there are some commitments that must be entered into totally and without reservation. But there are plenty of others that are bound to be blurred, that are redefined or amended as time goes on and that are capable of curtailment in emergency. As Heclo and Wildavsky point out, PESC may be 'a cost projection of existing policies. [But] it turns out that there is often disagreement about what each element – cost, projection and existing policy – actually means' (pp. 216–17).[3] The ambiguities of the projection inevitably multiply the further ahead one looks and there is no ideal time-period that will minimise these ambiguities. All one can say is that the period should be shorter the greater the uncertainties in assessing commitments and resources.

These uncertainties have obviously increased over the past twenty years, and it is therefore not surprising that in retrospect one should have doubts about a five-year rolling programme. In the early 1960s the errors of forecasting over a period of five years were limited because neither the rate of growth in real income nor the rate of increase in prices departed greatly from the experience of the previous five years. The growth in GNP between 1961 and 1966, for example, was 15.4 per cent in real terms and 36.0 per cent in money terms compared with 15.1 per cent and 32.4 per cent respectively in the previous five years. But in the ensuing five years these percentages became 12.5 per cent and 48.2 per cent while between 1971 and 1976 they were 7.3 per cent and 119.1 per cent.

This does not mean that the decade which is the subject of this book was one of smooth, predictable change in contrast to the wild, unforeseeable fluctuations of the succeeding decade. It was in the years 1956 – 66 that the great controversies over stop-go and national planning were at their height. Neither GNP nor public expenditure maintained an even pace and it was government policy for most of the decade to increase the pace of growth without much agreement about how this was to be done. The problem of fitting the control of public expenditure into the control of a fluctuating economy was more manageable than it has become, but still troublesome; and it was out of this very problem that the Plowden Committee and the apparatus of PESC came into being. The question remains how far it makes sense to talk of planning public expenditure for several years ahead when GNP undergoes violent and unpredictable fluctuations.

There are one or two other matters touched on in the book on which a brief comment may be useful. First of all, there is Otto's espousal of the case for a long-term taxation plan to set alongside the long-term plan for public expenditure. This would involve separating the short-term demand management aspect of taxation from its social and economic aspects by designating one or more taxes (VAT, or income tax) as short-term regulators and leaving the rest of the tax structure to be determined by long-run considerations. The advantages that he sees in this are that it would free the budget procedure from its excessive concentration on the short period and make it possible to discuss revenue and expenditure simultaneously, with debate focusing on long-term policy in the public sector, which is 'the most important economic responsibility and field of action of the government on the economic front'.

In pressing this case, Otto is dismissing the alternative procedure of weighing public expenditure against other claims on real resources and by setting targets for all of them except private consumption, narrowing down the choice to one between higher public expenditure and higher private consumption X years from now. This is the choice that emerges naturally from PESC exercises and it is the way in which the issue is presented first to Ministers and then in the annual White Papers. A forecast is made of the increase to be expected in GNP and of the residual rate of increase in private consumption if all targets are met and public expenditure follows the path suggested.

Otto argues that few people are capable of visualising the difference in public welfare between an increase of 2 per cent per annum and one of 2½ per cent per annum or of setting this difference against the benefits to be expected from an addition to public expenditure in four years' time of the equivalent of ½ per cent of private consumption or about £1000 m. He would prefer to weigh one set of government decisions (about expenditure) against another (about taxation) and, in terms of political responsibility, measure like against like.

But of course changes in private consumption *imply* certain tax levels. Underlying the choice as now presented are assumptions that remain unsettled as to how consumption will be kept within the limits indicated. It is not necessary to work out the precise rates of tax implied but if the calculation were made it would have to be based on assumptions (e.g. about the rate of inflation and its effects on tax revenue) that would have to be revised – perhaps drastically – before the time came to apply the tax rates foreseen. In other words if one sets out to do the calculation in real terms of the balance between expenditure and resources it is only possible to translate the calculation into cash terms, with taxes on one side and spending on the other, at the cost of introducing fresh uncertainties and holding out expectations about the rates of tax implied that may prove to be illusory.

It is also possible that Otto is too pessimistic about the persuasiveness of an argument couched in terms of what is likely to be left for private consumption. It appears to have been used by Chancellors in Cabinet with some success and to have shifted the discussion towards those longer-term considerations that, by common consent, are too often subordinated to short-term expediency. Ministers have been brought to see with increasing clarity that to use resources for the public sector is usually to forgo their use for other purposes of great importance economically and politically.

Suppose, however, that the argument *were* carried on in cash terms rather than in terms of real resources. Those who hold monetarist views might well regard this as an advantage since it would help to focus attention on the budget surplus or deficit, and hence on its monetary consequences. Those who hold Keynesian views of the budget on the other hand would regard it as retrograde to treat every £1 of expenditure as exercising exactly the same impact on demand as every other £1. There is a fundamental difference for example between welfare payments and other 'transfers' which put purchasing power in other hands without altering the load on the economy, and current government expenditure on goods and services which may add (except in conditions of full employment) to the total load. In assessing the impact on demand of changes in taxation and expenditure, an allowance has to be made for the different economic impact of different categories of revenue and expenditure. This point is made by Otto (para. 117) but the 'sophistication' of the calculations is intended to overcome a legitimate criticism of the use of crude aggregates for decision-taking and does not reflect, as he suggests, on the importance attached by economists to demand management as such. On the contrary, the calculations are intended to allow economically literate Ministers to examine and debate the growth of public expenditure in *demand terms*; and there have been times when the Chancellor has announced plans for public expenditure by expressing the maximum annual rate of increase intended in just those terms.

The fundamental issue to which the reader returns in the final chapter of the book is what difference PESC made to the control of expenditure.[4] On this Otto must be left to speak for himself. It is not in question that PESC made an immense difference if only because it furnished the Treasury with a map of total public spending without which navigation would have been far more difficult. It is rather less clear what PESC contributed to the relationship between the Treasury and spending departments, to the grasp within the Treasury of the policy options open to departments, and to the making of wise choices between these options. It is also not clear how expenditure was monitored nor whether the data available were appropriate to control over the *rate* of expenditure through the year as distinct from the total of expenditure during the year. The emphasis throughout is on the costing and approval of spending programmes and this reflects the weight of official effort. But what about the effectiveness of control? As we move from para. 185 (control by setting rates of expansion) to para. 213 (escalation of costings of existing policies) then to para. 218 (control by block allocations) and finally to para 336 (escalation still continuing) we are given a familiar picture of definition of policy followed by escalation of the estimated cost of the policy agreed. It is a picture that anticipates later complaints that public expenditure is out of control. But the picture is not filled in and the few references to the need to improve monitoring and control in the final chapter seem to pass too lightly over an issue that has come increasingly to the fore.

These brief comments, which owe much to suggestions from Sir Peter Baldwin, are intended to bring out some themes of the book which remain the subject of current controversy. It is important that the considered views of Sir Richard Clarke, with his long and creative experience of expenditure control, should now be available in this extensive commentary on that experience.

NOTES

1. Two articles that appeared originally in the *Political Quarterly*, 'The Number and Size of Government Departments' and 'Parliament and Public Expenditure' were included in *British Government in an Era of Reform*, ed. W. J. Stankiewicz (Collier-Macmillan, 1976). He also wrote a chapter on 'The Machinery of Government' in *The Modernisation of British Government*, ed. W. Thornhill (Pitman, 1975). Other papers written after his retirement from

the civil service include a report to the EEC Commission in July 1974 on
'Public Purchasing in the Common Market' and a paper given to an EEC
Conference in Venice in April 1972 on 'Aims and Means of a European Policy
for Technological Development'.

2. H. Heclo and A. Wildavsky, *The Private Government of Public Money* (Macmillan,
   1974).

3. Op. cit.

4. [On this point Otto expressed himself more pungently in a letter to Aaron
   Wildavsky than in the text that follows. 'The essential contribution of P.E.S.C.
   remains this', he wrote. 'Cabinets take their decisions on public expenditure in
   much the same way as they take their decisions on anything else – push and pull,
   threats and cajolery, bluff and counter-bluff, the day-to-day battle of the
   Cabinet room. P.E.S.C. can't change this at all, for this is the nature of political
   life.

   'But with P.E.S.C. they are now talking and bargaining about the right
   questions, and not about questions which are irrelevant – making real choices
   and not artificial ones. I think this is the real gain, and in my opinion, the
   important one.'

   In illustration of 'artificial choices' he refers earlier in the letter to the episode
   in 1955 (para. 14 below) when the Treasury forced the Ministry of Housing to
   get new legislation so as to replace capital grants to local authorities for water
   and sewage works (above the line) by loans to local authorities (below the line)
   with a grant (above the line) to pay the interest. He comments that had a similar
   item worth £50m been discovered in the economy crisis of January 1958 there
   might have been no Ministerial resignations! Ed.]

Personal Introduction

The Treasury was described by Lord Bridges in a famous lecture at Harvard[1] as 'the most political of all the departments'; and public expenditure is certainly the most political of all the Treasury's work; for the hopes and fears of Governments, and the pressures under which they have to live, are inextricably bound up with their spending programmes – social and environmental services, assistance to industry and agriculture, defence and economic aid – and with the counterparts of these in taxes, rates, insurance contributions. Moreover, so great has the scale of public sector expenditure become that it can be said that half the gross national product is determined in the last analysis by decisions by government. So the way in which Governments take these decisions are of first-class importance both to them and to the political process, and to the lives of the whole community.

It must be accepted that there is no 'scientific' way to handle public sector expenditure and receipts. It is a mixture of politics (sometimes of the crudest kind and sometimes of the most far-sighted), economics, and public administration. This book is mainly about the last of these, to which I devoted many years in the Treasury; but I hope the readers will see the rest of the mixture there too; for nobody of practical experience in public administration can ever claim more than that good administrative systems make it easier for good Governments to make good decisions, and more difficult for bad Governments to make bad decisions; and that on some occasions, such as the systems designed and operated by Lord Hankey in the First World War, these margins can mean all the difference between success and failure.

This book is centred on the system of looking ahead in the management and control of public sector expenditure known as PESC (named from the Public Expenditure Survey Committee) introduced following the report of the Plowden Committee in 1961. This has already generated a tremendous literature of Government publications, and some writings by academics and retired civil servants. Taking together the period of experiments in 'looking ahead' in the 1950s before the Plowden Committee was formed, the work of the Committee itself, and the first few years of the Treasury's action to implement the Report, until I left the Treasury in March 1966, I bear a large share of the responsibility; and I thought there might be advantage, many years afterwards, to write as clear and objective a narrative as I can of this time. I am reasonably confident that I am expressing the facts and opinions of the time without the benefits of hindsight; and on some occasions this will be painfully obvious to the reader. I have consulted neither other participants nor the official files; for this is my own narrative and not an attempt to write an official history, which would in any case need to be done by someone looking from the outside.

The narrative, I hope, maintains a proper professional attitude. It avoids disclosure of specific advice given to Treasury Ministers, and at no point indicates whether such advice was accepted or rejected; nor does it mention controversies between Ministers except where these have become common knowledge. It has no intention of entering into polemics with former or subsequent Treasury colleagues. I have mentioned the names of some who in my opinion made a major individual contribution; but this does not imply a failure to recognise the immense collective efforts of long nights and laborious days by scores of colleagues from the top echelons to secretaries and clerical officers.

It may help the reader, and avoid my having to use 'I' excessively, if this introduction sets out how I became engaged in public expenditure control; and how my successive posts contributed to it.

My first acquaintance with this subject was in October 1953 (aged 43 and an Under-Secretary in the Treasury since 1947) when I was moved from Overseas Finance (where I had been since coming to the Treasury in 1945) to be head of the division (SS) responsible for the control of social services expenditure. This was a heavy and varied division,[2] at the heart of the Treasury's 'Supply' work. This was a remarkable education both of Whitehall, and in finding the nerve-centres in this immense size and range of spending by central and local government. Coming from the fast-moving world of the balance of payments, I found myself in an arena in which today's decisions were determining the development and cost of the services several years ahead. So when in July 1955, the Chancellor of the Exchequer, Mr R. A. Butler, got his colleagues' agreement to a Five-Year Survey of the Social Services, we were ready, and it appeared in November. The sequel shows the hazards of public administration, for both Mr Butler and I were immediately transferred to different fields, leaving this unfinished business.

I was then promoted to Deputy Secretary,[3] as Head of what was misleadingly called the Home and Overseas Planning Staff (HOPS). This was the successor of the original Central Economic Planning Staff, under Lord Plowden; but whereas the latter's task was to manage a controlled economy, the controls no longer existed in October 1955. However, Sir Edward Bridges was determined to retain a unit outside the normal Treasury machinery, and to keep it powerfully staffed. The two Under-Secretaries (later Sir Burke Trend[4] and Sir Frank Figgures) and I worked out a programme and decided on the 'home' side (the 'overseas' was for co-ordinating overseas negotiations) to concentrate on the long-term structure and interests of industry and the public sector.

This led us through the next four years into four fields which turned out (together above all with the work that was being done in the Treasury and the Ministry of Defence to create a long-term defence budget) to provide the keys to the concepts of 'looking ahead':

(a) creation and operation of long-term public sector investment control (in the days of building control, this had been controlled on essentially similar lines to private investment: the introduction of long-term resources control needed a different approach);

(b) regular annual five-year 'Long-Term Economic Assessment' for the whole economy (mainly at that time to get guidelines on the scale of permissible public investment);

(c) nationalised industries (the development of the ideas of economic and financial objectives, ultimately agreed by Ministers and included in the 1961 White Paper: we regarded this as one of the biggest contributions to industry's long-term strength if we could get this right);

(d) studies on the long-term demand for steel, energy, scientific manpower, etc.

In the process of doing this, a lot of reorganisation took place, in the course of which 'HOPS' disappeared as an anachronism.

A reshuffle in January 1960 made me Deputy Secretary in charge of Expenditure, and I became an assessor with the Plowden Committee; and from then on I was totally engaged in expenditure activities. In the reorganised Treasury which came into operation in November 1962, I was promoted to Second Permanent Secretary in charge of what we called the Public Sector Group. So it went on until my departure from the Treasury to become Permanent Secretary of the Ministries first of Aviation and then of Technology.

Maybe this will give enough personal introduction, a little egotistical though this may appear, for readers to follow the text without my having to insert 'I's and 'my's all the time. It may also perhaps show how long it takes, both in the accumulation of knowledge and in experiment with new ideas, in order to get to a position in which major reform in public administration can be conceived and carried into effect. At the crunch in February 1960, when the question was squarely put to the Treasury 'Can this be done?', it could not have responsibly been answered 'Yes' without the five years' background: when I left the Treasury in March 1966, Governments of both parties had issued White Papers accepting it, but no real PESC system was in being. It took some years more before the PESC system could be said to be established. This illustrates the great time-scales in public affairs, because of the number of people to convince, the continuous and inevitable promotions and transfers of officials, above all the peripatetic nature of Governments; and the time-scale shows how project after project runs into the sand.

Lastly, I must thank the Civil Service Department for great help with this book, and above all HM Treasury, whose Permanent Secretaries, from Sir Edward Bridges to Sir William Armstrong, gave me the opportunity and the good fortune to devote the twelve years covered in this book to what I have always believed, whether events went well or ill, to be constructive work, to the full extent of my capability.

December 1974   R.W.B.C.

NOTES

1. Pollak lecture at the Graduate School of Public Administration, Harvard University, December 1961.
2. Just four Principals with a few junior helpers: Ministry of Housing and Local Government services and grants, and new towns, water, sewerage, rates, Ministry of Labour, etc.; National Health Service, Medical Research Council, etc.; Ministry of Pensions and National Insurance, National Assistance Board, etc.; Ministry of Education, University Grants Committee, Museums and Galleries; Fine Arts. Three of these four had the corresponding Scottish Departments too – I always had a notice on my desk, REMEMBER SCOTLAND.
3. I use throughout the current terminology; we then called this man a Third Secretary, whilst what is now called a Second Permanent Secretary was called a Second Secretary (the same Permanent Secretary rank and also the full pay!).
4. To be followed soon by Sir Matthew Stevenson.

Acknowledgment

Sir Alec Cairncross and Macmillan are grateful to the Controller of Her Majesty's Stationery Office for permission to reproduce the material in Appendix C, an excerpt from evidence given by HM Treasury to the (Robbins) Committee on Higher Education, May 1962, Cmnd. 2154-XI (1964), which is Crown Copyright.

1 The Background to Plowden

1. *The Estimates Committee.* The most convenient starting-point is the work of the Select Committee on Estimates on Treasury Control of Expenditure [H.C. 254, 1957–58]. This report, prepared under the chairmanship of Sir Godfrey Nicholson, was published in July 1958: it was based on four months' questioning of Treasury and other witnesses and substantial written memoranda: and its general tenor was critical but not unfavourable to the Treasury 'system'. The sting was in the tail:

> The aim of Your Committee was to find out whether the present 'system' of Treasury control is as effective as modern conditions demand. Your Committee cannot give a definite answer. The system appears to work reasonably well. But it would be idle to pretend that Your Committee is left entirely without disquiet . . .
>
> Because of all these doubts, and because of the constitutional significance of the subject, Your Committee have reached the conclusion that further enquiry, at once more detailed and more expert, is required. Accordingly they recommend that a small independent committee, which should have access to Cabinet papers, be appointed to report upon the theory and practice of Treasury control of expenditure.

2. The proposal for another enquiry was naturally unwelcome to the Treasury, which had devoted much work and time to the original one; but the Chancellor of the Exchequer, Mr Heathcoat Amory,[1] accepted the proposal of an enquiry, although in the different form of an internal enquiry (with outside people) under his own authority; and in July 1959, the appointment of Lord Plowden to take general charge of this work was announced.

3. *Trends in 1957–59.* The two-year period in which these things were happening may be regarded as a turning-point in Britain's post-war economic history. In this first of Mr Macmillan's administrations from January 1957 up to the Election of October 1959, we were passing from the expansionist economic liberalism of Mr Butler's time at the Exchequer towards the interventionist policies of indicative planning and incomes

policy which dominated both Conservative and Labour Governments in the 1960s.

4. There had been the sterling crisis of September 1957, with Mr Thorneycroft's measures to constrain public sector investment and bank advances to their existing money levels; and the Chancellor's resignation[2] (with his junior Ministers, Mr Nigel Birch and Mr Enoch Powell) in January 1958, when the Cabinet refused to apply the same formula to the Supply Estimates for 1958 – 59. Only a few months after 'Stop' came the pressure, particularly from the Prime Minister, for 'Go' to prevent the danger of unemployment, with most of Mr Thorneycroft's actions reversed by the summer, culminating in the large tax reductions in Mr Heathcoat Amory's 1959 Budget.

5. In terms of public expenditure, the Treasury in these years was facing three intractable problems. First, the long-term growth of Supply expenditure[3] (22 per cent of the gross national product, compared with 12 per cent in 1930, 6 per cent in 1910, 4 per cent in 1870). Second, the expansion of non-Supply public expenditure and charges on the Exchequer resulting from the development programmes of the nationalised industries (now beginning to take shape after the impact of nationalisation), the growth of local authority expenditure and the reorganisation and expansion of national insurance. Third, the fact that the great savings in defence expenditure following Sir Winston Churchill's cancellation of the 'Korea' rearmament programme in 1952, which had permitted big tax reductions as well as increases in social service spending, had now come to an end; and a massive momentum of social and environmental programmes was under way.

6. At the time, the concepts of public expenditure and their measurement against national resources were not clear enough to permit this to be expressed in simple figures: the following shows a rough-and-ready measure in up-to-date terms:[4]

Year	*Public expenditure* (£ '000 million)	*GDP* (£ '000 million)	*PE/GDP* 'Ratio''
1952	6.4	13.8	46.6
1956	7.5	18.3	41.2
1957	7.9	19.4	41.0
1958	8.3	20.2	41.2
1959	8.8	21.2	41.3
1960	9.4	22.6	41.5
1964	12.7	29.1	43.8

7. So we see 1957 as the last year of a period of falling 'ratio' and falling taxes: the next years with a 'ratio' edging upward; and then the rapid increase of expenditure in relation to resources in the early 1960s. It certainly cannot be asserted that this course of events could have been predicted in the late 1950s from the information available at the time; but it is certainly true that the forces confronting the Treasury (and threatening to confront it when the reduction in defence had worked itself out) were formidable, that the traditional system of expenditure control was not designed to handle the developing situation, and that the appointment of Lord Plowden and his enquiry was a constructive and timely step.

8. *The 'system' of the late 1950s.* The Treasury control system of the late 1950s was fully expounded in the written and oral evidence to the Estimates Committee. The report described it as 'a complex of administrative practices that has grown up like a tree over the centuries, natural rather than planned, empiric rather than theoretical'. Many people would think this comment more complimentary than may have been intended; for the ability of any organisation to survive even for decades and to adapt itself to changing circumstances would be regarded by many as an asset, the lack of which has been a source of weakness to so many 'planned' and 'theoretical' organisations in government.

9. In retrospect, the main characteristic of the system was its diffuseness and decentralisation. The management and control of Government expenditure was seen as the examination of a mass of spending proposals from departments, each to be considered 'on its merits', with a Judgement Day in January when the Estimates (over 2000 sub-heads) were added up and a view taken whether the Budget prospect called for special 'economy' action and if so (as in 1958), how much, and emergency action initiated accordingly. The responsibility for the work on the Departments' proposals was carried by the Principals in the Supply (and mixed Supply/Establishment) divisions of the Treasury, normally one Principal responsible for the work arising from each department, and the problem was referred to the Head of the Division or higher when it was particularly difficult and controversial or if agreement could not be reached.

10. The merits of this degree of decentralisation can be argued at length; but the crucial point in relation to what came later is that even in Supply expenditure ('public expenditure as a whole', about twice as much as Supply, was not yet a working concept) there was no process of reasoned judgement of the scale of aggregate acceptable expenditure, or its implications for taxes, or its allocation between the departments and services. Thus, although there was great expertise about individual departments' expenditure problems (and also on the procedures of

Parliamentary control) there was very little work done and knowledge about the role and impact and composition and morphology even of Supply expenditure, and virtually no information provided to Ministers about it.[5] The point at issue, easier to see now than it was at the time, was whether the Treasury and then the Government could develop a rational public expenditure policy (in this most 'political' of all the fields of government). If they were going to do this, a new system would clearly be required that treated 'public expenditure' as one subject and not as thousands of individual spending decisions.

11. *Public Expenditure and Supply.* The handling of different kinds of public expenditure in different ways (determined by different systems of Parliamentary control) created complexity, but more seriously, a lack of clarity and misunderstanding, sometimes even within the Treasury itself, often in other departments, and very frequently outside.

12. For example, it was never clear in dealing with national insurance whether the figure to watch was the gross expenditure from the insurance funds or the Supply figure, i.e. the Exchequer payments to the funds, which was the Exchequer contribution.[6] The choice gave a completely different impression of the scale of the expenditures (according to whether one regarded the employers' and employees' contributions as 'taxes' or 'receipts'); and could lead into different concepts of policy. Whenever a question came up for decision, the first point to decide was which was the criterion.

13. Again, the treatment of local authority expenditure simply in terms of Exchequer grants led to odd results when the grant structure changed. For example, when the general grant replaced the percentage grants for education, health, etc., in 1959 (a good reform in itself) the cost passed from the Ministry of Education Vote; and most of the Exchequer burden of education was taken on to Ministry of Housing and Local Government Vote.

14. The distinction between Supply expenditure ('above-the-line') and loans to local authorities and nationalised industries ('below-the-line') led to misunderstandings and interminable controversies. If the trunk roads could be built by a National Road Corporation instead of by the Ministry of Transport, could this not be financed 'below-the-line', like any other public authority, and so 'without cost to the Budget'? Sometimes these obscurities affected the Treasury itself: in 1955 the Ministry of Housing and Local Government was required to get new legislation to enable local authorities to borrow (and the Ministry to pay towards the interest on the loans) for building water and sewerage works, towards which the Ministry formerly made capital grants from its Vote: this was sensible enough, for

these are at any rate partially revenue-earning assets, but the ostensible purpose was to make savings 'above-the-line' at the expense of increased expenditures 'below-the-line', and so to contribute to an 'economy campaign'.

15. A comment apropos of a discussion in June 1955 in a committee of Ministers under Lord Swinton which was making an intensive review of expenditure:

> I am certain that a man from Mars would regard it as quite absurd for capital expenditure to be possible without any serious financial limitation in one part of the National Health Service (within the local authorities) whilst capital development of a cost-saving character (e.g. up-to-date boilers) cannot be undertaken for financial reasons in the hospitals.

16. *Longer-term Projections*. The 'system' was always criticised for being focused too exclusively on the single financial year, and means were devised for trying to lengthen it; but these were never successful, for the essence of the system was its being a part of the annual procedure of the Budget and the Parliamentary financial timetable, so that the emphasis on a single year was fundamental and not something that could be simply adjusted. Of course the Treasury divisions often needed to look three or more years ahead on specific projects, particularly in defence and aerospace and technology and infrastructure;[7] and there was enough sophistication throughout Whitehall to avoid the adoption of large expansions of services on the basis of small commitments in the first year or two. But this all had to be done *ad hoc*; and it became increasingly difficult to examine these projects (capital or current) with big long-term implications 'on their merits' and form a judgement whether they were acceptable from the national point of view, either individually or simultaneously.

17. Attempts were therefore made in the mid-1950s to develop 'forward looks' for particular sectors of public expenditure, notably as a guide for the planning of the department(s) concerned, to make sure that they were keeping their planning within the resources which were likely to be available for them, and so getting coherent programmes which would not be vulnerable to sudden cancellation, and give the best value for money.

NOTES

1. Throughout this work, people are referred to according to their style at the time of the reference.
2. The first by a Chancellor of the Exchequer on a public expenditure issue since Lord Randolph Churchill in 1866.
3. *Control of Public Expenditure* (Cmnd 1432), para 10.
4. The variation of the 'ratio' of public expenditure (as defined by PESC) and the gross domestic product (GDP) at factor cost is the relevant measure, which tends empirically to be reflected over the years in tax changes.
5. I remember when I first came into this field how difficult I found it to form any coherent image of 'public expenditure' which would help to discern patterns and to develop means of grappling with this growing amorphous mass, like a great cloud or a shapeless gasbag (which when gripped at one point would at once bulge out in another).
6. An increase in unemployment would reduce the Supply expenditure, for the unemployed men did not have to pay contributions, and therefore no Exchequer contribution.
7. There were also special enclaves, such as the universities, where the Treasury gave five-year grants, but this was done deliberately to reduce to a minimum the need to intervene in this sensitive area.

2 Long-term Operations: 1955-59

18. *Social Services.* The first of these, which failed to establish itself, was a five-year forward survey of the Exchequer cost of the social services (housing, education, health, national insurance, child care). It was begun in the last year of Mr Butler's Chancellorship, in mid-1955, and presented to Ministers early in December, just before Mr Butler was succeeded by Mr Macmillan. By our later standards, it was not a very sophisticated survey.[1] But it showed without any doubt that even on departments' expectations on the basis of their policy of the time, before the great expansions of the late 1950s had got under way, the cost would expand much faster than any expansion that could possibly be expected in the gross national product.

19. This was not the result of population changes: the growth in the number of pensioners was important, but not a decisive element in the growth; nor was the prospective growth of child population important. The programmes, even at underestimated cost, were expressing the continuing improvement in quality which is implicit in the development of the social services. But the dimensions of cost expansion were very much more manageable than they became in the next two or three years; and it might have been possible to develop a programme of planned expansion of the social services which would have established a pattern constrained within manageable limits.

20. Ideas current at the time, though never set up as a common programme, were, for example, (a) solving the rents/housing subsidy problem (much easier in the 1950s than the 1970s); (b) getting the local authority grant structure to put the onus for expansion on the local authorities, and not continually pressing them to spend; (c) determining a rate of development of the size and efficiency of the education services (schools, teacher-training, primary/secondary/further/higher), instead of plunging ahead simultaneously; (d) devoting much more resources to the planning of and allocations in the hospital service (huge discrepancies in cost, bed-occupancies, clerical and administrative apparatus, etc.); (e) establishing a formula for increased pensions (e.g. at rate of consumption per head of population). Then there were the problems of prescription and

other NHS charges, school meals, welfare milk, which have come up regularly for twenty years – which are significant but not in relation to the dynamics of unplanned growth of the services.

21. There may have been an opportunity at this stage to use the conclusions of this five-year survey effectively, with a new Parliament and the public expenditure/GNP ratio at its post-war minimum, leaving plenty of room for the creation of an expansive but manageable long-term programme. Certainly with every year that passed the problem of keeping these expenditures within reasonable dimensions became greater. But just as the survey was experimental, so was the expression of its conclusions inadequate to attract Ministers to the potentialities of the long-term approach. So nothing happened, for neither Ministers nor officials yet had the capability to move in this uncharted territory.

22. *Defence Budget.* There was more success in defence, where the Permanent Secretary of the Ministry, Sir Richard Powell, and the Head of the Treasury division, David Serpell, developed a 'forward look', which started in the second half of the 1950s and speedily developed a technique of forward analysis of programmes for five years ahead, and later even for ten years. At that time, before the great defence reorganisation pressed forward by Mr Macmillan in 1963, defence planning had to be seen as a co-operative task for the three Service Departments and the Ministry of Supply; and this 'forward look' system, the first step towards creating a real defence budget, proved indispensable for the linked planning of defence research and development, production, supply and manpower within the resources (then reckoned at about 7 per cent of the gross national product) that seemed likely to be available.

23. The problem was to build a self-consistent Navy/Army/Air Force series of programmes within a given total: the size of the total – first in the early 1960s to increase it, and then in the huge pressures of the middle and late 1960s to cut it right back – was not yet seriously at issue. But these later stages could not have been handled at all if this system had not been created; and the idea of getting the departments to frame self-consistent programmes (of which this defence work was the prototype) was as important in the original 'Plowden' thinking as the relation between the aggregates of expenditure and resources.

24. *Defence and Foreign Policy 1960-70.* This was a different kind of 'looking ahead', although it could be regarded as the first time the future concepts actually saw the light of day in Whitehall. In spring 1959, Mr Macmillan asked for an appraisal of our defence and foreign policy related to our economic resources over the period 1960-70. A powerful group was set up, including two future Ambassadors to Washington and one future Chief of

Defence Staff, to tackle this assignment – (i) the world background through the 1960s; (ii) the UK's resources for defence and other support of foreign policy (e.g. economic aid, diplomatic representation); and (iii) to draw conclusions for UK policy.

25. This assignment brought forward strikingly the different kinds of thought required for a ten-year appraisal. For example, in determining the 1960–70 world background, no secret or diplomatic information was relevant; the tendency (in all kinds of affairs) is to project what is thought to be the existing situation. This is bound to be wrong, and what is needed is to identify what might be regarded as the forces of continuity. If we had had to do the same task ten years earlier, in 1949, for 1950–60, we could not have predicted Korea, Suez, the Rome Treaty, Hungary, the reversal of the world dollar shortage, the consolidation of Chairman Mao, and all the changed relationships which followed. This was rather a solemn thought. Yet our defence apparatus (equipment, training, deployment etc.,) and our system of alliances and commitments depend on at least a 10-year view. So we had to seek 'ten-year' guidelines.

26. Perhaps the most important of these was what we called 'disposable power', a different concept from the old idea of 'economic strength', which recognised that in anything short of total war lasting several years (like World Wars I and II) what was important was the force that a country could actually mobilise; and that the high-income countries had a longer tail and more costly teeth, not only in their armed forces but in their whole economies, so that USSR, with only one-third of the 'economic strength' of USA, must be regarded as its equal in 'disposable power'.[2] This was demonstrated to the nth degree in the Vietnam war later on in the 1960s. The outlook for the 1960s could be summed up along the following lines:

(a) USA and USSR were the only countries with the 'disposable power' to provide a complete and self-sustaining defence and international power apparatus. EEC (the Six) could develop this strength in ten years if it pooled its resources and was determined to do so. No other country or group could be even near this situation by 1970.

(b) USSR's relative position compared with the West was likely to strengthen in those fields that they regarded as important.

(c) UK would be gradually weakening, both within the West and world-wide. Strength of sterling was fundamental to success of defence and foreign policy; partly because of the great damage to our political influence of repeated £ crises, and also because sterling is the reserve currency of African and Asian underdevelopeds from Freetown to Singapore.

(d) Whether EEC could in the 1960s become an effective political unit was something that would really count on the world political-military map.[3]

(e) China would still be far behind the West and USSR, but be strengthening production much faster than India.

(*f*) The immense and rapidly growing potential strength of Japan should never be ignored.

(*g*) The economic gap between the West and the Soviet bloc on the one hand and the underdevelopeds of Asia and Africa was likely to widen. Only India could in the 1960s reach the 'threshold' from which industrial expansion becomes possible (like, say, Russia in 1913).[4]

(*h*) The underdevelopeds would have formidable difficulties in making headway, and would be in danger of frustration. Improvement in their agriculture was the critical area, economically and politically; and how to help them to do this should be studied by the West. The economic relations of the advanced countries with the under-developeds (trade and aid) was of major political importance; but aid (on any scale then thought conceivable) could only supplement the underdevelopeds' own efforts.

27. As for the UK's resources for support of foreign policy, the cost appeared to be about 8½ per cent of GNP, and the two questions had to be posed – what effect the maintenance of this proportion would have on the rest of the economy; (notably the conflict with (*c*) above; and of at least equal importance over a ten-year period, whether the people would be prepared to accept this kind of defence/aid/diplomatic load as a continuing feature of our society. At this particular point of time (as explained earlier) the reduction of defence after 'Korea' rearmament had left the public expenditure/GNP ratio at its minimum post-war level, but there were now no declining programmes. The load was illustrated by two points – one, the defence load borne by other NATO and Commonwealth countries,[5] and two, the traditional peacetime defence loads borne by the British people.[6]

28. In the end, the analysis (though it wore quite well with time) could not lead to positive conclusions. It was evident that the UK could work only through alliances (with USA and with Continental Europe); that with the West/USSR balance, the area of economic and ideological confrontation was the underdevelopeds; that the UK effort was spread too thin; that the nation's willingness to sustain this effort at 8½ per cent of GNP was highly dubious, and that failure would react directly on sterling and make matters worse; and that whilst the defence of UK (i.e. membership of NATO) and the nuclear deterrent fitted well enough into the structure, the justification of our defence effort East of Suez was not clear.

29. But this book is not about defence and foreign policy, but about how the concepts of thinking seriously and systematically about long-term policy came into being; and it was not until the early 1960s that the

techniques came into being for allocating the total defence effort functionally (see para 90), which made it possible for the great debate about 'East of Suez' in the second half of the 1960s to be conducted on rational lines.

30. *Nationalised Industries.* By the mid-1950s, the nationalised energy and transport industries were established, and were being subjected to batteries of examination, committees, commissions, re-legislation, mostly involving more disturbance cost than ultimate benefit.[7] It was believed at the time that the problems were of organisation. But the true defect, both of the original and the revised statutes and of the intellectual approach (even by men as able and sophisticated as Hugh Gaitskell), was the failure to define the economic and financial objectives, for the statutory requirement that the industries should 'pay their way, taking one year [decade?] with another' provided no effective basis for management; and the failure to define the industries' independence from the Government in practice on the crucial elements of management – prices, wages, investment, commercial policy. Without clarity in the objectives and authority of the management of the industries, the organisational mix between central and decentralised control was of secondary importance.[8]

31. The immediate practical 'looking ahead' problems were bringing these immense deficiencies into the foreground. I will mention two, in no critical sense at all of the industries, departments, Treasury, etc., who were all in uncharted territory, but because they illustrate so clearly.

32. The first was in January 1955, when the British Transport Commission (BTC) published its Railway Modernisation Plan, to be completed in fifteen years at a cost of about £1200 million. In October 1953, the BTC, under Lord Robertson, had under the new Act taken over direct responsibility from the Railway Executive for the operation of the railways, and set up a planning committee at once. It cannot be said that this was a realistic course, for there were huge unresolved technological and commerical problems, with no integrated staff in depth to work out the best solutions to last for half a century. For example, the Railway Executive had been dominated by 'steam power' men, who had a long-term policy of replacing the 400 different kinds of locomotive by twelve standard locomotives. The BTC, however, decided to abolish steam power and to replace it by electrification (originally on the standard 1500 volts d.c. overhead system, changed a year later to the 25 KV a.c. system) and diesel traction (mostly preferring diesel-electric, but the Western, with its traditional independence since Brunel – and in this case like the Bundesbahn – diesel-hydraulic). There were similar problems at another of the central points of the plan – the introduction of continuous brakes for wagons, and the decision was still open between vacuum type and

compressed-air type and on the nature of the coupling.

33. So the Railway Modernisation Plan could not be regarded as a 'plan' in any business sense: moreover, the planning committee had made clear that there was no possibility of any contribution to revenue from the £1200 million capital expenditure until the whole plan had been completed and put into service – a sombre and factual warning which was at some point suppressed before the plan was published! The Government described it, however, as 'a courageous and imaginative plan'.[9] The immediate sequel was that the railways in 1956 for the first time in their history made an operating loss.[10]

34. The second case, of an entirely different kind, was the abortive nuclear power 'crash programme' of winter 1956–57. In 1955, an experimental programme had been determined to provide 1500–2000 MW by 1965. At the end of 1956, the AEA proposed a 'crash' programme to reach 8000 MW by end-1965: this had formidable political backing, seen as a massive riposte to Nasser.[11] The additional capital cost compared with conventional power stations was put at £800–1000 million. In the argument that followed, it soon became clear that 6000 MW was the practical maximum by end-1965; that the Central Electricity Authority (CEA), who had the responsibility for supply, could not accept a bigger programme than 3500 MW; and that no practicable nuclear power programme could reduce our dependence on oil by 1970. Nuclear power was seen as a great source of strength in twenty years but not in ten years (in which much larger energy savings could be made at a fraction of the cost). In February, Ministers had to choose between three programmes – for 5–6000 MW by end-1965, end-1966, and end-1967 – and chose the fastest. Extra long-term uranium purchases were made accordingly; a fifth consortium formed (which had to be given the contract for the fifth station), etc.

35. However, the practical difficulties proved great; and the contribution to the energy situation recognised as being trivial, and the extra cost of the end-1965 programme compared with the end-1966 so daunting at £150 million, that in the September 1957 crisis the end-1966 programme was substituted. Subsequently, after Lord Hinton had moved from the AEA to be chairman of the Central Electricity Generating Board, the merits of nuclear against conventional power appeared in a more sombre light; and in September 1958 a phased programme was agreed between the authorities, which ultimately yielded installed nuclear capacity of 4100 MW (including Scotland) at end-1967 – less than the lowest envisaged in early 1957. So the electricity authorities got what they wanted (with much reduced capital cost); the AEA lost prestige and incurred abortive expenditure (all paid for by the Exchequer); the nuclear plant industry,

having been induced to spend its own resources heavily in anticipation of a large continuing programme, was damaged and disappointed (and in fifteen years the five consortia had been reduced to one). We had not only failed to 'bash Nasser on the snoot', but when the true Middle East oil crisis came in 1973, our nuclear capability (still only 5100 MW at end-1974) was no longer seen as a dominant part of our response.

36. In both cases in retrospect, the Government's correct policy was clear. The 'Railway Modernisation Plan' should have been referred back for, say, three years' consideration, with some money for experimentation, and a provision that no new capital expenditures would be accepted that would not earn X per cent: alas, by then, the BTC was already deep in operating losses, and its days were numbered. For nuclear power, a decision could have been taken to build up to, say, 10,000 MW in the early 1970s, to proceed as fast as the electricity authorities (whose responsibility the reliability and safety and cost was) were satisfied to move.

37. For this book, however, the interest in these problems is their exposure of the Governmental apparatus. Ministers' love of 'crash plans' to deal with real or imagined dangers is well known and understandable for men and women working under the kind of pressure that is beyond the comprehension of people unfamiliar with it. But the relationship between the railway 'plan' and the developing concepts of a national motorway system was never clear. Nor were the fuel policy implications of the various choices in the railway 'plan'. On the other hand, the Ministry of Power's grasp of the country's future energy needs and the irrelevance to them of the 'crash' nuclear programme was fully adequate. In the Treasury, we were still a long way from being able to take these huge long-term programmes to pieces, establish the ground-rules and the rate of return that was tolerable, and judge whether the country could in any event afford long-term commitments of this scale without excluding more important other things. In 1958, we did bring all the nationalised industries work into one division under Matthew Stevenson (later Permanent Secretary of the Ministry of Power), which enabled us to extract the common experience. But as I said earlier, these were all uncharted territories for everyone concerned.

38. However, early in 1959, a seminal opportunity occurred, for a group of officials headed by the Treasury was asked by Ministers to report on changes in the organisation of the energy and transport nationalised industries and their relations with Government and Parliament. We had formed the judgement, as explained earlier, that organisation was secondary to economic and financial objectives and to freedom from Government intervention. So we persuaded our colleagues, so to speak, to answer the wrong examination paper; to begin by defining the obligation

on a Board to 'pay its way', to propose a definite business framework and standard of expected performance (earnings target) for each, and to give the Boards greater freedom from Government price control and intervention, except when they were failing to achieve their earnings targets. This was not before its time, for these authorities' net earnings after depreciation in 1955–57 averaged 3.2 per cent on net assets compared with 15.9 per cent for manufacturing industry. The organisational proposals were designed to fit into this pattern.

39. Our fears at having answered the wrong question were relieved by some consummate diplomacy by Sir Thomas Padmore, the chairman, who persuaded the relevant Ministers of not only the validity but the necessity of this approach; and after lengthy argument and negotiation the White Paper *The Economic and Financial Objectives of Nationalised Industries*, Cmnd 1337 (April 1961) was published, widely welcomed in the industries as providing (except in the railways) an effective basis for business management for the first time, and the targets were fixed for five-year periods.[12] This was only a first step, and in 1962 we started on the next (on investment criteria) and could have published in autumn 1964, but did not do so until 1967. Nevertheless the system of financial objectives was firmly endorsed by the Labour Government.[13] So the system continued (with the inevitable occasional wobbles) to the great benefit of this vital industrial sector, until 1970. However it was then a casualty of Mr Heath's Administration; and these 'commanding heights' of industry, nationalised because of the supreme importance of energy and transport to the health of the economy, became the 'sunken quicksands' into which hundreds of millions of pounds of taxpayers' money disappeared without trace - and the reclamation of which will be one of the biggest and most pressing tasks of some Government in the next ten years.

40. *Steel.* The 1953 de-nationalisation Act set up two bodies - The Iron and Steel Holding and Realisation Agency (ISHRA), brigaded with the Treasury and with the duty of selling back the shares to the companies: this proceeded fast, until the 'hard core' of Richard Thomas & Baldwins (RTB) was left with no buyer in sight (10 per cent of the industry) and in effect had to be treated as a permanent State company (see Chapter 12). The other was the Iron and Steel Board, which had a supervisory capacity for prices and investment. The 'looking ahead' aspect was that the Board moved in five-year development plans, into which it tried to fit the companies' projects; and these had to be based on some concept of the future course of demand.

41. The custom was for the Treasury, the Department concerned with steel (a bit of a shuttlecock), the Iron and Steel Board and the industry to conduct a major analysis. The work for the third of these (1957–62)

started at end-1955; and we arrived at figures of capacity rising from about 22 million tons in 1956 (only 14 million in 1945) to figures ranging between 27 - 30 million in 1962 (never absolutely clear, for the rate of installation of new capacity was the vital thing, and the failure to eliminate obsolete capacity the bugbear). The figures illustrate the expansiveness of the time (everyone agreed it was better to have excess capacity than steel shortage); and the programme was at least £100 million a year (another big chunk of future investment).

42. Another and rather paradoxical feature was that we could have an entirely friendly discussion with the de-nationalised industry and its supervisory authority, involving not only the expectations of the rate of growth of the economy but, at least equally important, the likely development of the steel-intensity of the economy, and the relationship of new capacity to obsolete capacity, etc., in a manner which would have been impossible with any nationalised industry!

43. The third plan was ultimately disrupted by the problem of the fourth strip mill, to provide for the expanding motor industry. Its location was vigorously contested, and RTB at Newport was a natural choice (inevitably 100 per cent State-financed); but the prospective return was far below the levels to be established later for the nationalised energy industries, and much farther below what was implied in the Iron and Steel Board's price formula for the steel industry. There was hue-and-cry from Scotland, where the Board of Trade was trying to establish a motor industry on grounds of regional policy; so Colvilles (at Ravenscraig) were (not very willingly) in the field too (also with Government money). In the end, Ministers made a Judgement of Solomon at end-1958, and both projects went forward: the sums allocated by Parliament in 1960 were £70 million and £50 million respectively - but these were wholly inadequate, and RTB had to go on with ISHRA money 'off the cuff' and Colvilles to the grave detriment of their whole financial situation.[14]

44. These notes about steel are included partly because they are an illustration of 'looking ahead' between the industry and the Treasury over a considerable period of time; and partly because of the industrial and financial danger that it shows of not having a disciplined nationalised industry policy (RTB) and of using the power of the purse to induce companies to undertake projects that they do not believe to be sound, and which by striking at the company's profitability and financial resources, weaken, not strengthen, the regional policies that they are intended to promote.

45. *Other Long-term Studies.* In the nuclear power case above, an important element was a report on the balance of energy demand and supply up to

1975, produced in December 1956 under the leadership of an Under-secretary of the Ministry of Fuel and Power (later Sir Goronwy Daniel, future Principal of Aberystwyth University College) with strong Treasury participation. We tried a similar operation with the Ministry of Transport in 1956–57 on the future demand for transport services, in order to begin to get some statistical framework between road and rail and coastal shipping, but this proved too difficult and ran into the sand.[15]

46. Another interesting case was a study by Sir Solly Zuckerman and myself on the future requirements for scientific and engineering man-power: Christopher Saunders exerted great ingenuity to find relations over time and in different countries between economic growth and the stock of scientists and engineers; and we arrived at results that were reasonable in establishing a dimension for the next few years,[16] but when mechanically extrapolated, particularly by people who did not view the subject as one for objective analysis at all, soon got the figures too big and this led to waste of resources.

47. The Crowther Report of 1959 on the Raising of the School Leaving Age[17] led to a useful ten-year estimate of the future expenditure on education. The report to Ministers on the Crowther Report was something of a breakthrough, for it was the first time that a relation had been accepted between education (essentially a process of developing the individual) and the national economy, except of course in the field of further education. Oddly, the universities had been pressing their case for massive expansion on the opposite (economic) argument; and I have for several years believed it to have been a mistake in the national educational interest for the universities (after their expansion had got under way in the mid-1950s) to have continued in their Treasury-financed enclave and not been brought within the aegis of the Ministry of Education, so that there could have been a better allocation made of the available resources between primary, secondary, further and higher education.

48. In 1959, the Society of Motor Manufacturers and Traders invited us to join with them in examining the implications of the great expansion of car population upon which their members' production plans were based. We of course accepted this constructive and socially responsible move; and with them and the relevant departments produced what must have been the first official report on 'living with the motor car', one of the important factors which led to the commissioning of the Buchanan Report.

49. Finally, one must mention a very-very-very long-term report on afforestation, which clearly had to extend into the twenty-first century (unless it was solely concerned with ten-year conifers). It became rapidly clear that at any conceivable rate of interest, the idea of afforestation (i.e.

creating new forests) could find its justification only as a social service (or perhaps, we would now say, an ecology) project with no economic return. But it was not necessarily the worse for that.

50. Some of these studies were initiated by ourselves; in some we were invited by other people; in some we participated in projects in which others had taken the initiative. The point of listing them here is not their intrinsic interest; though in many cases this was considerable and indeed had a notable effect on affairs. But the relevance is that over a very wide range of industrial (nationalised and private) and social service problems we were becoming accustomed to think in terms of five, ten, twenty or even more years; which is an altogether different kind of discipline of thought from what is required in the ordinary political market-place, but on which the real successes and failures of government will ultimately depend.

51. *Public Sector Investment.* The problem was how to establish financial control over public sector investment (central Government, local authorities and nationalised industries) when physical controls were removed. From 1948 to 1952, both public and private investment were centrally controlled by a system analogous to building licensing, operated by a committee managed by Lord Plowden's Central Economic Planning Staff. In 1953, this weakened as the building situation improved, and at the end of the year building control was abolished. For the Treasury, the result was that apart from direct central Government expenditure (e.g. hospitals, roads, atomic energy) there was no established system of control, and the divisions had to handle the cases as best they could. In all these fields, short-term control was obviously futile: the Treasury had to create a capability to look ahead for several years.

52. The administrative problems, overcome successfully by Matthew Stevenson and later by Peter Vinter, were formidable. For example:
  (i) What period? We collected five-year programmes with specified control figures for the first three.
  (ii) Should we control gross investment or borrowing from the Exchequer? A profitable nationalised industry or a local authority could understand why the Government should want to control its borrowing from the Exchequer, but if it got its money some other way, why should the Government worry? The difficulty was, of course, that if the Government can afford to lend only X, how can it rationally allocate the X, without going behind the borrowing to the investment? So we went for the latter.
  (iii) If you make allocations, how can you define and police them? A statistical apparatus is needed, to compare 'actual' with 'allocation'. But, apart from price changes, can you expect a big organisation to get its actual capital expenditure, through

hundreds of spending points, 'right' within 10 per cent? If one outruns the constable, what can you do about it? This assumes moreover that there is goodwill, but in one classical case in the early 1950s, a powerful Cabinet Minister overran his allocation by £400 million!

53. The Government's constitutional right to exercise control was subject to argument. The Ministry of Education had to approve local authorities' school-building; but the historical basis of this was to maintain standards, not to control a programme. Local authorities had to get the Ministry of Housing and Local Government's sanction for borrowing from any service, but this was to satisfy the Government (and thus the lender) that the local authority's financial position was strong enough to accept this additional obligation. Even in nationalised industries, the statutory right of the Government was obscure: the Minister had the duty of approving a long-term development programme, but some authorities thought they were entitled then to borrow what they needed from the Exchequer (or with Exchequer guarantee). This sorted itself out, for the power of the purse is persuasive, but it took time.

54. The worst difficulty, however, was the political one, which was the discontent by public sector authorities of all kinds (shared indeed within the Government) that public sector investment should be controlled whilst private investment went free. Why should Council housing be limited whilst private developers (shops, houses, offices) could go ahead? The country had been living under a State-controlled system for fifteen years, and although the removal of food rationing was popular, the implications of building de-control were less clearly understood.[18] For some years, this problem of building control reverberated round Whitehall; and the stronger the evidence became that the aggregate of the public sector programmes under way (both basic investment for the national economy and the development of the social services) was due to increase much faster than the gross national product, the more difficult did this argument become; though in actual fact in the economy the issue was not between public and private investment but between both and consumption.

55. The first of these public sector programmes was produced in 1957: it had taken since February 1956 to overcome the problems and get it into being. We were helped to get the allocation system off the ground by the sterling crisis which was developing in July following the collapse of the 'price plateau', and the report proposed rephasing of the nuclear power, railway, telephone development, and education programmes, a new policy for housing (taking public and private together), more self-financing for nationalised industry.

56. On 18 October, the Chancellor (Mr Thorneycroft) announced the

decision to keep public sector investment at the same aggregate in 1957 - 58, 1958-59 and 1959-60; with the detail in much the same areas as indicated above.[19] So the annual review of three-year programmes of public sector investment was instituted; and these were subsequently published a year at a time in the Economic Survey for 1959 and then in a regular annual Public Investment White Paper from 1960 [Cmnd 1203] onward.

57. It must be added that a major examination was simultaneously being made of private investment, with particular emphasis on the scale and health of the basic industries, capital goods and manufacturing industries, and what the Government could do to help where the obstacle was either shortage of capital or inadequate investment. The sadness is that twenty years after exactly the same report could be written, with exactly the same possible courses of action adumbrated; and no advance made as a result of Government action.

58. The structure of public sector investment control was established by end-1957. The biggest difficulty was then 'stop-go'. No sooner had the programmes of October 1957 been determined, and the 'little local difficulty' of the resignation of the Chancellor and his colleagues completed, when forces built up for reflation, and by October 1958 I was reflecting that:

> ... to protect discipline and Treasury control of public sector investment operations, we are trying to bring into being a system that operates this control – the lack of which was a contributory factor to the crises of 1955 - 56 - 57. If these programmes are opened and reopened at every puff of wind, we cannot sustain any effective control. It is not really a question of disciplining the departments – it stretches right through to the nationalised industries and the local authorities. With this large number of clients dealt with by remote control, we cannot conduct complicated and sophisticated manoeuvres of economic management.

I have never been enthusiastic about attempts to stimulate and depress public sector investment in the short term. I have too much experience of the frustration to all concerned of having to apply the ice-packs before the hot fomentations have cooled off. But as we shall see throughout this book, and at least ten years later, the attraction of 'stop-go' persists; for when the economy is seen to be moving up or down, Ministers must be seen to be taking action.

59. *Long-term Economic Assessment.* In order to make a judgement of how big a public sector investment aggregate the economy could bear, we had

to create a forward-looking view of the course of the economy. In 1957, the first of these annual assessments was prepared under Peter Vinter's chairmanship, to try to establish the prospects of the growth of the economy and the development of the other claims on it. The original purpose of this was to provide the 'resources' background for the public investment operations; and it was tailor-made for this purpose. But it became used much more widely for the specific operations discussed in this chapter. At this stage, therefore, the long-term work on resources was arising directly from the need for Government decisions on specific industrial and related expenditure issues. These were business decisions, subject to risks about the future and the costs of these risks, and the only merit of the 'long-term planning' arithmetic was to clarify these risks and costs, and enable Government to make better decisions accordingly. We were still a long way away from the 'macro' models of the future, seeking to illuminate the problems of general economic policy.

60. By the middle of 1956, when some of the studies described above were approaching completion, our thinking had developed along the following lines. We must avoid at all costs making 'models' for the future on arbitrary assumptions and building a superstructure of 'requirements' of steel or whatever. Still less should we call this 'the best estimate we can make'. The 'assumptions' assumed away all the uncertainties of the future. For Whitehall, this provided a convenient alibi: we could fill our papers so full of reservations that we should never be caught out. But if we wasted hundreds of millions of pounds, or 'planned' ourselves into devaluing the currency, this alibi was not entirely satisfying. We didn't want to know how much steel would be required on one assumption and how much on another, and be asked to make an agonising appraisal of which was more likely. Nor did we want to have to choose between 'optimistic' and 'pessimistic' assumptions. What we needed was the long-term production plan that made most sense on most interpretations of the future. We had to weigh the risks of having too much or too little, and the corresponding costs. In primary fuels, for example, we needed to consider the minimum requirements for which we must provide (in coal and other indigenous fuels, or imports) in, say, 1965, on almost any rational hypothesis. Then we had to consider in what circumstances we might need more (and what would be involved in getting it) and also consider our plight if the Middle East was cut off. From these assessments would emerge some pretty definite judgements (not related to particular hypotheses but to the whole complex of them) on actions which seemed to be definitely required and worthwhile; and another series of actions for which the case was less strong. But we were opposed to saying that on these assumptions you must do this, and that on those you must do that, or that 'our best estimate of the 1965 requirements is X.'

61. *Preliminaries to Plowden.* The intellectual and administrative 'jump' to

the ideas of the Plowden Committee came when it became necessary to move from the specific and limited long-term operations described in this chapter, where even the largest, such as defence and public sector investment, were only 6 or 7 per cent of the national economy, to the wider concepts of public expenditure as a whole – at that time just over 40 per cent of the national economy. If we were considering the economy's future needs for steel, for example, we could ignore the possibility that the economy would expand by less than, say, $2\frac{1}{2}$ per cent a year, because it was a major objective to avoid steel shortage: even in public sector investment, if after a critical examination of the programme it became clear that the aggregate would have to expand faster than GNP, this did not call for undue alarm. But when we came to look at the whole of public expenditure, the margins for manoeuvre were very much less: the totals were up against the hard facts of the balance of payments needs, private investment, and above all private consumption, notoriously difficult to influence (for if people are taxed they may respond by reducing their rate of saving).

62. We first began to speculate on the possibilities here in August 1958. This arose from a request which had been made to the Chancellor (Mr Heathcoat Amory) to examine the possibility of long-term saving in civil Government expenditure in order to contribute to strengthening our external financial position. This remit was part of the re-thinking that was going on about the position of the United Kingdom in world affairs, which led into the study of Defence and Foreign Policy 1960 – 1970 (paras 24 *et seq.*)

63. After considerable discussion, we formed the view that this could be seriously considered only in terms of the whole deployment of resources and thus of the 1958 Long-term Economic Assessment. So this developed into a long-term strategic paper, based on a $2\frac{1}{2}$ per cent growth rate for GNP, exports and investment (public and private) growing much faster, defence and overseas political expenditure given; and then the problem of how the rest (consumption and civil public expenditure) could be fitted in. The four areas chosen as being strategically vital may be of interest nearly twenty years later:

(a) Policies to increase the 'savings ratio' – the crucial point in con-straining growth of consumption.

(b) National Health Service: general grant to local authorities (mainly education): size of civil service.

(c) Long-term policies to stop misapplication of resources: agriculture; rents and housing subsidies (on which a beginning had been made); prices and investment in nationalised industries (i.e. proper economic and financial criteria).

(d) Expansion of basic productive investment in the private sector.

64. This was a first run over the course; and it was a long hard road from these thoughts among a handful of very senior people in Treasury Chambers to the creation of an apparatus on the resources (Long Range Economic Assessment) side that would carry conviction to Ministers and departments, and an apparatus of expenditure control throughout the public sector which would be accepted and effective · especially when in both cases the answers would be neither pleasant nor popular.

65. On the resources side, Mr Vinter and Mr Hopkin (in 1974, Sir Bryan Hopkin, the Treasury's Chief Economic Adviser) were becoming more confident. We decided that we could use the 1959 LREA more widely and also began to use it in Whitehall (as in Defence and Foreign Policy 1960 70). On the expenditure side, we had only the fragmentary experiences already described; and thinking about it many years later, there was always in my mind some conflict between the 'defence budget' concept, of getting the best programme from a determined limited amount of resources, and the 'public sector investment' concept, of establishing an allocation of resources. Of course these are complementary; but as the narrative proceeds, the emphasis can be seen swinging from one to the other.

NOTES

1. For example, what was later known as 'Clarke's Law', now in the system as RPE (Relative Price Effect) had not yet been introduced. [It was first enunciated in *Public Expenditure in 1963-64 and 1967-68* (Cmnd 2235, December) p. 10n. Ed.] It provides that when forecasting expenditure on public services at constant value of money, you have to allow for an increase of pay of soldiers, teachers, nurses, etc., in line with the expected increase of pay and productivity in the private sector, for their productivity is not measurable (or even conceptually clear) but their pay rises generally in line with the private sector. So if you are projecting, say, defence or education in relation to GNP, the proportion, even with the same manpower, will rise. Before this was understood, all forward projections of public services 'at constant pay and prices' significantly underestimated how the charge on resources would appear in five years' time.

2. The direct antithesis of the French slogan of 1939 – 'nous gagnerons parce que nous sommes les plus forts'.

3. Two years after the Rome Treaty this was still a question of controversy. My recollection is that many thought that the momentum to unity would go quite fast: others that it would fail because of French recalcitrance, followed by German determination for reunification: not many would have thought then that by the mid-1970s, the EEC would still be firmly linked together, but as very little more than a Customs Union, and no military and political unity at all.

4. Latin America did not appear in these conclusions, illustrating a decline of British interest there after World War II. But Brazil was classed as having great expansion possibility, and possibly an important political significance by 1970.
5. Defence (NATO definition), as percentage of GNP, 1958: UK 7.9; USA 11.5; France 8.2; Canada 6.5; Holland 5.7; Germany 4.2; other NATO generally around 4; Australia (1956 - 7) 3.3; New Zealand 2.5. [Five years later, in 1963, UK was 7.2; USA 10.0; France 6.4; Germany 6.1; Holland 4.9; Canada 4.6; Australia 3.1; New Zealand 2.0].
6. Defence as percentage of GNP: 1870 - 90 2 - 2½; 1900 (Boer War) 6.6; 1905 3.3; 1913 3.1; World War I; 1930 2.7; 1938 4.9; World War II; 1949 6.9; 1952 (Korea rearmament peak) 9.8; 1960 - 64 around 7; and in the early 1970s about 5. In the early years particularly, much of the Army (not Navy) cost of 'East of Suez' was covered by the Indian Army, paid for by India, and not by UK; but if this had been financed by UK it could not have affected these percentages much.
7. Ten years later, in its first six months in 1964 - 65, the Ministry of Technology was in similar plight. The Permanent Secretary, Sir Maurice Dean, pointed out that when the Ministry was repeatedly asked 'What have you actually done in the last six months?' the honest answer would often have been, 'Much of our time is taken up with answering questions about what we are doing' (*Mintech in Retrospect*, p. 29).
8. The clearest description of this phase was in Sir Ronald Edwards's Graham Clark lecture on 'Objectives and Control in Nationalised Industry' on 7 March 1963, published by the Electricity Council.
9. There are two good sources on this, the *Report of the Select Committee on the Nationalised Industries on British Railways*, HC 254 - I (HMSO, 1960) - the Committee then in its palmiest days under Lord Aldington and Austen Albu; and the autobiography of the railwayman A. J. Pearson, *Man of the Rail*, (Allen & Unwin, 1967), who had served on the planning committee.
10. Admittedly partly because of Mr Macmillan's 'price plateau', the first time that control of nationalised industries' prices was used to keep the cost-of-living down and so discourage wage increases.
11. In the reconstruction of the Government when Mr Macmillan became Prime Minister in January 1957, Lord Mills was given special responsibility for the nuclear power programme, and the Prime Minister himself took over responsibility for the AEA in April 1957.
12. E.g. Electricity Boards 12.4 per cent and Gas Boards 10.2 per cent (before depreciation); Post Office 8 per cent (after depreciation), etc.
13. Answers in Parliament by Mr Callaghan on 22 Dec 1964 and by Mr Brown on 4 Feb 1965.
14. The four development plans (1945 to 1952 - 53, 1953 to 1958, 1957 to 1962 and 1961 - 65) - the work on the future of demand for steel for the second and the fourth was handled just the same as described for the third - are described well in pages 160 - 3, and the extraordinary events about the fourth and fifth strip mills on pages 169-74 of Professor Vaizey's *The History of British Steel* (Weidenfeld & Nicolson, 1974).
15. It was always possible to compare individual rail and road projects, as Beesley and Carter did; but the Ministry had not got as far as the Ministry of Power in its capability in these fields. Every department really needed a 'Resources and Finance' Division to handle all these subjects.

16. *Scientific and Engineering Manpower in Great Britain* (HMSO, 1956).
17. From fifteen to eighteen. *Report of the Central Advisory Council for Education (England)* (HMSO, 1959).
18. One Prime Minister, for example, was so incensed on his weekend visits to Chequers at seeing petrol stations being built on the road, that there was a regular flow of minutes on Mondays saying that this waste should be stopped.
19. An important illustration of a key principle of public administration. Without the intensive eighteen months' work to get this diffuse series of programmes of about £1200 million a year (plus housing) identified and classified and organised, the Chancellor and his colleagues would have had to take purely *ad hoc* and arbitrary action: the obverse is that if you have done the staff-work on a problem of first-class importance, however difficult and apparently unacceptable, an opportunity will arise sooner or later to bring it into effect.

3 The Plowden Report

66. The Plowden Committee began to work in October 1959. The chairman was supported by Sir Sam Brown, Sir Jeremy Raisman and Mr (later Lord) John Wall, all of whom had had much experience in public administration; with six permanent and deputy secretaries from the Treasury and other departments, who were more properly described as assessers, for they could not sign the reports. It must be recalled that this was an internal Treasury enquiry, responsible directly to the Chancellor of the Exchequer; and it proceeded by making interim reports to him, the first of which, covering the fundamental issues before the Committee, were presented at the beginning of June 1960. One must note from these dates that the Committee moved with effective speed: when I became an assesser in January 1960, the discussion of the basic principles was already well under way, and the questions of what could practically be done, rather than what was desirable, were beginning to dominate the situation. As the enquiry proceeded, it became clear that it would be necessary to produce a published report, and this was of course done [Cmnd 1432 of July 1961]: it covered the whole range of the Committee's deliberations, and only omitted those points that the Committee wished to keep confidential to the Chancellor and his senior colleagues.

67. The Committee's first preoccupations were with the fundamental questions of how governments can best determine their policies affecting public expenditure; for the level of public expenditure ultimately (sometimes after many years) follows from these. The first conclusion was that the traditional system, which made this the sole responsibility of the Chancellor of the Exchequer (subject of course to the collective assent of the Cabinet), carried out by a process of piecemeal decisions with no central review by Ministers collectively, was no longer likely to be effective in curbing expenditure or keeping it within the prospective resources available; and that a reconstruction was necessary.

68. Three principles were laid down:[1]

   (1) Effective collective responsibility of Ministers for public expenditure, so that the Chancellor no longer carries the weight alone.
   (2) Regular Ministerial appraisal of public expenditure as a whole, over a period of years ahead, and in relation to prospective resources.

Decisions involving substantial future expenditure should be taken in the light of these appraisals.

(3) The greatest practicable stability of decisions on public expenditure when taken, so that considerations of long-term economy and efficiency throughout the public sector have the best possible opportunity to develop.

69. *Collective Responsibility of Ministers.* The Committee put this first;[2] for public expenditure is the most 'political' of all the business of government; and the problem arises (just as much in the late 1970s as in the 1960s) because the political attitudes towards public expenditure, in government, in Parliament and in all important elements of public opinion, are radically different from what they were when the traditional system was built up.[3] It followed from this that the first need was a change of balance at the political end, in order to strengthen the position of the Chancellor of the Exchequer.

70. The Committee suggested that this should be done by setting up a Public Expenditure Committee of senior Ministers to examine the expenditure/resources appraisals and to consider particular large long-term expenditure proposals. This would not be an executive committee that would lessen the Chancellor's own responsibility for the decision (and to defend it if necessary in the Cabinet): its purpose would be to give the Chancellor the support of senior colleagues' opinions, and to bring more collective judgement into the process. So the appraisals would be seriously considered by an informed and influential group of Ministers, as indeed the spending priorities and the relation with the nation's prospective resources should be; and there is no reasonable doubt that, if certain large spending proposals of the last fifteen years had been submitted to a procedure of this kind, the decisions might well have been different. The Committee made no recommendation on the composition of the proposed group,[4] whether of non-spending Ministers or spending Ministers or a mixture of the two: most emphasis was laid on seniority.

71. Two attempts were made on these lines for *ad hoc* groups of non-spending Ministers, one in 1961 by Mr Macmillan, under Mr Selwyn Lloyd's chairmanship, and one in 1965 by Mr Wilson, with Mr George Brown and Mr Callaghan. These experiments were not repeated, which suggests that they may not have given much satisfaction to Ministers generally: the adverse comments of 'participants' quoted by Heclo and Wildavsky suggest that some spending Ministers found themselves at a disadvantage in this environment;[5] and it would not be surprising if they then persuaded their colleagues that this should not happen again! Nevertheless, so experienced a judge as Sir Samuel Goldman has since his retirement from the Treasury expressed himself against this concept,[6]

attributing the 1965 success (from the Treasury point of view) to a considerable extent to 'the accident of personalities'; and his view must be given great weight.

72. In October 1961, Mr Macmillan tried to strengthen the Chancellor by a different route, appointing Mr Henry Brooke (to be followed in 1962 by Mr Boyd-Carpenter) as Chief Secretary to the Treasury, a full member of the Cabinet, with responsibility for public expenditure. In the following Labour Government, Mr Diamond was Chief Secretary, but was not brought in to the Cabinet until 1968. In Mr Heath's Government (and in Mr Wilson's 1974 Government) the idea of a second Treasury Cabinet Minister was dropped. In my opinion, the concept was a good one, provided that the Chancellor firmly refused to act as court of appeal against the Chief Secretary's decisions, and insisted that such appeals should be made direct to the Cabinet. This full Cabinet membership is of course the essence of the concept: otherwise, the Chief Secretary is no more than the traditional Financial Secretary - indeed, rather less, because he is only one of a number of junior Treasury Ministers; whereas fifty years ago the Financial Secretary was normally regarded as being on the doorstep for promotion to the Cabinet. It could be argued, indeed, that the Treasury Ministerial teams in the 1920s and 1930s were a stronger segment of the available Ministerial timber than after the war; and if this is so it reinforces the argument for strengthening, and indeed for the second Treasury Cabinet Minister.

73. Since the experiments ten years ago with an Expenditure Committee, the big expenditure and PESC operations have been handled in the Cabinet; and this in itself has been a step forward compared with what happened before, and has introduced at any rate formally more effective collective responsibility. It takes a lot of Cabinet time, but this is not unreasonable for decisions of this political and economic importance. It excludes collective participation by permanent secretaries. It does nothing to strengthen the Chancellor's hand, except to the extent that the logic of the PESC operation and the overt requirement on the Cabinet table to balance programmes against resources achieves this.

74. There is always the written Treasury answer, written by the head of a Supply division in the 1960 discussions:

> there is an answer - a strong Chancellor with the highest batting average in the Cabinet, strongly supported, above and below.

So may the files of the Florentine Signory in the early sixteenth century have contained little notes in the margin signed 'N. M.' saying: 'What we really need is a new Prince.'

75. But I am sure that no former Chancellor of the Exchequer will take umbrage when I say that not all Chancellors are Princes. Indeed, for a Chancellor to make the sustained contribution to the public expenditure problem that is needed to offset the built-in forces against him, two overriding qualities are called for:

both   (i) to regard long-term public expenditure control as being equally important to the Chancellor's other tasks – the short-term management of the economy, overseas finance and sterling, taxation, inflation, etc.;

and   (ii) powerful political standing, and the continuous support of the Prime Minister.

Some have (i), and some have (ii); but only rarely can Chancellors have both at the same time. In the 29 years from Dr Dalton in 1945 to Mr Barber in 1974, there were twelve Chancellors (excluding Mr McLeod): it would be difficult to argue that in more than seven of these years were both conditions (i) and (ii) satisfied. If this assessment is accepted, and if this generation's experience is regarded as representative, progress is likely to be made in only one year in every four; and 'progress' will normally be to offset some of the setbacks of the previous three years, so that we continue to slip downward.

76. In my opinion in retrospect, the Plowden Committee was certainly right in wanting to take some institutional action to tilt the balance in the Chancellor's favour. I think that the second Treasury Cabinet Minister is valuable; and I would favour further experimentation with the Public Expenditure Committee idea (possibly a standing committee of two or three plus the Treasury Cabinet Ministers, chosen for seniority – including former Chancellors if any; to consider big single expenditure issues, such as Concorde, the Channel Tunnel, Maplin in early 1974, as well as the PESC appraisals). If the opinion is held that the Government's long-term expenditure strategy and its relation to resources is so politically sensitive that it cannot be considered by any Ministerial body junior to the Cabinet, I would propose that Prime Ministers should make this one of their major preoccupations, in which they would be mastering the detail and operating themselves, in very much the same way as Mr Eden, Mr Macmillan and Mr Wilson identified themselves with and bore much of the working load on matters of foreign and commonwealth policy. The combination of the Prime Minister (or First Lord of the Treasury) and the Chancellor of the Exchequer is the only one with the political muscle to hold these weighty and slippery subjects in a firm grip.[7]

77. *Long-term Appraisals.* As soon as the Committee began to see these appraisals of expenditure and resources as its main technical desideratum, attention centred on the practical considerations; for (as subsequent appraisal showed all too clearly) a bad or misleading appraisal would be

worse than none at all. In the early days of the Committee, the Treasury had difficulty in seeing a way through the practical problems; but at the end of February it crossed the Rubicon, and produced for the Committee a cautious but entirely positive paper, which provided the basis for the next phase of work.

78. The emphasis was on 'appraisals' and 'surveys', and not at this stage on the creation of new administrative control systems for public expenditure. The concept was to get a background to decisions five years ahead – a gradually developing frame of reference into which specific problems for decision could be fitted as and when the decisions had to be taken. If such a background could be provided; Ministers when confronted with a new spending programme involving rising expenditure over the years – an expansion of teacher training, a hospital building programme, a new military aircraft, a nuclear power development – would at the same time have a rational guide to whether the nation would be able to afford it when the heavy spending got under way, and what the implications might be. This seems far away from the PESC operations of the mid-1970s, but it was the point of departure.

79. Alongside this was the development of well-thought-out long-term programmes for the big spending departments – the equivalent for education, health, etc., of the defence and public sector investment 'forward looks'. This was seen as desirable in its own right; and the dimensions of all these 'forward look' long-term programmes would be related together (and to prospective resources) by the expenditure/resources appraisals. The Treasury regarded the speed with which effective 'forward look' programmes could be worked out and discussed with the Treasury as a major limitation on the whole operation; and proposed to take as the first step:
  (i)   public sector investment;
  (ii) defence, together with economic aid and other expenditure on security and support of foreign policy;
  (iii) education; ⎫ in alternate years, local govern-
  (iv) National Health Service. ⎬ ment current expenditure as a
                                   ⎭ whole
These totalled 85 per cent of public sector expenditure on goods and services.

80. There would then be a continuous cycle (rolling forward a year at a time) with the 'forward look' programmes discussed by the departments and the Treasury in May–July; and then the expenditure/resources appraisals in autumn, if necessary amending the programmes; and then the new 'forward looks' (consistent with the amendments) next spring, and so on. Other 'forward looks' would be brought in as soon as solid

programmes had been worked out; but the Treasury wanted to limit the operation to the big programmes. With more programmes, there would be no significant improvement in the quality of the expenditure/resources appraisal – basing it on 90 per cent of expenditure is hardly better than 85 per cent; and the ability of Ministers and officials to grasp them simultaneously, and the quality of the work on them would be much reduced (as the German proverb says, 'The devil is in the detail'). But these doctrines ran into difficulty later.

81. It was decided that the expenditure/resources appraisal should be conducted in terms of national income analysis at constant value of money and not in terms of Government revenue. Projections of revenue would have to be derived from national income analysis in any case (with further vagaries in the translation); and taxation is a 'money' concept and not a 'physical' concept. But the greater difficulty was the Chancellor of the Exchequer's fear that his independence in deciding tax policy would be weakened; and the practical fact that the simultaneous use of taxation for short-term management of the economy and for social policy means that any conclusion from the appraisal in terms of tax rates would be vulnerable. This decision was certainly correct at the time; but the experience has been that the only really effective political argument against an increase of public expenditure is the impact on the taxes, and these are the terms in which the alternatives before Ministers have to be expressed.[8]

82. As we have seen in para 65, the resources side of the appraisal was not regarded as presenting formidable problems. With the 1957 and 1958 Long-term Economic Assessments, and the 1959 Long-term Resources Review just completed, in which the prospects of economic growth had been reassessed favourably,[9] it was thought that the ground had been cleared well enough, and the experts were cautiously confident.

83. Transfer payments – social security pensions and benefits, launching aid for civil aircraft, agricultural and industrial subsidies and grants, debt interest, etc. – were not included. Except for social security, these were clearly not predictable five years ahead. Social security payments have always been a subject for long-term planning, but it had not yet been decided how best to fit them into this resources analysis (a problem that would recur).

84. In retrospect, one can detect most of the future elements of PESC (and of the 1970 PAR as well). There were two closely linked objectives – the first, to get much better articulated departmental programmes with clearer priorities and sharper planning (the objective of the 'forward looks'; and the second, to build an apparatus which would sound the alarm

and provide a basis for action, if the growth of public expenditure was likely to outrun future resources. The existence of good long-term programmes was obviously a precondition, for without this there could be no meaningful appraisal of how expenditure was likely to develop. Great weight was therefore placed on the educational work that would be required to get a full understanding in the departments of the new concepts involved in these operations; and it was always true that the limitation on their successful introduction and development was the rate at which this understanding could grow.

85. One gets the impression, fifteen years later, that the Treasury was underestimating the momentum of growth of public expenditure implicit in the policies which the Government was developing; and was framing a system which was designed to make moderate adjustments in programmes, continuously over a long period of time, rather than to prepare the way for a major surgical operation – but this was still in the future.

86. The Committee made a wrong judgement on one point, which was its conclusion that Ministers would be unwilling to publish the expenditure/ resources appraisals; for this would involve disclosing the Government's future intentions (e. g. on pensions) and expectations (e. g. on wages, employment, etc). However, first Mr Maudling in December 1963 [Cmnd 2235] and then Mr Callaghan in February 1966 [Cmnd 2915] decided to publish; and after then a regular annual series started, beginning in 1969 [Cmnd 4234]. It must be recalled, however, that those that set the pattern were in the period here called 'anti-PESC', in which the expenditure projections were matched with a 'target' rate of growth of resources, to which the Chancellors were irrevocably committed with their Governments, but which were far above the rates of growth which would have been judged reasonable on a realistic assessment; and this removed the obstacles to publication which were in the Committee's mind. Nevertheless, in my opinion, both at the time and in retrospect, both Chancellors were right in proceeding with publication, for it was right to begin to acquaint Parliament and the public with the dimensions of public expenditure, and with the necessity that programmes and promises should be matched with future resources.

87. *Stability of Expenditure Policy.* The views expressed in para 58 show the expenditure controllers' hostility to 'stop-and-go', for it frustrated the planning of departmental programmes and reduced value for money. Moreover, it was believed to be counter-productive in terms of its own objectives: the chain of command from the Cabinet to the building site in departments, local authorities and nationalised industries was at least six to nine months, so that in the two-year cycle which was typical of the 1950s the attempt to stimulate or dampen down spending was likely to take effect

at just the time when the tide was turning.[10] But this was never readily accepted by those who were responsible for the short-term management of the economy, whose instruments were inadequate for carrying out their task within the tolerances which had been prescribed; and the idea of varying public expenditure (particularly investment, which is the slowest to react) had a respectable parentage going back to the 1909 Minority Report on the Poor Law and the 1944 Full Employment White Paper (for the old trade cycle of double the length); and the 'rational' view could not be expected to carry great weight.

88. The Committee recommended that a list of 'fast-moving' items should be selected, and that nationalised industries should have some margin in their programmes, to be used (or to remain unused) for this purpose. It is probably true to say that over the years the short-term operations have been improved accordingly: Sir Samuel Goldman[11] is of the opinion that the scope for conjunctural variation of departmental expenditure, if planned effectively in advance and not as an emergency response to sudden 'stop-and-go' decisions, is larger than had been believed at the time of the Plowden Committee. If Sir Samuel is right, this would indicate considerable progress in the last fifteen years in departments' control and management of their programmes, not only in this respect but in general, and this could certainly be regarded as a success for the objectives of the Committee.

89. *Improved Tools and Quantitative Methods.* The Committee advocated more widespread use of quantitative methods for dealing with public sector expenditure, which was hitherto singularly lacking; and this has had a considerable response. The annual Public Expenditure White Papers covering the next five years; and the Methodology Handbook;[12] and the material given in Sir Samuel Goldman's book[13] and its appendixes speak for the existence of a powerful statistical apparatus behind them, all of which has been created in this period, and all integral to the PESC operations in their mid-1970s form.

90. From the earlier years, however, I would mention two quantitative innovations, which had major (perhaps even decisive) effects on important Government decisions. One was the development by the Ministry of Defence in the early 1960s (closely related to Mr McNamara's reforms at the Pentagon) of the system of functional costing, dividing the whole defence expenditure into 700 functional or programme elements, which could be used as a new kind of building-block, to permit the costing of the whole defence effort by function, or by mission or by geographical area. This provided the technical apparatus (which had never existed before) to guide the 'East of Suez' policy decisions in the mid-1960s. In my opinion, the fact that the Ministry of Defence was the first department to develop its

own statistical and financial techniques to guide its decision-making (years before Health and Education) may be related to the fact that it was the first department, several years earlier, to develop the 'forward look', and to organise itself rigorously to think out its expenditure strategy.

91. The other was the appraisal system for new investments developed by the Treasury in the early 1960s for the application of 'discounted cash flow' and related techniques which were coming into use in industry. Other departments developed this for their purposes, and of particular importance was the work of the Ministry of Aviation (and then Technology) on the most difficult of all kinds of evaluation – that of civil aircraft projects, with their huge time-scale; and continuous technological and commercial uncertainties. In the end, there is bound to be a broad judgement taken. But when a decision has to be taken between some people whose 'broad judgement' on an aircraft project will always be 'Yes', and others whose 'broad judgement' will always be 'No', the most rigorous analysis of the aircraft's prospects must be helpful, and this appraisal system broke new ground.

92. *Estimates and Accounts.* The Committee endorsed the Treasury's project for the first reform of the Form of Estimates since they began in the late 1860s. The proposal was a major simplification, involving a saving of about-two thirds in space for the Civil Estimates (so that they could all be accommodated in one volume) and about 40 per cent in the number of sub-heads. A corresponding reduction was made in the Defence Estimates. This was worth doing, and it is relevant to note that there was not a single question raised, from Parliament (after the Estimates Committee's agreement) or from public opinion, about any part of the vast masses of demolished detail, although every item of this had at some previous time been insisted upon as essential.[14] However, ten years later the detail had begun to grow again, and the Treasury is considering another reform.[15]

93. The Committee attached weight, also, to the reform of the Form of Accounts, to remove the misunderstandings about the 'line' once and for all; to enable the Exchequer Accounts to be related to the accounts of other public authorities (to make Public Sector Accounts) and to the national income and expenditure accounts; and to achieve a simplification. This proved more complicated than the Form of Estimates, but a series of major reforms were made, beginning with the Financial Statement of 1965, and the basis is now clear. In this, as in the Form of Estimates, it cannot be said that the changes have had a revolutionary effect: but misunderstandings that used to be important (and sometimes damaging) no longer occur.

94. One part of the Committee's decisions which now seems less controversial than it did at the time was its endorsement of the cash system

of accounts.[16] This, following the report of the Crick Committee in 1950, may be said in retrospect to have closed a controversy which had been active from time to time since the accountants brought into Government service in the First World War pressed hard for the introduction of commercial accounting; and under the influence of the adoption of separate capital budgets in some other countries. Fashions change and the accountants now attach much more importance to cash flow than used to be the commercial practice. In the public service, experience has shown conclusively in my opinion that apart from trading and quasi-trading activities (which can always show separate trading accounts, and which are increasingly hived off from departmental control), the cash basis is the most realistic as well as possessing its traditional merit of being much the easiest for accountability: the distinction between 'current' and 'capital' in defence and social services, where there is no clearly measurable 'output' can only be arbitrary when measured in financial terms.[17]

95. *The Treasury and the Departments.* The second half of the work of the Committee, through the autumn and winter of 1960–61, was no less important than the first in many respects, though it is much less tangible. This was the problem of the relation between the Treasury and the departments, and the role of management in the civil service [Part II of the published report]. For the development of PESC this was fundamental, for the change in the concept of public expenditure from thousands of individual transactions to 'expenditure as a whole' and allocation of resources on long-term programmes carries with it wide implications for the relations between the Treasury and the departments.

96. This aspect of the Committee's proposals has had less acclaim than the 'regular surveys of public expenditure as a whole, over a period of years ahead, and in relation to prospective resources'; but the conclusion that:

34. The relationship between the departments and the Treasury should be one of joint working together in a common enterprise: it should be considered not in terms of more or less 'independence' of departments from 'control' by the Treasury, but rather in terms of getting the right balance and differentiation of function . . .

is hardly less striking, especially when followed up, as it was, by a clear series of statements of these distinct functions:

35. The primary responsibility of a Department is to conduct its policy effectively within the limits laid down by the Government. The Department is itself responsible for the efficiency with which it does its work: the Permanent Secretary, as Accounting Officer, is responsible for the financial management. It is important that these responsibilities should be clearly understood, fully accepted, and reflected in the Department's relations with the Treasury.

36. The Treasury is the Department with the central responsibility for

economic and financial policy, the custodian of the Exchequer, and the authority for Civil Service and establishment matters. It bears the responsibility:

(a) for allocating the amount of money and economic resources to be made available for each purpose to each Department;

(b) for advising the Departments on economic and financial matters, and for assisting them to maintain proper practice in the expenditure of public money;

(c) for the overall efficiency of the public service, and thus for seeing that the Departments are staffed, particularly at the top levels, with the best available officers drawn from the Service as a whole;

(d) for the development of management services throughout the public service; for taking the initiative in the introduction of new management techniques; and for keeping an oversight over the management practice of all the Departments;

(e) for the settlement of pay and conditions of service, and grading of staff throughout the Service.

It is important that these responsibilities of the Treasury, like those of the Departments, should be clearly understood, fully accepted, and reflected in the Treasury's relations with the Departments.

97. This layout throws light on a paradox of the time, that some departments criticised the Treasury[18] for intervening too much, and some for intervening too little. This did not show that the Treasury was doing just right: it was interfering too much in the field of departments' responsibility, and not doing enough in its own field of responsibility. The traditional decentralised system of expenditure control tended to push it this way; for the working relationship between the Treasury and a department was conducted by a Treasury man who was normally concerned wholly with that department; so that the subject of the dialogue would be the department's activity, and not what the Treasury's wider outlook and knowledge could contribute to it. Progress was made during the Committee's discussions (e.g. in extending departments' delegated powers) as far as departments could be persuaded to seek it – it is always easier for a Finance Officer to tell an operating division, 'I'm certain the Treasury wouldn't agree' than to say 'No': and it is always easier for the Treasury to go on asking more and more detailed questions about a project than to think how it would really impinge on the national economy, and whether the return is worthwhile.

98. One cannot say how far this part of the Committee's work was successful. Following the Committee's recommendation [para 59 of the published report] there was a major reorganisation of the Treasury announced in July 1962, with Sir Laurence Helsby and Sir William Armstrong made joint permanent secretaries on the management and

financial/economic sides respectively – the biggest reorganisation since 1919, planned to enable the Treasury to carry out effectively the functions laid down by the Plowden Committee and the new tasks for the chief economic department involved in the 'interventionist' Government policies that were getting under way ('Neddy', incomes policy, etc.). The reorganisation was a formidable task (and an interesting subject in itself, for it involved linking together responsibilities for the short-term and long-term development of the national economy, the control of public sector expenditure, home and overseas finance, and the management of the civil service) but the reorganised Treasury had only a two-years' run, before being split up in November 1964 for the creation of the Department of Economic Affairs; and then again in 1968 for the separation of the Civil Service Department. When DEA was abolished in October 1969, some was redistributed to the Treasury; but by this time the Treasury was developing anew.

99. If the reorganised 1962 Treasury had been allowed to continue through the 1960s and early 1970s unchanged, would the nation's economic performance have been better? This is a question worth pondering. Is the large effort deployed on machinery of government and departmental organisation, both by Ministers and by top officials, to be regarded as wasted, or at best of marginal importance?

100. After all these changes, the state of the relations between the Treasury and the departments and between the Civil Service Department and the departments is outside my experience and the scope of this paper. These two sets of relationships will inevitably become distinct. In the early years after the fission, the Civil Service Department was very much like the old management side of the Treasury (same people and same offices), and as the two sides of the Treasury had never been very closely integrated, Whitehall could see little difference. But this was bound to change in time; and the two departments are now housed at the opposite ends of Whitehall, with independently constituted staffs; and a time will come (it may have come already) when the two will be thought of as being quite separate, with different images and different networks of relationships.

101. It will then in practical terms be necessary to go back to the 1961 Treasury's functions as listed above in paragraph 35 of the published Plowden report, and see how these are divided between the Treasury and the Civil Service Department. Perhaps the most important role of the central department(s) of government is to satisfy itself that the departments are working well and efficiently, particularly in their deployment and use of resources, in their financial control systems, and in their relations with outside bodies (such as local government, nationalised industry, and indeed their contacts with the private sector). The virtue of

handling men and management and money together is that the knowledge and contact with departments' performance can come through the 'money' channel – it is the dialogue between the Treasury and an operating department which gives the clear impression of how the department is performing – as well as through the much narrower and less significant dialogue with the Civil Service Department.

102. With divided responsibility at the centre (divided in fact as well as in form) how effectively will the central role of appraising departments' performance and efficiency be carred out?[19] This does not necessarily imply that the decision to create a separate Civil Service Department was mistaken, for there were many considerations to be taken into account: what is odd is that there is no evidence in the Fulton Report that this vital issue of the central management of government was considered when the Committee made its recommendation; and there was hardly any mention of it (except for some admirable articles in *The Times* by Peter Jay) in the public discussion which preceded and followed it. This again has a bearing on my earlier comment doubting the efficacy and desirability of changes in the machinery of government except after very lengthy and well-informed consideration. To the extent that there was merit in the long deliberation and recommendations of the Plowden Committee on the relations between the Treasury and departments (or, if one prefers it, the centre and the periphery), which were fundamental to its proposals for management and control of public expenditure, it cannot be said that this has been absorbed into the governmental system.

103. *Permanent Secretaries' Responsibilities.* The emphasis on 'management' in the report, however, may be said to have had effective results; for this has been a great theme of the 1960s and 1970s. The recommendation that permanent secretaries should regard management as a part of their responsibilities, equal in importance to policy advice to their Ministers on the one hand and finance on the other, would now be almost universally regarded as axiomatic; and to the permanent secretaries of the very large departments which came into being in the last ten years, management is clearly the first task. The contribution of the Committee was less, in my view, in its insistence on the importance of management (and management services) than in its firm expression of opinion on the priorities in the use of a permanent secretary's time between this and the traditional re- sponsibilities for policy advice and finance.

104. *Enquiry Technique.* It is generally accepted that the Plowden Com- mittee, rare among public committees, did succeed in pointing out a new course in an important field of public affairs, which has been followed by a succession of governments and has become part of the structure of public administration; and it has often been asked how far its composition and

method of working contributed to its success, and therefore whether such a formula – an internal enquiry by a mixed group of outside people and civil service assessers, working primarily by discussion with permanent secretaries, with confidential reports to the responsible Minister – could be used with good prospects in other cases.

105. Another occasion on which an analogous technique was used, with results of similar long-term importance was the wartime Beveridge Report on the reconstruction of the social services, an enquiry carried out by Sir William Beveridge (as he then was) with a group of civil service assessers.

106. These enquiries had three points in common:
  (i)   they dealt with practical questions, in which the requirement was to find a course of action that would break through an administrative tangle – not the usual kind of 'Royal Commission' subject in which the purpose is to ascertain and weigh the views of many different interests and sections of the community;
  (ii) the enquiry was conducted by a man of great standing and authority and with deep knowledge and experience of the subject-matter: Lord Plowden's position about governnment was unique in these respects;
  (iii) the civil service assessers wanted to get positive answers; and so the enquiries could formulate recommendations which (if accepted) could lead at once to Government action. When individuals (or small committees) have been asked to conduct enquiries on their own, without civil servants participating, they have often found difficulty at this last, but most important, stage.

107. In these conditions, the combination of distinguished independent people and civil service assessers has been shown to be potentially powerful. The conditions do not come together very often; and the opportunities are therefore few. But the conclusion that I draw from the experience is that when an opportunity does arise for using this technique of enquiry it should not be missed.

NOTES

1. A fourth was subsequently added in the published report, reflecting the next phase of the Committee's work; calling for improvements in the tools for measuring and handling public expenditure problems.
2. In the published report it was put last, because only a summary of the advice given to the Chancellor could be made public at that stage.
3. Only the senior citizens can now remember that in 1931 what was essentially a balance of payments and sterling problem was presented to successive Cabinets

as a public expenditure problem, with the solutions focusing on the unemployed and on public sector employees' pay, endorsed by an unprecedented election majority.

4. H. Heclo and A. Wildavsky, in their otherwise well-informed book *The Private Government of Public Money* (Macmillan, 1974) state erroneously (pages 184–7) that the Committee recommended that the group should consist of nonspending Ministers.

5. 'It meant you did not have a friend! Then the thing would get to Cabinet and the supposedly objective Ministers would not hear of any alteration . . .' (op. cit., p. 187).

6. Sir Samuel Goldman, *Public Expenditure Management and Control* (HMSO, 1973) p. 11.

7. See also para 401 where a rather different view is expressed[Ed.].

8. See my article on 'Long-Term Planning of Taxation', in *Taxation Policy*, edited by Crick and Robson (Pelican, 1973). The size of the figures in national income analysis, and the remoteness of the concepts from day-to-day experience neutralises them.

9. The conclusion was that to postulate an annual rate of long-term growth of GDP per worker of less than 2 per cent (GDP 2¼ per cent) might turn out to be unduly cautious: whilst to base Government action on an annual increase per worker of more than 3 per cent (GDP 3¾) might well turn out to be inflationary. In fact, the average annual increase of GDP in 1958–63 was 3.4 per cent; in 1959–64 3.7 per cent, bumping along the top of the range in the Review.

10. See *Public Investment in Great Britain*, Cmnd 1203 (Nov 1960) paras 9 and 10.

11. Op. cit., p. 54.

12. *Public Expenditure White Papers: Handbook on Methodology* (HMSO, 1972).

13. Op. cit., 37–40 and 61–89.

14. The Committee also made recommendations on other technical questions of Parliamentary control, which resulted in simplifications.

15. Sir Samuel Goldman, op. cit., p. 38. [The projected reform was brought into effect in the 1974–75 Estimates and passed virtually unnoticed, partly because of the general election in March. It rearranged the whole of the Civil Estimates on the basis of the same set of sixteen main programmes as were adopted for the White Paper (Cmnd 5519) in December 1973. The reform of the Estimates on this functional principle was carried through to the components of the main programmes also. As a result comparison can now be made directly between the Estimates and the White Paper. Ed.].

16. When I joined the Treasury in 1945, and had my introductory interview with the Permanent Secretary, Sir Richard Hopkins (memorable particularly for his epic struggle with Maynard Keynes before the Macmillan Commission in 1930) told me, 'You'll find our accounting system very easy: it's just like a schoolboy's cash book (producing one from his pocket): you put the money coming in on one side, and the money you pay out on the other; and then add up each side'.

17. It is by no means obvious why the building of schools should be 'capital' while the training of teachers is 'current' – the human capital is just as important for the educational 'output', and lasts as long as the building.

18. In 1961, 'the Treasury' covered the field now covered by both the Treasury and the Civil Service Department. The financial/economic and the establish-

ment sides of the Treasury tended to be run in separate compartments, but the criticisms generally applied to both alike. The establishment side had to insist upon a greater uniformity, because pay and conditions and grading had to be standardised throughout the civil service.

19. This was one of the considerations that led me, *New Trends in Government* (HMSO, 1971), to speculate (pp. 62-71) whether a new rearrangement of the departments at the centre might become necessary: four years later, this is still an open question, though there may well be other solutions than those that were there discussed.

4 The Initial Operations: 1960-62

108. While the Plowden Committee's interim reports had been going through their final stages in the early summer of 1960, the next steps were being developed. There were three essential things to be done:
  (1) to make a statistical apparatus for the 'Plowden' operations – definitions, classification, accounting conventions – and find the people to do it;
  (2) to educate the departments in the concepts of the new system, and to persuade them of its value – without this, it was impossible to imagine carrying out operations of the seriousness and complexity that were envisaged;
  (3) most important of all, to persuade Ministers to accept the implications of the new system – the prospectus was straight common sense, which nobody could sensibly resist, but the implementation was certain to be full of difficulty, and probably disadvantageous for the interests of some Ministers.

109. *Definitions.* It was decided at the beginning to have a wide definition of 'public expenditure' – all the expenditure of central government, above and below 'the line', current and capital expenditure of local authorities, gross outgoings of the national insurance funds, the capital expenditure of nationalised industries and other public corporations. This was to be a consolidated statement, in which grants and loans within the public sector appeared only once, referred to the substantive expenditure and not to financing: local authorities' education expenditure shown, and not central government grants; nationalised industries' capital expenditure, and not Exchequer loans.

110. This 'wide' expenditure definition was adopted in order to avoid any danger that questions of expenditure would be turned into questions of financing (so avoiding the crucial issue of the reasons for the expenditure). This of course implied that on the corresponding receipts side, taxes and local rates and national insurance contributions and nationalised in-dustries' surplus would be brought into account. In fact the definition could have been made a little wider, if for example health expenditure had been struck gross of prescription charges, or law court expenditure gross of

fees, and so on: but the income from these charges could not in practice be regarded as analogous to taxes, so the net figures were taken. In general, the lines were drawn according to administrative sense.[1]

111. It is necessary for the aggregate to be equal to the total of public expenditure in the National Accounts in order to permit an easy translation from one to the other, and with a few minor exceptions, well known to the experts, this is so. This constraint determined the inclusion of certain items of expenditure (e.g. central and local government debt interest) which proved extremely difficult to handle and sometimes had to be dropped. Another difficult item was nationalised industries' capital expenditure: at the beginning this was included with schools and hospitals as 'public investment'; then separated, on the grounds that the criteria should be entirely different (and control exercised differently) if they were running as commercial enterprises; and in the 1970s, with the abandonment of commercial criteria for most of them, it has been reasonable to bring them back again into the public expenditure competition for resources. In this and other matters, the treatment of individual items has changed since 1960, but the definition has stood up to experience.

112. *Public Expenditure Panorama.* All these forms of public expenditure had to be brought together from diverse sources; and the most important single issue was how this should be classified. For operational purposes, it had to be divided into blocks which made political common sense, and which, generally speaking, represented one department's expenditure (or two, including Scotland). At that time, this aggregation of public expenditure was uncharted territory: David Burdett, the talented and original Treasury statistician who broke this new ground, and whose tragic death a few years later was a terrible blow to this work, called it the Public Expenditure Panorama; and those of us who were engaged in it at the time can still remember the excitement of seeing the first map of this new world which we were seeking to reduce to order.

113. At that time expenditure was divided into eighteen blocks as shown in the following pages.

114. Each of these eighteen blocks was subdivided, and the total number of subdivisions was about 80. With the passing of time, there have been additions and rearrangements, and the corresponding number of 'main programmes' is now sixteen (including debt interest), and nearly 200 'subprogrammes' are distinguished in the returns. The most important change has been the distribution of 'other civil public investment' (C2, housing, hospitals, roads, etc.) among the functional programmes, so that schoolbuilding is treated as part of 'education' and not as 'investment': the previous treatment was of course derived from the existence of a civil investment 'forward look', and the change was a great improvement, for it

	Total public expenditure, 1959–60 (£ million)	Expenditure on Votes, 1959–60 (£ million)
I SUPPORT OF EXTERNAL POLICY		
A Defence (defence budget, civil defence, strategic stocks)	1506	1534
B Civil operations overseas (diplomatic administration, information, aid programme, international subscriptions)	199	135
II CIVIL INVESTMENT*		
C 1 Fixed investment of public enterprises	912	28
C 2 Other civil public investment	677	150
	1589	178
III OTHER CIVIL EXPENDITURE		
D Industry and transport (assistance and loans to industry; BTC and civil airports deficits, etc.)	118	28
E Agriculture (including fisheries and forestry)	289	281
F Civil science (AEA, research councils, etc.)	115	74
G Arts (museums, libraries etc.)	22	6
H General and rate deficiency grants to local authorities	–	512
I Education (including universities)	730	82
J Health and welfare (NHS, local services, child care, welfare foods, school meals and milk)	885	627
K Other local services (housing subsidies, water and sewerage, road maintenance, parks, etc., local administration)	489	148
L Law and order (Parliament, justice, police, prisons)	148	78
M Benefits and assistance (national insurance and assistance, family allowances, etc.)	1351	567

* Investment included in C1 and C2 and not in individual blocks.

Table continued

	Total public expenditure, 1959–60 (£million)	Expenditure on Votes, 1959–60 (£million)
N Central administration (includes accommodation, stationery etc.)	318	248
IV DEBT INTEREST		
O 1 Central Government (payments less receipts)	518	
O 2 Local authorities	268	
O 3 Nationalised industries, etc.	275	
	1061	
V MISCELLANEOUS		
P 3 Northern Ireland	116	
P 1, 2, 4–9 Miscellaneous services (post-war credits, BBC, repayment of debt to overseas governments, etc.)	179	32
Q Cost adjustment		
R Statistical adjustments	35	
GRAND TOTAL	9150	4530

was clearly right to make e.g. school-building compete for resources against teacher-training and university grants instead of against roads or housing (a competition which could make sense only if the scarce factor of production was not economic and financial resources generally, but building capacity, which could hardly be so for more than a short period – shorter indeed than the time taken to plan the buildings). This change removed a continuous source of misunderstanding, and indeed a red herring that was often introduced into Ministerial arguments.

115. In substance, the important fact that appeared from this classification (particularly when the social capital investment was added in with the social current expenditure) was the significance of a very few large programmes. The biggest for 1959–60 was defence (A: £1506 million); with benefits and assistance (M: £1351 million) just behind. There were four programmes around £1000 million: education (I); health and welfare (J); housing and other local services (K, which then included roads); investment of public enterprises (C1). These were about five-sixths of the Great Britain total, apart from debt interest. The next items in the list were around £300 million each – agriculture, costs of central administration, civil operations overseas. And so down to the small items.

116. As soon as the classification of public expenditure had been well done, giving an entirely different picture from that of expenditure on Votes, it became clear that the ability to contain the growth of public expenditure and to relate it to resources would depend upon (i) the ability to limit the expansion of these large programmes and (ii) to prevent the emergence of other expenditure programmes to this size. Throughout the 1960s, after the rundown of the 1950s, the defence budget was contained; and the investment of nationalised industries remained within the rate of growth of GNP. The driving force to increase public expenditure was therefore provided by the big social and environmental services, all of which expanded much faster than resources; and in addition in the second half of the 1960s there was the great expansion of regional grants and other industrial and employment expenditures (including Concorde) which rose to considerable dimensions (and outstripped support for agriculture, which in real terms remained very stable throughout the period). The point to emphasise here, however, is not what actually happened, but the fact that for the first time it had become possible to identify the areas which would be decisive – the large numbers; and these were the areas where successive Chancellors of the Exchequer and Chief Secretaries were subsequently continuously engaged.

117. *Economic Impact.* The classification was set up so that it could readily be converted into the 'economic classification', which divides the expenditures into the 'economic' categories of the national income and expenditure accounts. The purpose was to use the data for the forecasts made for the short-term management of the national economy; and estimates were made of the impact of each kind of expenditure upon the immediate demand for resources. For example, it was reckoned that 80 per cent of grants to persons (e.g. pensions) would immediately result in demand on resources, whilst 90 per cent of current expenditure on goods and services (other than wages and salaries) and 93 per cent of investment expenditure would so result.[2] In each package of expenditure changes it was therefore possible to estimate what would be the effect upon the demand for resources as a whole – about 85 per cent of total public expenditure might be expected to have an immediate impact on demand; so that expenditure cuts of £100 million might consequently reduce demand by £85 million, or in order to get an impact of £100 million on demand, cuts in expenditure of £118 million would be required. The sophistication of these calculations illustrates the importance which economists have attached throughout to the problems of short-term demand management; with results over twenty years which can only be described as disappointing.[3]

118. At the beginning of PESC, the economic impact of different elements of public expenditure was seen more in terms of the growth of resources. The investment of nationalised industries was clearly economic-

orientated. A powerful case of economic benefit could be made for roads
and indeed for most of the social infrastructure. The place of education and
health in this spectrum was difficult to determine, for although there
are national economic benefits to be derived from both these services, these
are very long-term, and the structure of these services may easily result in a
negative national economic return. Assistance to industry and agriculture
is likewise a mixture of beneficial and damaging effects upon the national
economy. At the bottom of the spectrum were defence, and overseas aid
and administration, where the public expenditure impacts immediately on
the balance of payments.

119. At the root of the thought on this matter is concern whether public
expenditure, which absorbs a very large part of the country's economic
resources, tends to increase the output from these resources or to reduce it.
Some expenditures are favourable to the growth of resources and some are
unfavourable; but for about two-thirds of the total of public expenditure,
no real judgement can be made on whether it is better for the growth of
productivity and the national economy for the public services to be
developed in one direction or another. The variety of impacts of public
expenditures upon the supply of resources (and thus upon income) is
certainly much greater than the variety of impacts upon the demand for
resources. The fact that much more effort has been devoted to the latter
than to the former in the last twenty years illustrates how the 'macro'
problems of short-term demand management have dominated the economic scene at the expense of the 'micro' problems of the most efficient use of
economic resources.

120. *Revenue and Resources.* For reasons already described, it was decided to
relate prospective expenditure to resources in terms of the national income
and expenditure accounts. However, it must always be recognised that
taxes are the political counterpart to expenditure, and the table on page 47
showing the sources of revenue in 1960–61 matches the 'panoramic'
expenditure table.

121. This 'panoramic' table of revenue brings out clearly why it was
necessary to handle the material in terms of 'resources', not 'revenue'. Such
a table explains at a glance the great importance, in relation to taxes and
local rates, of national insurance contributions, nationalised industries'
trading surpluses, and local authority rents – these three lines in the table
add up to £2050 million, or nearly one-third of taxes and local rates. But
the difficulty would always have been to establish how much borrowing
from outside the public sector would be possible and desirable; for if the
Chancellor could not establish a maximum borrowing figure for the years
ahead, and get his colleagues' agreement to it, he would be unable to tie
the expenditure estimates to their tax implications. Indeed, the need to

	Sources of Revenue 1960 – 61 (£ million)		
	Central government	Local authorities	Public corporations
Taxes	5823	—	—
National insurance contributions	894	—	—
Local rates	—	780	—
Trading surpluses	113	45	560
Rental income	68	370	
Dividends and interest	36	32	65
	6934	1227	625
Borrowing from outside public sector	465	409	– 2
TOTAL	7399	1636	623
GRAND TOTAL		£9658 m.	

demonstrate a maximum borrowing figure would have come back again to the national income and expenditure accounts.

122. Nevertheless, more work in this field might have eased some of these problems of bringing the tax consequences of expenditure policy more into the foreground; and might have helped to relieve the Chancellor's dilemma between the risk, if he brings taxation policy into the Ministerial arena, of losing control over it, and the risk on the other hand of failing to get the right public expenditure decisions because he cannot expound the taxation implications in convincing detail.

123. *Three Years or Four or Five?* The idea of a five-year programme followed naturally from the previous 'forward looks' on defence, public investment, etc.; and hardly any thought was taken about what was the best practical period to take. If the matter had been argued out at the beginning, a shorter period might have been found better.

124. First, from Ministers' point of view, five years is a very long time, always after the next election, somewhat unreal except for the political optimists who would bank on having two terms. When Ministers are asked to take difficult decisions (and all public expenditure decisions are difficult), they must be related to a nearer crisis (or an earlier pay-off) than five years. In my opinion, this outrides any technical consideration.

125. Second, the size and composition of public expenditure can change

in significantly less than five years. Of course some elements need much more than five years to mature, particularly those which depend heavily on research and development and on capital expenditure. In 1960, 'the supersonic airliner' was already taking its place (but the cost at that time was thought of as around £100 million). The 'forward look' in defence increased fast from three to five to ten years. From the decisions to build new hospitals or teacher-training colleges to the impact upon the employment of more health and education staffs (this future current cost, not the capital cost, is what is important for public expenditure) is more than five years. For pensions, we must think in decades. It was the awareness of these time-scales that led to the adoption of a five-year period. But for most of these particular items, five years is too short: a four-year period might have been hardly less satisfactory for these, and easier to estimate and less unreal for the items with a shorter lead-time.

126. Third, in the national economy as we now have it, nobody can judge the fluctuations for more than a year or eighteen months ahead. For the PESC concept, the last years of the run must be 'neutral' years in terms of the immediate situation of the national economy, so that the resources estimates require neither an inflationary nor a deflationary operation by government. But the fourth year, and probably the third, satisfies this condition as well as the fifth.

127. Fourthly, a shorter period requires less paper at all stages in the operation; and more time in the departments, in the Treasury and in the Cabinet to examine the smaller amount of paper. The original intention was to have a major discussion between the Treasury and each department on its long-term programme before the latter were aggregated; but the scale of operation and the constraints of the timetable cut this much shorter than was desirable. Programmes with three or four years' figures instead of five might have made this easier.

128. Finally, these arguments require to be considered in relation to the purpose of the operation and the method of conducting it. At the Plowden Committee stage, the thought was in terms of relating the growth rate of public expenditure to the growth rate of resources; and the concept of a 'growth rate' involves a considerable period – certainly not less than four years: the purpose was to look well ahead. But as the operations developed, a programme pattern appeared in which expenditure would be rising fast from the first two or three years and then flattening out. This lacked credibility, so that the control operation had to be shortened, and the Treasury began to regard the third year as the crucial one, and to concentrate the operation on this: so the importance of the fourth and fifth years' figures inevitably declined, and there was a shift in the purpose as originally conceived.

129. If the original project had been framed for a four-year period (e.g. for the first report which was presented to Ministers in June 1961, covering the years 1961 - 62 to 1964 - 65 instead of including 1965 - 66) there could thus have been quite considerable practical advantages; and with a four-year programme, the task of making a credible path to the fourth year might have been accomplished without the anomalies which forced the Treasury to concentrate on the third year. In my opinion, a three-year programme would have been too short to implement the 'Plowden' concepts, but a four-year programme would have been better than a five-year programme. This is in the light of what actually happened; and I do not recall anyone proposing this at the time. It would have been necessary to reinforce a four-year programme with 'forward looks' going well beyond four years for those programmes which depended heavily upon research and development and upon capital expenditure and upon population growth; but a five-year programme requires this also. There are many time-scales in public expenditure; and universal four years' planning, with individual 'forward looks' for those, like defence and education, with longer time-scales, may be the best system.

NOTES

1. The up-to-date definitions are set out in *Public Expenditure White Papers: Handbook on Methodology* (HMSO, 1972).
2. *Methodology*, pp. 30 - 2.
3. See, for example, Sir William Armstrong's Stamp Memorial Lecture (1968).

5 The First PESC Report: 1960 – 61

130. *Ministerial Action.* Mr Selwyn Lloyd became Chancellor of the Exchequer in July 1960, arriving at the same time as the Plowden Committee's first set of interim reports. Mr Lloyd was probably unique among post-war Chancellors in bringing with him into office his own ideas about how to handle public expenditure: he favoured long-term planning of public expenditure and taxation, so found the Plowden Committee's advice welcome. He also wanted to simplify the Estimates and Accounts, and the Plowden Committee's advice fitted well with this. He wanted to create a single tax for companies, instead of income tax and profits tax, and set the studies on foot that led to Mr Callaghan's corporation tax in 1965; and he wanted to merge income tax and surtax, an extremely difficult reform to accomplish, ultimately done in Mr Barber's 1971 Budget. Mr Lloyd took the unpopular step of bringing the surtax threshold into line with the fall in the value of money, raising it from £2000 to £5000: he began the removal of Schedule A tax on resident owner-occupiers: he introduced the short-term capital gains tax. He introduced the 'regulator' to permit changes in indirect taxes between Budgets (and the abortive 'regulator' to change employers' insurance contributions, quickly abandoned).

131. Finally, Mr Lloyd set the pattern for Conservative and Labour Governments alike by the combination of incomes policy and the commitment to economic growth in discussion with industry ('Nicky' and 'Neddy', forerunners of many later organisations). These are remarkable and original achievements in two years as Chancellor of the Exchequer; and Mr Selwyn Lloyd has a strong claim to be regarded as the most innovative of the post-war Chancellors, and the first in the activist style of the 1960s.

132. The new Chancellor was confronted with an uneasy economic situation. The reflationary action of 1958 and 1959 was working its way into the system, and 'we are up against the old conundrum of how to achieve growth without inflation'. He was much impressed with the continuous bids for more Government spending, and soon identified this as

a crucial area. Meanwhile, the Treasury had been completing its first drafts of the five-year relationship between expenditure and resources, and was ready to go.

133. In the autumn, the Prime Minister set up a Ministerial group to help the Chancellor, on the lines proposed by the Plowden Committee. It was a group of three - one a big spender [Mr Brooke, Minister of Housing], one a second-level spender [Mr McLeod, Colonial Secretary] and one a non-spender [Mr Hare, Minister of Labour]. This group had several meetings around the turn of the year and had full discussions of the diagnosis and strategy submitted by the Treasury. They were not considering individual projects and programmes or interviewing other Ministers, but were applying themselves to the five-year prospective situation.

134. There followed a submission to the Cabinet by the Chancellor, with the outcome that the Treasury was instructed to work out, in collaboration with other departments, a public sector plan on the assumption that the ratio of public expenditure to GNP should remain at the then current level of 42.5 per cent, and to report on its implications for economic growth, taxation, and the balance-of-payments. This put the responsibility squarely on the Treasury to do what the Plowden Committee had said should be done; and although it did not represent a decision in favour of pegging the public expenditure/GNP ratio to 42.5 per cent, it made this the starting-point.

135. It would have been unreasonable for the Chancellor to have expected his colleagues to be more forthcoming at this stage; and the general opinion at this point was that the existence of the Ministerial group had been valuable in getting this positive reaction from the Cabinet. Mr Lloyd announced the decision to make this study in his Budget speech on 17 April:

Nowadays, all political parties are committed to a high and rising level of expenditure on education, public health and numerous other public services. But although this is accepted, public expenditure must not be allowed to outrun the prospective growth of our resources. It should not take too much of our resources from other forms of economic activity where growth is most likely to come. . . .

This calls for new methods. We need increasingly to look at all public expenditure together instead of piecemeal, and to look at it for a period of years in relation to prospective resources. I have recently set in hand a study of the whole problem of public expenditure in relation to the prospective future growth of our resources for a period of five years ahead. . . . The object . . . is to see how we can best keep public expenditure in future years in proper relationship to the growth of our national product.

136. *Public Expenditure Survey Committee.* The challenge was welcome to the Treasury, which saw its task as being to produce a realistic plan by a procedure which would involve the maximum practicable amount of participation by the rest of Whitehall, in order to spread the new style of thinking as widely as possible and to carry the responsible officials (Deputy-Secretaries and Under-Secretaries) in every department with us in the analysis of the whole situation and in the facts relating to their own work. So a Committee of 24 departments was set up (the original PESC), with special sub-groups for investment, defence, civil operations overseas, assistance to industry and agriculture, social services.

137. The Committee was set up early in April, and completed its report in June, covering the period 1961 - 62 to 1965 - 66: it was a report of some 20,000 words, deliberately made very full and comprehensive in order to ensure that the course of the argument, the nature of the estimates and the conclusions that could legitimately be drawn from them would be permanently available to all Ministers and officials concerned with this work. It was described as having been prepared by the Treasury - not agreed between the departments nor committing them, but prepared with their full knowledge and co-operation. In the event, the report proved to be more of a genuinely collective effort than could have been expected at the start;[1] and in the months of discussion which followed, it was accepted as being fair and objective; although some Ministers (reasonably enough from their point of view) were determined not to accept the Treasury's proposals.

138. *The First PESC Report: 1961 - 62 to 1965 - 66.* The objective of the report had been laid down by Ministers - to create the framework for a public sector expenditure plan working within an aggregate of 42½ per cent of GNP and paying special regard to economic growth and the balance of payments. This went far beyond the Plowden Committee's recommendation for a regular survey of expenditure against resources: we were asked for specific proposals within the constraints stated by Ministers; and in calling for such a report, as the Chancellor had said in his Budget speech, the Government was moving into new territory.

139. The report began by insisting that although it covered a five-year period, it was concerned entirely with immediate action, for Ministers' present decisions (together with those of the past) are in fact determining the level of public expenditure five years ahead: either the Government takes new decisions now, or the development of public expenditure follows implicitly from the momentum from past decisions. The appraisal was meant to help Ministers to take these decisions - to make judgements on the best assessment that could be provided of future resources and future risks.

140. The first step was to appraise the prospective growth of resources. This was put at 3 per cent a year, an increase of 2½ per cent a year in GDP per worker (higher than the average for the 1950s of around 2 per cent a year), and ½ per cent a year in working population. This was regarded as being highly vulnerable on balance-of-payments grounds; and justifiable as a basis for public expenditure planning only if all government policies (including the size and composition of public expenditure) were directed to strengthening the competitiveness of the economy.

141. Particular stress was laid on the role of the public sector from this point of view: employing 25 per cent of the working population and 40 per cent of the capital expenditure, the efficiency of the public sector itself in its use of resources is crucial; and this led to recommendations endorsing the new policy just promulgated for the nationalised industries (the February 1961 White Paper, Cmnd 1337) and proposing stringent criteria for Government assistance to private industry, and limitation of support for agriculture. Stress was laid also on the disadvantageous effect on competitive power and the balance of payments of direct overseas expenditure for military and civil purposes and of the heavy use of advanced industry for defence and related purposes. This theme of the interrelationship between the efficiency of the public sector and the composition of public expenditure on the one hand and the growth and solvency of the national economy on the other was very strong in this report.

142. In the event, the increase of GDP from 1960 to 1965 was 3.2 per cent a year, so that strictly, over the period, the 3 per cent a year estimate was soundly enough based. But so of course were the fears about the balance of payments; and the continuing balance-of-payments crisis from 1964 reduced the growth rate to 2.2 per cent a year in 1965–70. In retrospect, the appraisal in the report appears to have been sound; and one would not argue now that a lower growth rate than the 3 per cent should have been recommended as the basis for public expenditure planning. What does emerge, however, is the fact that the problem of making a realistic five-year estimate of future resources was successfully solved on this first occasion, but that this was not enough. The growth calculation could not express the true limitations on the national economic prospects which had to be taken into account; and the report had to qualify itself accordingly.[2]

143. The second step was to appraise the future expenditures and to fit them within the aggregate of 42½ per cent of gross national product. The objective here was to establish policies in all the main fields that would generate expenditures of the right aggregate scale. In some cases this was defined as a quantitative limit for the year 1965–66; in others as a specified rate of expansion through the period; in others again, in which the nature

of the programme excluded the idea of a quantitative limit, policies were framed in qualitative terms. The concept was a tailor-made arrangement for each programme. The proposals were confined to the large programmes – twelve blocks and subdivisions of blocks, totalling nearly 80 per cent of the aggregate public expenditure (except debt interest): if the large programmes could be settled, this would set the tone for decisions on the remaining 20 per cent.

144. At this first PESC operation, therefore, the whole emphasis was on the policies to be carried out in 12 large and important programmes; and the terms in which these would be expressed and carried out would be arranged between the department(s) concerned and the Treasury. The development of this into a universal financial allocation for each of five years ahead came later. At this stage, indeed, there were no 'bids' from the departments, but estimates of what would be involved in 1965 – 66 under existing policies; and the Treasury did not seek to apply 'cuts' in these figures, but started the other way round by writing down estimates of the financial resources that would be needed in 1965–66 with alternative and less expansive programmes.

145. The Treasury's proposals added up to an increase of nearly 11 per cent (constant pay and prices) from 1961 – 62 to 1965–66, an increase on the £10,280 million total of £1100 million. This was a little above the 42½ per cent limit; and given the doubts about the balance of payments (failure in which 'would undoubtedly enforce a major reappraisal of the plan sooner or later') it was clearly a maximum (unless the Government was prepared to envisage higher taxes, having reduced them two years before). The proposals were presented in groups.

146. (1) Emphasis on the new nationalised industry policy; on stringent criteria for assistance to private industry (and better procedure for collective examination); and stopping the open-ended commitment for agricultural support. This whole area was seen as very important for competitiveness, and one in which the power of the Government purse could be decisive; and after the nationalised industry losses of the 1950s (worse in the 1970s when the 'new policy' had been abandoned), and a flood of public money for the private sector (Colvilles' steel mill, the new Cunarder, cotton industry reorganisation, launching aid for civil aircraft, the motor industry expansions on Merseyside, etc.), and the continuing risk of an uncontrollable bill for agriculture, the danger of more subsidies for inefficiency loomed large.

147. (2) In the public services, quantitative limits were proposed involving substantial increases from 1961 – 62 to 1965–66 in local authorities' education running costs, hospital and local health and welfare

services running costs, the bill for state pensions (arising from the increasing numbers) and defence. A number of possibilities were suggested for specific economies in the social field (e.g. family allowances, nutrition services) which could give more room for manoeuvre in the development of the main social programmes.

148. (3) The other specific item was civil public investment (about £900 m. nationalised industries and £800 million other, including schools, hospitals, housing, roads, water and sewerage, etc.), which had its regular July review and allocation for the next two years, followed by the autumn White Paper. This was essential for the proposals above, for the growth of education running costs was mainly attributable to the expanding numbers of teachers (following the expansion of teacher-training colleges) and the cost of maintaining and operating and financing the new buildings being provided; and in most of the social and environmental services field the effective means of moderating the growth of current expenditure is to reduce and postpone the expansion of capital facilities by public investment. The investment in 1962–63 and 1963–64, to be decided in July, was therefore decisive to whether the education and some of the health current programmes could be constrained as proposed.

149. (4) Finally, the report envisaged the next steps if the Treasury's proposals were accepted as the basis for a 'plan'. This would involve working them into specific policies for implementation and public announcement and action to build up public understanding; reviewing the expenditures not yet considered; developing the timetable and organisational pattern for future operations.

150. In retrospect, the report had two weaknesses, neither of which could have been avoided at the time. First, it proved beyond any reasonable doubt that unless the Government (and any other Government in sight) were prepared to make fundamental changes in their social policies, it would be impossible in the long run to contain public expenditure at around 42½ per cent of GNP. The momentum was such that a substantial increase in this ratio in the 1960s was by 1961 inevitable. The true conclusion was that the Government was already in fact committed to increases in taxation in the long run. The issue of taxation versus social services had already been decided. If this had been widely appreciated at the time, the course of policy might have been different. But the report could not easily have said this.

151. Secondly, as an immediately practical matter, the treatment of public investment as a subject for special determination, instead of bringing the capital expenditure items in with the current expenditure programmes, led to confusion, for there were two separate operations,

very closely related together. But it was still too early to change this. As it happened, a third subject came into the picture – Supply expenditure in 1962–63 – and the combination of the three related subjects complicated the operations of the next six months, and much reduced their effectiveness.

152. *The July Measures.* While the PESC report was being prepared, an acute sterling crisis had been gathering strength. It was a crisis not unlike that of September 1957, with our fundamentally weak balance of payments and our vulnerable reserve situation making sterling the target for attack in any period of world currency instability and speculation. Throughout June and July, the Chancellor was preparing the 'package' of measures to restore confidence in sterling, and to enable us to reinforce the reserves by borrowing from the International Monetary Fund. For this purpose, Government expenditure was an indispensable part of the 'package': as the Prime Minister recorded it:[3]

> If we are to get our 'drawings' from the International Monetary Fund, we shall have to make – or pretend to make – large savings on Government expenditure. This is (in the short as well as in the long run) more difficult than extra taxation. It is also very hard to achieve quickly . . . But if the package is not good enough, the international usurers – bankers – will turn us down. Then sterling will go.

153. The Chancellor accordingly decided to include in his statement of 25 July an undertaking that the 1962–63 Supply Estimates would be kept within 2½ per cent (in real terms) of the original Estimates for 1961–62. This was a formidable commitment. It was probably as difficult as it would have been to get the last £50 million off the 1958–59 Estimates (to keep them to the same figure as 1957–58) – the Cabinet's refusal to do this had led to the resignation of Mr Thorneycroft and his two junior Treasury colleagues. At the same time, a special effort was announced to reduce Government overseas expenditure – military expenditure (the cost of our troops in Germany and commitments elsewhere), a ceiling on overseas economic aid, and a reduction in the diplomatic, administrative and information services overseas.

154. For effective action to align expenditure with resources, these measures were of mixed value. It had been possible sometimes in the past to bring about long-term savings of expenditure by prompt and relevant action in an atmosphere of crisis. But the fundamental weakness is that if the need to deal with public expenditure is associated with a time of crisis – and even more if it is attributed to the need to satisfy 'foreign bankers' – the impression is created that the need to act effectively in this field will no longer exist when the crisis is over, and everything can go on merrily as before.

155. On this particular occasion, following the work done on the PESC report, there was no doubt at all about the nature in detail of the action that was required to get public expenditure into a much better relationship with prospective resources; but this could be put into effect only by a Cabinet which was convinced that this was necessary in its own right in the long-term national interest; and could not be done as a quick reaction to an immediate short-term situation – even less as measures designed to appease our creditors. In my view there are two ways of introducing a 'plan' for public expenditure:

    (i)   In case of a balance-of-payments crisis, rush a detailed policy through; or

    (ii) patiently argue it out in relation to growth, competitiveness and solvency, with White Paper, etc.

There is a danger of falling between two stools, and failing to get either the advantage of a long educational process (to convince people about the problem) or the advantage of operating in real crisis and being able therefore to drive ahead. In June/July 1961, the crisis was manifestly not deep enough for (i), but it was obviously impossible to leave it at (ii).

156. The upshot was that, for the next few months, there were three public expenditure operations proceeding together:

    (i)   1962 – 63 Supply Estimates (to carry out the Chancellor's undertaking);

    (ii) public investment for 1962 – 63 and 1963 – 64 (for White Paper to be published in October);

    (iii) action on the PESC 1961 – 62/1965 – 66 report.

To this was added a fourth, of major public expenditure importance though not handled as public expenditure, i.e. the 'pay pause', in many respects the most important part of the Chancellor's July statements.

157. It soon became clear that the public sector was the key to the incomes problem, and this has been so ever since, partly because of the ambivalent position that the Government as an employer is bound to adopt, partly because the one-quarter of the national labour force in the public sector contains very important people in the running of society, and partly because the private sector employers will always follow the Government, and blame it if it gives way. So in the Chancellor's statement, the provisional agreement on teachers' salaries was revised (nevertheless, still a 14 per cent increase); and immediately following were the problems of delaying the application of awards made to public sector employees under compulsory arbitration agreements – civil servants, health service, police; and then in November the real breach of the pay pause, as a result of a muddle. Muddle was not surprising, for in many of these issues, particularly with local authorities and nationalised industries, the Government's legal power to intervene at all was wholly uncertain. But as

Mr Macmillan said, there was a tremendous amount of money in all this.[4]
Indeed, it is readily arguable that successive Governments' failure to
handle the public sector pay problem, where Government has ultimate
executive responsibility, has been the main contributory reason for the
failure of each of the rounds of incomes policy from 1961 to 1974.[5] But it
can equally be said that failure to handle the public expenditure problem
in the hope that success of incomes policy would in some way solve all
problems is just as reprehensible!

158. *July 1961 to February 1962.* The three expenditure operations were in
continuous play from the Chancellor's statements in July to the publication of the Vote on Account – i.e. the total of the Estimates – in the
following February. They were handled without any special Ministerial
machinery; the group to assist the Chancellor was designed for the strategy
rather than to intervene in the struggle between the Chancellor and the
individual spending Ministers. From October, the Chancellor had the
support of the new Chief Secretary to the Treasury, Mr Henry Brooke,
who took all the day-to-day work on public expenditure on to his
shoulders. The existence for the first time of an inter-departmental
committee – PESC – covering the whole field proved useful – and the
committee was given a great deal of work; but all the important substance
was handled by Ministers themselves.

159. The outcome of the campaign as a whole, as it appeared at the end of
February 1962, was indecisive. It could not be said that the prospective
balance between public expenditure and resources had improved over the
year since Mr Selwyn Lloyd had first brought this problem, with the
Plowden interim reports, to his colleagues. On the other hand, the
Treasury had made gains in important sectors; and, above all, the issues
were already being discussed and argued about much more realistically
than hitherto. Hardly any time was wasted by Ministers on unreal and
artificial expenditure issues (such as in pre-PESC days, whether road-
building should be put 'below the line'). Where there were misunderstandings and confusions, they were largely due to the fact that three separate
operations were being conducted at the same time.

160. The Chancellor's undertaking to keep the 1962 - 63 Estimates within
2½ per cent in real terms of 1961 - 62 was sadly frustrated: the actual figures
were £111 million above the mark, and the increase was 4½ per cent. It
could have been argued that the Chancellor was unlucky: two open-ended
commitments, one for agricultural support and the other the railways
deficit, added up to £109 million -- but this, after all, is why it is wrong to
have policies which involve open-ended commitments. A very thorough
review was made of administrative costs, saving £15 million; but the
Chancellor was unable to point to specific major policy savings.

161. The conclusion that one is bound to draw is that this kind of commitment - announcing a target of this kind even as little as seven months ahead - is viable only if the Government has already decided upon measures which are virtually certain to give effect to it: the range of real uncertainty is too great. Moreover, it was very noticeable on this occasion that neither Parliament, nor the media, nor indeed the foreign bankers regarded the failure to meet this undertaking as being a matter for concern: this may well be another illustration, sharper than ever, of the basic doctrine of the Plowden Committee that there are now no forces outside Government to check and criticise public expenditure - and the corollary that the Chancellor's hand must be greatly strengthened inside Government.

162. Civil public investment was divided in the course of the campaign between nationalised industries' investment and public service investment. The adoption by the Government of the 'new' policy on nationalised industries in February 1961 implied different criteria for their investment; and this process was being introduced, with reservations, for coal and railways. Moreover, the role of public service investment as the creator of future current expenditure was becoming understood; and the argument was very keen, particularly on education and housing. The Chancellor announced as part of his 27 February statement that in 1961 - 62 public service investment was increasing by about 13 per cent; in 1962 - 63 it was planned to increase by 6 per cent;[6] and the Government planned to hold the aggregate rate of increase in 1963 - 64 at 6 per cent. These programmes were still rising much faster than the GNP, and still too fast to be consistent with a viable level of future current expenditure. But the pace was being slowed down.

163. For the five-year programme for 1961 - 62 to 1965 - 66, some progress had been made. The Chancellor had announced on 26 July 1961 the policies on nationalised industries and assistance to private industry, and good progress was being made in spelling out the criteria in both. The great increase in agricultural support costs, both for 1961 - 62 and for 1962 - 63, was underlining the danger of the open-ended system. In defence, intensive work was proceeding to clarify the strategic implications of the lower long-term resources limit - the argument that in the end led to the debate about 'East of Suez'. Overseas aid was being held down. Agreement had been reached for a five-year growth rate for national health service current expenditure; and a five-year building programme had been agreed for roads. Current expenditure on education and the rest of the social and environmental services was being approached through the public service investment decisions. In total, some advance; but certainly none of the events of the period since the first PESC report was issued were making the problems look easier.

NOTES

1. As chairman of the committee through this period, I cannot however refrain from quoting Heclo and Wildavsky, op. cit., p. 240: 'A departmental official recalled that "no one had much interest in the beginning. Clarke was regarded as something of a figure of fun. What a bore, people would say. We left it to the Principal Finance Officer to deal with. Eventually it got so far it couldn't be stopped." ' An acceptable epitaph for a Treasury official!

2. The balance-of-payments problem in the 1960s, and the combination of the inflation and balance-of-payments problems in the 1970s, were so overriding and so intractable that the answer to any practical piece of business in government extending for more than a year or two ahead always had to be based on an assumption that these problems would be 'solved', although (as the 1961 report bluntly stated) no solution was in sight. This practice was unavoidable, for otherwise the business of government would have been paralysed. But it may nevertheless have contributed to the failure over decades to cope with these intractable problems; for it enabled Government and everyone else to carry on calmly on the conventional lines; and to treat the minatory assumptions and reservations as common form which could be taken as read before proceeding to the main business.

3. Harold Macmillan, *Pointing the Way* (Macmillan, 1972) p. 376: note of 23 July 1961.

4. 'What is the use of our scraping and scrounging to get £50–150 million of "economies", if the extra wage and salary bill of £1000 million or more is presented again?' Note of 9 August, Harold Macmillan, *At the End of the Day*, (Macmillan 1973) p. 36.

5. See Sir Richard Clarke, *Incomes Policy in Phase IV* (Manchester Business School, 1973).

6. *Civil Public Investment in Great Britain*, Cmnd 1552 (October 1961).

6 PESC in Reflation: 1962 – 63

164. Very soon after the Chancellor had made his expenditure and investment statement on 27 February 1962, the pressure for reflationary action began to build up again. Mr Selwyn Lloyd made no concession to this in his Budget speech on 9 April, but in the next few weeks it became insistent. The Prime Minister, as in 1958, was in the lead in this and, writing of this period, records:[1]

> I had been continually pressing on the Chancellor of the Exchequer and the Treasury the need for a substantial reflation. . . . On 8th March 1962 Bank Rate was reduced from 6 to 5½ per cent. But I was not satisfied and kept pressing for further expansionist moves. On 22nd March, Bank Rate came down to 5 per cent, and to my great delight the Treasury and the Bank agreed to a further reduction to 4½ per cent on 16th April. . . . I was also anxious for the system of Special Deposits to be modified with a corresponding increase of the total sums available for credit: this was done on 31st May when £70 million of these deposits were released.

165. The Ministers in charge of some of the big spending departments were quick as always to take advantage of the changed wind from No. 10 Downing Street, and at once submitted proposals for additional spending. This was the inevitable consequence of concentrating in 1961 on short-term cuts in expenditure, for reasons of the short-term economic situation. So the change of atmosphere developed; and indeed apprehensions were widening by June to the fear of world-wide deflation.[2]

166. *PESC Reports for 1962.* The PESC reports were being prepared during the spring, as in the previous year, and were completed in June. This time, there were two reports, one entitled 'Public Expenditure and Resources 1961 – 1966', and the other entitled 'Public Expenditure to 1966 – 67'. The first showed the economic background for the five-year period – the growth of resources and the development of the economy – in which 1962's public expenditure programme decisions would have to be taken. The second was described as a 'costing' of specified policies and programmes, both as an aggregation of departments' estimates (covering virtually all the departments' programmes) and in relation to what was

described as a 'pattern' rate – fundamentally the levels proposed by the Treasury in the 1961 report, with some adjustments. This 'pattern' rate involved an increase of 3¼ per cent a year (compared with a 3 per cent a year growth in GDP) without allowing for the relative price effect. The departments' figures were about £225 million (or about 2 per cent, i.e. a ½ per cent higher annual growth rate) higher for 1966–67 than the 'pattern rate'. This was the same practical conclusion as in the 1961 report: unless the defence and social and environmental policies were radically changed, higher taxes were inescapable.

167. The growth rate for resources was still put at 3 per cent a year, heavily qualified with reservations about incomes policy, avoidance of over-heating the economy, and the balance of payments. The actual growth from 1961 to 1966 was 3.1 per cent a year, the collapse to an average of 2.1 per cent a year in 1966–71 reflecting the substance in the qualification. Nevertheless, the performance of the Treasury economists and statisticians was remarkable:

	1961 to 1966 annual % increase 1962 PESC	*(constant prices)* Actual*
Private consumption	2.6†	2.75
Private investment	2.5	2.8
Public sector purchases of goods and services	3.2‡	3.9‡
Exports of goods and services	3.8	3.9
Imports of goods and services	3.2	3.7

* From *National Income and Expenditure 1972*, (HMSO, 1972). There may be differences of definition between the Central Statistical Office classification in 1972 and what was used in 1962. The price basis of the 1962 PESC was 1961, and that of the 'actual' was 1963.

† Assumed on the basis of 2 per cent a year increase per head (apart from State benefits and assistance), the same as in 1954 to 1961.

‡ The 1962 PESC figure was the Treasury 'pattern rate', for current goods and services and public sector investment (not transfer payments): the excess in the 'actual' is due entirely to investment, particularly public service investment.

168. The PESC report had been based on a current account balance-of-payments surplus of £200 million in 1966, estimated (optimistically) to be enough to finance net investment abroad, and keep the external monetary position in balance. The actual 'surplus' in 1966 (if one can so describe it in the circumstances) was £40 million: the growth of imports, not the failure of exports, made the difference. The inadequate external performance, plus a rundown of stocks (instead of an expected increase, again a

weakening of national liquidity) in effect financed a slightly higher growth rate for private consumption and investment and much more public sector investment than had been envisaged in 1962.

169. I have made this comparison of the 1962 report for 1961–66 with what actually happened, for this was the best of the appraisals of resources that was made: after this, they began to reflect the Government's political commitment to a 4 per cent growth rate. It would be unreasonable to expect anyone to look five years ahead, and for these to turn out to be such years as 1961 to 1966, nevertheless to get as near the actual result as these appraisals did. That public sector expenditure would substantially exceed the Treasury 'pattern rate' was hardly surprising; and the outcome of the balance of payments was even less so (the interesting point is that our poor competitive power was seen in imports, not in failure to export).

170. The outcome justified the experts' earlier confidence in their ability to make reliable projections. But do they show conclusions for policy which would be different from what informed and experienced people would make without any such analysis at all? In 1962, two policies were clearly essential – to concentrate on the balance of payments and to stop public expenditure from rising too fast; and what happened in 1961–66 showed this clearly; but it cannot be said that the resources analysis gave a lead in this direction. It showed that you couldn't get a quart out of a pint pot; but it did not give a clear message on whether the right conclusion was to try to increase the size of the pint pot, or whether we should be actively reducing the claims to the quart, and if so which; or how to put the balance of payments right.

171. *Problems of Presentation.* The 1962 PESC report showed that we were getting on very well on the technical and administrative side – both in the development of the resources analysis and in the collection and collation of the departmental programmes, and in relating these together. But no method had yet been found of relating them to the world of politics and politicians. At the first round early in 1961, the idea of the ratio of public expenditure to GNP had been used as a yardstick – and with success, for Ministers made it the starting-point in their directive for the first PESC report. But as Ministers and others became used to it, they said 'Why 42.5 per cent?'; and with experience, changes in definition became necessary, so that the definite yardstick was muddling, for once one figure was in people's minds, there was confusion if it was changed. So in the 1962 report, it was dropped: it would in any event have run into bigger figures than the previous year (for purely technical reasons). But the resources analysis concepts, with their culminating conclusions on the practicable levels of private consumption were always too sophisticated to carry ready understanding, as I have explained elsewhere.[3]

172. To my mind, the specific tax consequences are the only yardstick that could carry the same kind of clarity (and political weight) as the popular expenditure programmes. Although this raises prodigious problems, both political and technical, this still seems to be the indispensable course, so leading to the concept of a long-term expenditure-taxation Budget.[4] Treasury Ministers could of course and did make general statements to their colleagues about the tax implications of the expenditure programmes, but the real counter-weight would be a specific Government tax reduction programme (like education or pensions) which would have to be sacrificed if the expenditures were accepted.

173. The 1962 reports were completed too early to accommodate the change in the atmosphere to reflation. Once the economy was no longer thought to be over-heated, the subject was at best an uninteresting one to departmental Ministers; and if it could be argued that the economy was becoming underloaded, there were immediate pressures for extra spending. There has always in fact been overwhelming Ministerial support for "stop-go" policy, despite all criticism. The taxation approach is essential for these circumstances too, for the only answer to the wish for extra expenditure (apart from the practical one, right nine times out of ten, that the desired expenditure will be so slow to take effect that it will be counter-productive for the reflationary purpose) is to show that this is competitive (if the economy needs a boost) with tax reductions (which take effect much more quickly). So changes up and down in the economy can be accommodated in a long-term expenditure-taxation Budget; but are very difficult to accommodate otherwise. As soon as the 1962 reports appeared, they were at once in difficulty accordingly.

174. An entirely different approach that was floated in June 1962 was to publish an annual Public Expenditure White Paper, giving the five-year figures and a description of growth and prospects of each block of expenditure. This ultimately happened in November 1963, in February 1966, and then annually from 1968;[5] but it was then new, and had been rejected by the Plowden Committee. In relation to the problem of how to work PESC into Government philosophy and practice, there were the well-known risks of having to declare the Government's intentions earlier than is necessary, but there were potential political advantages for all Governments alike:

(i) In actually having a five-year plan for the public sector, with priorities – at worst, more clarity and fewer muddles in the Government's operations

(ii) Making a comprehensive presentation of the achievement of expansion of social and community services in the past and of the development intended for the future. It is a common belief of Governments that their public relations are weak;[6] and certainly this particular Government in spite of its unprecedented expansion of expenditure in all these fields, had acquired a reputation for 'meanness'. Such a White Paper would give it a good opportunity to dispel this;

(iii)   If it was publicly known that the Government's forward spending programmes (which would in fact have their impact on the economy and taxes during the period of the next Parliament) were the most the nation's resources could afford, this could be a factor moderating the tendency for General Elections to become auctions for the highest bidder with new expenditure programmes and tax promises.[7]

The merit of this idea, in the circumstances of that particular time, was to bring to the surface the political content of the PESC operations, which are the real meat of politics.

175. The report was presented as being the background for the decisions which the Government would have to take in the second half of 1962 – defence budget, negotiation with local government for general grant, the next round of pensions, public service investment (1963 - 64 to be finalised in July for October White Paper, with the material now included in the PESC report to avoid the previous year's confusion); as well as in handling the 1963 - 64 Estimates, which seemed likely to show a further increase at least as great as in the previous year.

176. *New Treasury Leadership.* In the latter part of June and early July, Treasury Ministers were considering how to handle the PESC report, and in particular how much reflation to introduce into the final public investment decisions for 1963 - 64. This was suddenly ended by the dismissal of Mr Selwyn Lloyd on 12 July and his replacement by Mr Maudling; and Mr Boyd-Carpenter took Mr Brooke's place as Chief Secretary, the latter moving to the Home Office. Moreover, two weeks later, the Treasury reorganisation came into operation, with Sir Laurence Helsby and Sir William Armstrong heading the management and the economic and financial sides respectively. This complete change, both at Ministerial and at official level, was of course fortuitous, for the retirement of Sir Norman Brook and Sir Frank Lee had been timed long before; but it nevertheless represented a most unusual course of events.

177. I was sad to see Mr Selwyn Lloyd go. He had been responsible for getting the Plowden proposals and PESC off the ground; and had done this with great success; and never missed an opportunity to drive home the principle in his speeches. Indeed, in the light of our practical experience, his original idea of a long-term expenditure-taxation budget became in my opinion the most promising way to proceed.

178. Mr Lloyd's undertaking (para 153 above) on the 1962–63 Estimates, part of a short-term defence of sterling, must be called unfortunate; for it never got near success; and no Chancellor of the Exchequer can afford an open failure in public expenditure (for it weakens him against all his colleagues). Suppose that all the time and energy and political capital that Mr Lloyd (and later Mr Brooke) expended on the Estimates 'pledge' had been applied to getting the effective long-term decisions on defence, education, public service investment – the three items needed to establish the first PESC pattern – might they have scored a real historic success in the handling of public expenditure? No one can say, but certainly the atmosphere of 1961, with the sterling crisis, and with a novel imaginative project trying to get away from the traditional 'economies' (and therefore much easier for the Prime Minister to support) was a better opportunity to get a PESC pattern established than ever recurred during the Conservative Government.

179. Mr Maudling was well known in the Treasury and very familiar with it, although he had not previously had to deal with public expenditure. I had personally had the opportunity of working with him in 1956–58, when he was in charge of the negotiation with the Six to create a free trade area of the Community and ourselves (and preferably other European countries), and I was the chairman of the committee of officials that was advising him. Mr Boyd-Carpenter had been Financial Secretary, and had also been in charge of important spending departments; so we had an experienced Treasury team. As I explained earlier, the Treasury reorganisation had been designed with the implementation of the Plowden Report very much in mind; and it settled down quickly under the new political and official management.

180. *The First Reflationary Spending.* The new Ministers' first task was to settle the public service investment for 1963–64, for the usual October White Paper. Mr Selwyn Lloyd and Mr Brooke had got quite a long way with this, and had consulted the group of 'Chancellor's friends'; and the outstanding points were quickly settled. The outcome was a £70 million investment programme (£40m. housing, and the rest education and local authority investment). This was for reflationary purposes, with £15 million estimated to be spent in 1962–63, £40 million in 1963–64 and £15 million in 1964–65: it involved a large proportion of fast-moving programmes, and it was to be specially concentrated geographically. The effect was to increase the 1962–63 programme so that it was about 9 per cent above 1961–62, and the 1963–64 programme about 9 per cent above 1962–63. In his statement on 27 February, Mr Selwyn Lloyd had given both of these figures as 6 per cent (which had been presented as an offset to the failure with the 1962–63 Supply undertaking); but the excess was readily explained as 'reflation', and the White Paper (Cmnd 1849) gave rise to no

difficulty. Nevertheless, in terms of size and duration and industrial impact, this programme was certainly as big a reflationary move as could reasonably be regarded as compatible with the Plowden Committee's thinking on 'short-term flexibility'; i.e. the most that could be done without becoming counter-productive from the point of view of reflationary effect, and simply an addition to long-term spending programmes.

181. Up to the end of the year, apart from some release of post-war credits, the further reflationary measures were on the taxation, not the expenditure, side – reductions in purchase tax (at the beginning of November and on 1 January), and an improvement in investment allowances. On the other hand, a decision by Treasury Ministers (in practical terms, unavoidable) not to seek an 'economy campaign' on the 1963-64 Estimates, which were in the end 9.4 per cent or over £500 million above the previous year,[8] illustrated the size of the contribution to 'reflation' made by the increasing momentum of public expenditure.

182. The increase in the Estimates had been a record since the Korea crisis; and the build-up of the momentum was indeed remarkable:

	% increase over previous year
1952 - 53 to 1955 - 56	+ 1.7 average
1956 - 57 to 1959 - 60	+ 3.9 average
1960 - 61 to 1963 - 64	+ 7.6 average

This illustrates the change which had taken place in Conservative thinking somewhere in the late 1950s. It also illustrates most forcibly the dangers in the reflationary situation, for the loss of a year's corrective action made it certain that the momentum would sweep on to 1964-65 and later.

183. *Block Expansion Rates.* Treasury Ministers began a new initiative to contain the risks ahead; an important development of the earlier 'Plowden' ideas. The new approach was to take seven major elements of expenditure – the defence budget, roads, education, health and welfare, police and prisons (all these including both current and capital expenditure), housing and general local government investment, and national insurance benefits – and decide for planning purposes on an approved annual rate of expansion for each of them for three or four years ahead. Departments would plan their expenditure accordingly: if a Minister wanted to embark upon a course of policy that would involve going faster, he would have to seek his colleagues' agreement, which would involve argument both on the project and on the implications for total expendi-

ture. Nationalised industries' investment, assistance to industry and agricultural support would be controlled by qualitative criteria.

184. For the first time, this plan introduced specifically an apparatus of long-term allocation and control. The original plan had been to get long-term policies in each of the critical areas which would in the aggregate be consistent with the expected growth of resources; this involved quantitative limits, but the emphasis was on the policies, not on the limits, for all the evidence (particularly in defence, which had been the bell-wether of the 'Plowden' concepts) showed that the prior condition for living within long-term financial limits was to have compatible departmental policies. The new approach was to establish financial limits for planning purposes (annual rates of expansion in real terms), so that the pressure from them would Contain the policies and enforce changes in them; and this was a lasting change in the development of the PESC system. Moreover, it rightly brought the main items of public service investment into their own service blocks (roads, housing, schools, hospitals, etc.); and it also brought new areas of public expenditure into the central allocation (roads, Home Office).

185. It was decided to set rates of expansion which would be broadly equivalent to those laid down by departments in the 1962 PESC report (or agreed since) as the costings of present policy up to 1966–67. This abandoned the possibility of taking policy action (except on defence) to keep the growth of public expenditure in line with the growth of resources; and implied tax increases later on (Mr Callaghan had them on his plate later). Nevertheless, if these limits could have been established effectively, this would have been a great step forward.

186. This approach was discussed fully with the Ministerial group of 'Chancellor's friends'. Once again, the existence of a group of this kind proved to be a valuable sounding-board, and helped to get the Treasury Ministers' proposals accepted in principle, subject to the specific determination of the expansion rates. But the course of events tended to confirm the development of opinion in the Conservative Party from the late 1950s that expansion of social and environmental services was more important in political and electoral terms than the possibility of tax reduction. This view was expressed strongly by Mr McLeod at that time; but it did follow after a great tax reduction in 1959; and perhaps it was difficult to take a different view about the needs of the 1970s from this widely held view of the 1960s. Nevertheless, the philosophies of the 1960s were what led inexorably to the actual situation in the 1970s.

187. The details of the expansion rates, and indeed of the operation of the scheme, took longer to complete than expected; and by the time this was

done, the estimates for the 1963 PESC report were becoming available; which were involving much larger expenditure than was provided in the 1962 report; and so the determination of the figures presented new problems, and had to be postponed until later in the year.

NOTES

1. Harold Macmillan, *At the End of the Day* (Macmillan, 1973), p. 67. In this period, Mr Macmillan's activity was heavily focused on incomes policy, and like Mr Heath (Mark II) after him, was insufficiently aware of inconsistency between this and a reflationary policy. He noted (op. cit., 59, 24 March 1962) that 'the pay – the Government's policy – has offended dons, schoolmasters, school-teachers, civil servants, clerks, nurses, public utility workers, rail-waymen and all the rest. But perhaps it is most resented by the doctors, dons, nurses, etc., who feel that they are relatively ill-paid compared to the high wages which they hear about coming into the ordinary artisan's household'; but, of course, incomes policy or no incomes policy, it has always been the Government's job (never in fact done) to fix (or negotiate) the relativities within the public sector, and the public sector has always been the Achilles' heel of incomes policy.

2. 'A talk on 20th June with Lord Cromer, the Governor of the Bank of England, convinced me that there was a real risk of world deflation.' Harold Macmillan, op. cit., p. 89.

3. 'Long-Term Planning of Taxation' in *Taxation Policy*, edited by Crick and Robson (Penguin, 1973).

4. Note my Stamp Memorial Lecture 1964, Appendix B below, p. 183; *New Trends in Government* (HMSO, 1971) pp. 43 - 47; and article in *Taxation Policy*, n. 3 above.

5. [The annual series of five-year White Papers did not start until December 1969, following the plan announced in a Green Paper, *Public Expenditure: A New Presentation*, in April 1969 (Cmnd 4017). The White Papers of 1968 and 1969 did not look so far ahead. Ed.].

6. Harold Macmillan, op. cit., p. 62 (note of 7 April 1962): 'The general view is that [the loss of confidence in the Government] is based not so much on the policy mistakes of Ministers as to their failure in public relations. Of course this is the usual excuse . . . The traditional form was to blame the Conservative Central Office. Now (rather more fairly) it is Ministers who cannot 'put over' their cases. The back-bench M.P.'s (who don't seem to realise that this is their job) join in the general scare . . .' In July, he brought Mr Deedes into the Cabinet as Minister without Portfolio with this problem in mind.

7. Facts get lost in the electoral rough-and-tumble; but if such a White Paper had been on the table at the time of the 1959 General Election, Mr Gaitskell might have fought a better and perhaps a more successful campaign.

8. An increase over the 1962 - 63 Estimates of about £325 million (5.6 per cent) at constant pay and prices, compared with 4.7 per cent in the previous year.

7 The Impact of NEDC

188. A new and important dimension was introduced by the decision of the National Economic Development Council ('Neddy') on 6 February 1963 to approve the objective of a 4 per cent a year growth rate for the economy. This committed the Government up to the hilt, for the Chancellor was chairman and there were two other Cabinet Ministers there: indeed, only the Government could truthfully be said to be committed to any action by the decision, for the industrialists and trade unionists could not be regarded as delegates committing their organisations. The General Council of the TUC had specifically made this a condition for accepting Mr Selwyn Lloyd's invitation to be represented. In their letter of 24 February 1962 to the Chancellor, they said:

> [In accepting the invitation] they wish to emphasise that they attach great importance to the right of the members of the NEDC to report to the organisations which they represent, and that they would not regard association with NEDC as debarring those organisations from expressing in public such reservations as they might hold about government decisions on economic policy.

The members from the management side of private and nationalised industry were representing themselves, though many were closely associated with the original constituents of the present CBI.

189. *The 4 per cent Growth Rate.* For public expenditure, the consequences of the commitment of the Government to 4 per cent was twofold. First, the electricity investment programme and those of other public services required by industry had to be expanded to match the higher assumed growth rate; for the Government could not allow itself to risk having the objective frustrated by lack of electric power or other public sector services. There are only a few public services (of which electricity is much the most important) of which the requirements are linked closely to the growth of the economy, so this was a limited problem. The industrial outcome, however, was damaging; for the large increase in orders overloaded the heavy electrical engineering industry, therefore frustrated its export business, and led inevitably to the protracted depression in the amount of new ordering when the growth rate for the economy failed to rise at all towards the promised 4 per cent and then fell to 2 per cent.

190. Second, and damaging over the whole public sector, it was

impracticable to conduct long-term public expenditure planning on any other estimated rate of growth of resources than 4 per cent p.a. It would have been theoretically possible to do so: the Government could have said reasonably and legitimately that it would continue to plan expenditure on a 3 per cent growth rate for resources until the various obstacles listed in the NEDC report[1] had been sufficiently overcome to make it reasonably assured that the 4 per cent objective would be achieved. Indeed, the formal position was covered by Mr Boyd-Carpenter in an answer in Parliament on 1 March.

191. But the overriding consideration was that the 4 per cent had become a fundamental ingredient of the Government's (and indeed Mr Maudling's) policy, both to refute the political charges that the Government was restrictive and hostile to growth, and to provide a basis for a possible bargain with the trade unions linking together economic growth and incomes policy (as Mr Heath sought to do in 1972). To have adopted a different basis for its own public sector policy would have unquestionably been violently attacked as evidence of the Government's insincerity in accepting the 4 per cent objective.

192. Moreover, within the Government, it would have required a Chancellor of the Exchequer of extraordinary authority to be declaring outside his conviction of the 4 per cent objective and to be insisting inside (and forcing this to difficult and unpopular decisions) that expenditure planning should be based on a 3 per cent growth rate. The 'Plowden' system depended upon Ministers accepting the resources limitation; with the 'Neddy' economists describing 4 per cent as a possible objective for 1961 – 66 (i.e. a higher rate in the later years) and the senior economic Ministers having accepted this as the Government's objective, no agreement could have been reached on a lower figure.

193. The sums involved for spending Ministers in the difference between 4 per cent and 3 per cent p.a. in growth rates of GNP were over five years the difference between feast and famine. The defence budget, for example, was being limited to 7 per cent of GNP - a rough-and-ready measure of what the Government was prepared to allocate to defence. In five years, the difference between an annual growth rate of GNP of 3 per cent or 4 per cent meant a difference of 5 per cent in the defence budget – a sum equivalent at the time to the cost of the nuclear striking force, or the whole defence electronics research and development, and a great deal more than the whole cost of our Middle East defence effort.[2] The Secretary of State for Defence would have to think about his responsibilities and policy in a different dimension if the annual growth was 3 per cent rather than 4 per cent. For education and other services there was no formula relating their allocation to a proportion of GNP (they were growing much faster) but the

implications were the same. A difference of dimension in the rate at which their services could grow; for in all these programmes, perhaps 90 per cent is committed ahead by existing policy, and whether your financial resources are enough to give you an extra 15 per cent for 'improvements' in five years' time, instead of 10 per cent, makes a fundamental difference to the kind of programme of new developments that you can undertake. This is the true outcome for individual Ministers if the total of allocations is related to 4 per cent a year growth rather than 3 per cent. If there was genuine doubt about the assessment of the prospective growth of resources, no spending Minister could reasonably be expected to support the lower figure.

194. In fact, experience showed that the 3 per cent figure would have been right over the five-year period, just as the 3 per cent figure turned out to be right as recommended in the 1961 PESC report (3.2 per cent actual for 1960–65) and again in the 1962 PESC report (3.1 per cent actual for 1961–66). The actual for 1962–67 turned out to be 3.0 per cent; and that for 1963–68 was 3.1 per cent. So the concept that the rate of growth could be levered up to an altogether new level within a period that was relevant for immediate Government decisions (e.g. on public expenditure) turned out to have been terribly wrong. Moreover, the ten-year period at about 3 per cent a year (from, say, 1958 to 1968), which had been quite a good advance on the 2½ per cent a year of the 1950s, was succeeded by a return to lower figures.

195. It is not argued here that the Government was wrong to accept the 4 per cent growth objective, for the handling of public expenditure is only one of the responsibilities of government, and not always the most important (although any Government that underestimates its importance will pay sooner or later). Moreover, a harsh and realistic analysis might suggest that the combined effect of the reflationary pressure early in 1963 (reinforced by the severe winter and the frightening unemployment figures that accompanied it) and the approach of the General Election (expected in spring 1964, though in fact delayed until the last possible day in October) had such a powerful effect on the Government's expenditure planning that the acceptance of the 4 per cent growth rate made very little difference to what happened.

196. '*Anti-PESC*'. But in terms of the long-term control of public expenditure, we certainly ran into a period early in 1963 which I can only call 'anti-PESC', in which the whole idea of 'Plowden' was stood on its head. The long-term expenditure plans were related, not to the best and most serious appraisal of prospective resources that could be made (at which the Treasury economists and statisticians proved themselves to be remarkably adept), but to a 'target' or 'objective' of growth of resources,

determined for entirely different purposes. So the fact that expenditure was threatening to outstrip resources very fast was concealed by hope that eventually a miraculous growth of resources would save the situation.

197. At its first meeting on 7 March 1962, NEDC had set on foot a study of the implications of a 4 per cent growth rate, from which the February 1963 decision ultimately followed. It was always clear that the 'anti-PESC' difficulty was there in the background. It seemed to me from the beginning that we should be stoking up for a catastrophe of quite unprecedented dimensions if we proceeded to lay on public expenditure on the assumption that the rate of growth of GNP was going to accelerate sharply. The dangers were known in advance, but I cannot see how this dilemma could have been avoided, though it might have been mitigated.

198. *Beginnings of NEDC.* When once the Government had decided to set up NEDC and it had been decided that NEDC should make its main task to explore the economy's capability for growth, the appearance of some kind of 'plan' carrying with it inevitably some Government commitment was at the least very likely; and this was of course the point that leads straight into 'anti-PESC'. Mr Macmillan has explained[3] that there was some difficulty in getting Cabinet approval for setting up NEDC, and this required two long meetings to resolve. Mr Selwyn Lloyd's plan to create NEDC revealed:

a rather interesting and quite deep divergence of view between Ministers, really corresponding to whether they had old Whig, Liberal, *laissez-faire* traditions, or Tory opinions, paternalists and not afraid of a little *dirigisme*.

When NEDC was approved, the Government was launched on this course of action, and economic growth was coming into the forefront of Government policy, both in substance and in the shop-window.

199. Moreover, when one goes back to the beginnings or even the pre-natal stage of NEDC, one must recognise the intimate relation between this idea and the problem of incomes. The trade unions of course recognised this very clearly; and this was why it took several months, until the end of February 1962, to persuade them to participate, and then only on the specific condition that this could not commit them to support the Chancellor's views on the desirability of a policy of wage restraint.

200. But before Government had any intention of intervening in income determination at all, it still seemed desirable to many people that there should be a place where Government, management and trade unions could discuss the capability of the economy – and so conduct a mutual educative process which would prevent the adoption of policies by any of the organisations involved which would be manifestly impracticable and

incompatible with the common objectives for the development of the economy. It is not easy from our vantage-point in the mid-1970s to cast one's mind back to perhaps a less sophisticated period, say in the late 1950s, when it seemed simple common sense to provide such machinery for tripartite discussion, not in relation to any tactical situation of Government statements or industrial relations, but in order to get a meeting of minds which would have its repercussions on the way in which all the day-to-day business was conducted. This now looks rather naive, but it was not entirely unreasonable.

201. Perhaps an opportunity was missed in the 1950s by failure to make effective use of and develop the Economic Planning Board. This had been set up by Sir Stafford Cripps in 1948 as a body under the chairmanship of the Chief Planning Officer, then Sir Edwin Plowden, with permanent secretaries and representatives of management and trade unions: when there ceased to be a Chief Planning Officer, the Permanent Secretary to the Treasury took the chair. The Board never established a role for itself; for none of the three 'sides' could see a ready purpose for it, or advantage to be gained from it. The nature of permanent secretaries is to seek practical results from their hard-pressed working time; and not to cast their scarcest resource – time – upon the waters in the hope of an ultimate return. The industrial representatives were first-rate people, who welcomed the opportunity to get discussion and confidential information about the economic situation, but did not invest time and effort in it: in the last analysis, they were representing themselves and nobody else. Much the best contribution made by the Economic Planning Board was in a discussion on economic growth which occupied several meetings in the winter of 1960–61 – Sir Frank Lee in the chair, with on the industrial side Sir Hugh Weeks and Len Murray, among others – and Treasury papers which set out the essential facts and considerations: the millions of words and the hundredweights of paper in the following several years added virtually no substance to the conclusions of this discussion (nor to action within industry or between Government and industry to overcome the obstacles); and the Board was dissolved when NEDC was set up. In many respects, the Economic Planning Board had the best potential ability of all the tripartite institutions to develop the purposes above, for it was informal and expert and non-political; and thus could have been a nucleus for subsequent expansion if conditions justified it.

202. In my opinion, successive Governments and the two sides of industry have been at fault throughout the post-war period in failing to establish organisations which made it possible to get a meeting of minds: and this may have been an important political and economic weakness in Britain's development in this period; and one which helps to explain the virtually unique (among advanced countries) lack of understanding and even

hostility between government and industry which characterises our economic affairs, whatever may be the political colour of the Government. I was for many years a member of the Economic Planning Board, and have seen a lot of other Government/industry advisory bodies, some more and some less successful. What has been most lacking throughout has been the will and creative power to make an effective relationship and community of interest between government and industry. NEDC provided another opportunity to do this, and for this reason alone many welcomed it warmly outside the context of economic growth and incomes policy with which it was originally associated.

203. *NEDC and 'Planning'*. In the seven months between Mr Selwyn Lloyd's initial statement in Parliament and the first meeting of NEDC at the beginning of March 1962, it became clear that there was no possibility that the Council would become a powerful 'planning' organisation, seeking to stimulate industrial reorganisation and expansion, and initiating realistic Government-industry negotiations to remove the obstacles. Apart from the three Ministers, the members (six from trade unions, six from private industry, two from nationalised industry and two academics, and the director-general, Sir Robert Shone) had no authority or mandate to commit anybody. The staff was 'independent' and not 'governmental' – a sensible enough arrangement if no action was intended to flow from the Council's work: if there had been any intention by any of the participants to use the Council as an instrument for attacking the nation's industrial problems, there would have had to be a 'governmental' staff (no doubt manned with 'temporaries') just like the French *Commissariat du Plan*, which was and is wholly part of the governmental machine. But the analogy that was often drawn with the French *Plan* at the time never had any substance.

204. Within its very limited scope, 'Neddy' and its staff was heavily concentrated on economic and statistical analysis and model-making (exactly the same function as was carried out very successfully and with much more experience within the governmental machine) and not at all upon industry (on which work was developed very slowly through the 'little Neddies'). Here too it was exactly the opposite of the French *Plan*, which was wholly industry-orientated at the start in the 1940s, and did not concern itself with economic model-making for several years. This anomaly led to inevitable difficulties of duplication; and further difficulties because the Government could not release to an outside agency any material which it did not provide for Parliament: and, obversely, the departments were not getting the lively flow of industrial information that they had hoped would be a great gain from the existence of 'Neddy'.

205. In the end, these problems were resolved when the Labour

Government took over in October 1964. They were clearly going to be responsible for their own 'National Plan', and from the outset took over the economic and statistical analytical staff from 'Neddy', and merged it with the departmental staffs. It would have been much better if this function had been left within the departmental machine when 'Neddy' was set up, serving the Chancellor of the Exchequer in both his roles, one in Whitehall and one as chairman of NEDC.

206. *Was 'anti-PESC' avoidable?* If the organisation of NEDC had been set up in this way (as the Labour Government did do it) it could in my opinion have much reduced the 'anti-PESC' dilemma. Admittedly the crux of this dilemma was the Government's own wish to foster and identify itself with the 4 per cent objective; and given this, it could not in political practice (both inside the Government and outside) be seen to be planning its public expenditure on a lower (though much more realistic) assessment of the future growth of resources. If the economic and statistical apparatus used for the NEDC 'plan' had been part of the departmental machine, the Chancellor would certainly have had better balanced advice on the risks and opportunities of reaching the 4 per cent than he was getting from the two sources.

207. We now know that what happened in the next five years was 3 per cent a year, but there were persuasive arguments for regarding 4 per cent as possible, especially if one was not too particular about the year by which this could be achieved. It seems to me possible that if this work had been designed and done as a unified effort from March 1962 onward, and removed from the area of 'political' conflict, an assessment of the feasibility of 4 per cent could have been made by early 1963 which would have enabled the Government to espouse the mystique of 4 per cent without at the same time making it impossible to handle the Government's own business on a more solid and realistic assessment. Later on in the 1960s, techniques were elaborated which avoided some of these difficulties.

208. However, as events went, it was certainly unwise from the point of view of public expenditure control to adopt the 4 per cent objective so completely and unreservedly. Whether the benefits in other aspects of Government policy outweighed this damage is indeed difficult to say. But it does seem very likely (especially when one thinks, for example, of the consequences for the heavy electrical industry) that the effect was to intensify the future crises of the economy.

NOTES

1. *Growth of the United Kingdom Economy to 1966* (HMSO, 1963). See especially pp. 58-60.
2. See *Statement on the Defence Estimates 1966*, Cmnd 2902.
3. *At the End of the Day*, p. 37, note of 21 September 1961. . .

8 PESC in 1963–1964

209. The first half of 1963 was a difficult period for expenditure decisions. The reflationary policy and situation had greatly weakened the brakes: any relaxation of the normal Treasury pressure against expenditure is bound to have this effect, even if it is supposed to be highly selective (e.g. for short-term projects only). The Government's adoption of the 4 per cent growth objective had similar effect. The General Election was coming into sight. The terrible weather in January and February, with the interruption of outdoor work, led to high temporary unemployment and mistaken fears that the Government's reflation policy was failing.

210. This atmosphere affected all decisions, rationally or not. At end-January, the decision on national insurance pensions and other benefits (to come into operation on 27 May) was announced. These were very favourable to the pensioners – an increase over the last figure fixed in April 1961 of 17½ per cent, compared with increases in wages and earnings of 7½ per cent in the same period, and a 'real' increase of about 4 per cent a year, compared with a national average increase of about 2 per cent per head in real consumption. 'Generous' decisions here are very expensive, partly because of the large numbers involved, and also because each decision is the starting-point for the next, so that a 'generous' decision does not only affect its own lifetime, but raises the whole structure permanently.[1] Mr Maudling, like many others before and since, worked hard to bring the new benefits into effect earlier (the best of all reflationary expenditures, all spent and strictly limited in time), but it could not be done.

211. Mr Maudling's Budget was modestly reflationary, with tax reductions of about £250 million (mainly personal income tax, following purchase tax reductions already made). Its real interest was in an array of imaginative assistance for the development districts ('free depreciation' for industrial plant and machinery, and standard grants of 25 per cent for buildings and 10 per cent for plant and machinery, and new social infrastructure programmes on the way for the North-East Coast and Scotland; and the first of a sad series of aids for shipbuilding and shipping); and in the enactment in detail of the improvements in all investment allowances announced in the previous November.[2]

212. This was part of the 'modernisation' theme (which later included

measures for industrial training and for redundancy payments) which the Prime Minister and he were developing, linked up with the 4 per cent growth objective and incomes policy. This was an attractive theme, which like most of Mr Macmillan's, reverberated through the rest of the 1960s: the real difficulty, then and later, is that to tackle seriously the modernisation of the British economy (private and public sector) involves both a scale and a time-scale and a priority of operations of an entirely different dimension from the customary procedures of government. Mr Maudling's measures involved great work and effort and resourcefulness, and like many of their successors were well directed. But in relation to the requirements of modernisation of the British economy, they like their successors were a drop in the ocean.

213. *The 1963 PESC Report.* The usual reports came forward during the spring. By this time the assumption of a 3 per cent p.a. growth rate had been abandoned in favour of an assumed 4 per cent p.a. rate of growth (for the years 1962-67 the rate actually turned out to be 3 per cent p.a.). The public expenditure costing report showed that on existing policies there would be an even large increase than had been envisaged, running well ahead of the prospective growth in gross national product.

214. There were three factors of major importance:
  (i) the pensions decision referred to above;
  (ii) large increases in public sector investment programmes – both nationalised industries (responding to the 'Neddy' 4 per cent) and public service investment (exaggerated by the big shortfall in the 1962-63 investment because of the weather);
  (iii) over the programmes generally, more 'realism' in the estimates of the continuing growth in the later years implied in 'present policy' – there had been from the start a tendency to underestimate the future growth (and so make the situation appear better than it really was), and departments were now improving in this respect.

These costings were salutary; for they showed very clearly the knife-edge on which the management of public expenditure was resting, and always does rest. The biggest and most important single decisions are the pensions decisions: in January 1963, the difference between a 'generous' pensions decision, and one which increased pensions according to the increase in manual workers' earnings was of the order of £150 million in 1967-68; or about 1¼ per cent (or ¼ per cent growth rate a year from five years before) in total public expenditure. This is the only expenditure where the scale is so great that the difference between two plausible decisions in one field can change the total of public expenditure by over 1 per cent every year ahead (though these decisions do normally carry with them offsetting decisions in increases of contributions, i.e. of taxation).

215. The 1963 report did illustrate how easy it is for the figures established in one year to be left far behind by the figures in the next year, sometimes as a result of actual decisions taken and sometimes by better and clearer estimating of how present policy will involve additional expenditure in the future. Moreover it was known that pressures were building up for many new expenditures – the Robbins report on higher education, which would inevitably lead to claims for extra spending on all kinds of education; the infrastructure programmes for the North-East Coast and Scotland; the Buchanan report on urban road renewal; the ideas which were beginning to be examined on wage-related unemployment benefit; the increasing indications that the existing defence policy was going to need much more. None of this was allowed for in the costings.

216. Meanwhile, the economy was recovering in lively style from its winter troubles; and it seemed reasonable to say that the Government's economic policy since mid-1962 had been successful, and that the turning-point had come again, and that the danger was no longer underloading but overloading in 1964–65 – a diagnosis with important implications for the 1964 Budget, the last before the Election.

217. *A Step towards Long-term Control.* In July, Mr Maudling and Mr Boyd-Carpenter presented this situation to their colleagues, and during summer a series of conclusions was reached:

   (i)   the reflationary period was at an end, and there should be no more projects for this purpose; and the Estimates for 1964–65 should be constrained accordingly;

   (ii) the departments' investment proposals for 1964–65 were reduced (but still represented a high figure, both in money and in terms of the prospective load on the construction industry);

   (iii) the 'block allocation' proposals which had been approved at the end of 1962, subject to agreement on the figures of the allocations, should be put into operation, using the figures for each of the six civil blocks from the 1963 PESC report, and a lower figure for defence: new proposals which could not be contained within these allocations to be decided by the Cabinet.

218. The introduction of the 'block allocation' was a first practical step towards long-term control (as distinct from the determination of long-term policies consistent with resources). The use of the 1963 PESC report figures, high though they were, and incompatible with a 3 per cent p.a. growth rate, was inevitable at that stage; the advantage was to get the system started, and in particular to have a framework into which to fit the new proposals (e.g. Robbins) that were now coming forward.

219. Another conclusion could very readily be drawn from the situation as

it was developing. The Government was becoming increasingly committed to spending programmes which were developing on a scale that could not be reconciled with a programme of tax reduction (except, of course, as opportunity might offer – and then withdraw again – on short-term economic policy grounds).

220. *The Political Controversy.* On Saturday 9 November,[3] the subject was brought into party-political controversy in a speech at Wembley by Mr James Callaghan, then leading for the Labour Opposition on finance:

I ask the Government to publish a White Paper setting out in detail the total additional expenditure they propose to embark upon over the next five years . . .

We know that thousands of millions of pounds are to be spent on electricity, roads, housing, schools, hospitals, universities, the North-East and Scotland. In addition they propose to lend hundreds of millions of pounds to local councils. On top of that there are to be new plans for the RAF, a new aircraft carrier, a new airliner flying at twice the speed of sound, which together will cost at least £1000 million.

This will be the biggest spending spree ever by any Government in peacetime; and yet two years ago they were unable to find an extra sixpence for the nurses. If they carry out this programme without the capacity to pay we shall be in for a period of galloping inflation.

As for the Labour Party, . . . we shall embark upon expenditure only when we have the capacity to pay. We shall match our policies to our resources, and by planning choose our priorities from those urgent measures that are needed to modernise Britain. Above all, we shall get away from this atmosphere of pre-election recklessness that the Tories have embarked upon.

221. In the debate on the Address on the following Wednesday, 13 November, the Chancellor gave detailed figures for the main programmes, and linked them to the 'Neddy 4 per cent':

We accepted in the Budget the NEDC target of 4 per cent growth rate. As I have said, all our calculations of social expenditure are reckoned on acceptance of that growth rate. . . . Having accepted that objective, we base our programme on it . . . because all the parties in the NEDC accept that a 4 per cent growth rate is achievable . . . The 4 per cent growth rate is the basis of our future plans; it is accepted by NEDC including the trade union representatives; I think it is acceptable to the party opposite; it is the only coherent basis on which to operate, and we prefer on this side of the House to have a coherent basis upon which to operate.

222. Following the debate, the Chancellor decided in favour of publishing a White Paper. The arguments for doing this were formidable – to inform

public opinion, to show the Government's ability to tackle a major problem of government, and to warn of the perils of trying to go faster. The first PESC White Paper, '*Public Expenditure in 1963-64 and 1967-68*' [Cmnd 2235] was published accordingly just before the Christmas Recess.

223. *The First Published PESC.* The White Paper was launched in an atmosphere of political controversy, and there is something wrong if a highly political subject does not generate controversy. By subsequent standards, it was a short paper – only ten pages. Part I expounded the history, starting from Mr Selwyn Lloyd's 1961 Budget speech and the Plowden report, and defining the classification and method: Part II gave 1963-64 and 1967-68 figures for twelve blocks, and a description of the programme for each: Part III explained how the public expenditure relates to the national economy, both on a 'physical' and on a 'fiscal' approach; and came to the final conclusion:

38. For the aggregate of public expenditure the White Paper shows the total, at 'Survey 1963' prices, increasing by 4.1 per cent a year between 1963/64 and 1967/68. The Government are aiming at a rate of growth of the Gross National Product at constant prices of 4 per cent a year on average. This rate of growth, if maintained between now and 1967/68, should be enough to support public expenditure on the general scale foreseen in this White Paper; and implied by the Government's policies. But if these policies seemed likely to make a larger claim on resources than is here envisaged, or if the prospects for economic growth substantially worsened, it would clearly be necessary for the Government to review their policies accordingly.

39. If public expenditure and the Gross National Product developed over the next few years as set out above there would in the event be an increase in the ratio of public expenditure (excluding debt interest) to Gross National Product from the present figure of something like 40 per cent to around $41\frac{1}{2}$ per cent.[4]

40. It is unlikely that a development of public expenditure on the scale implied will leave much scope for a reduction in the burden of taxation. The level of taxation will, of course, be closely affected by the level of savings. The higher the level of savings, the less the need for taxation. The rate of personal saving has risen in recent years to very high levels, and the Government's policies will continue to be directed to encouraging still higher levels of saving. Provided these are achieved, and a 4 per cent rate of growth of the economy is maintained, the level of total public expenditure implied in this White Paper should be reasonably related to the needs and resources of the community and to the possibilities of the nation's growth.

224. The layout of total public expenditure in the White Paper is as follows:

| | £ million at 'Survey 1963' prices | | |
	1963/64	1967/68	Change (%)
* Defence	1,905	2,170	+ 13.9
Aid and other overseas			
expenditure	310	365	+ 17.8
* Roads	360	470	+ 29.2
* Housing and environmental			
services	1,135	1,315	+ 15.9
* Education	1,260	1,570	+ 24.0
* Health and welfare	1,020	1,160	+ 13.8
* Benefits and assistance	1,745	2,105	+ 20.6
Children's services	290	315	+ 8.6
* Police and prisons	200	230	+ 14.9
Assistance to industry,			
transport and agriculture	665	620	− 6.8
Investment by nationalised			
industries and public			
corporations	1,135	1,330	+ 17.2
Administrative and other			
services	705	725	+ 2.8
Contingency allowance	. .	250	. .
Adjustments	180	200	. .
TOTAL PUBLIC EXPENDITURE	10,910	12,825	+ 17.6

* Programmes for which there were "block allocations" (for housing and environmental services, only investment was allocated - £555m and £695m, i.e. plus 25.0%, in the two years).

The increase of expenditure was put at about £1900 million, which was probably about £500 million more than could be readily accommodated by the national economy on a realistic estimate of the prospective growth of resources. The conclusion stated in paragraph 40 was therefore very optimistic. It must be said, however, that no Government, or political party, had ever made such a lucid statement of the taxation situation on the eve of a General Election; and even if in the light of subsequent events the judgement must be that it was optimistic, it was in a different class of realism and rationality from the kind of statements which had been the usual contribution of the political parties previously. The White Paper probably had a constructive effect, indeed, for nobody argued seriously in 1964 that a higher level of spending was practicable.

225. From the point of view of those who were responsible for thinking about the long-term control of public expenditure, the publication of the

White Paper was a real gain. It clearly committed the Conservative administration to the PESC system, although it had not yet been applied in practical control terms within the administration itself. Moreover, it was such an obviously sensible way of handling the public expenditure problem that once it had been made public, a future Labour Government would have found great difficulty in abandoning it; and so it turned out. No system can itself solve any governmental problem: but having a good system instead of a bad one (or none at all) can offer possibilities of finding solutions if Ministers (and the public opinion behind them) wish to do so.

226. *Growing Pressure on Demand.* In the second half of 1963, the economy moved sharply forward; and it became clear that the second half of 1964 would be a period of heavy demand, continued strongly in 1965. The Chancellor had brought the 'reflationary' period to an end in the previous July, but the time was now approaching for the opposite course, a particularly difficult situation and the test of 'expansion without inflation', and no reversion to 'stop-go'. Moreover, not all of the members of the Cabinet in 1964 (nor, for that matter, in 1974) had fully appreciated the injustice (or justice?) of the demand management policies that as soon as the Government had succeeded in bringing about economic recovery and active business conditions, the time had come for unpopular measures – taxes and public expenditure cuts: one Minister was heard to say that now that private housing was increasing it was obviously unacceptable to cut back public housing.

227. The first area in which to move was clearly public expenditure; for it was the decisions to start things in 1964 that would create the overload of work in 1965; and the error to be avoided at all costs was to stoke up the 1965 boom by adding to the public expenditure programmes which had already been publicly stated (and without contradiction) as the maximum that the economy could afford, even if the 4 per cent growth rate was achieved. In the early months of 1964, the Chancellor and the Chief Secretary pressed hard. The Supply Estimates for 1964-65 were up by 6.7 per cent, at any rate a relief from the higher figures in the previous two years (when there was some reflationary justification). The 1965-66 public service investment programmes were significantly cut down or postponed). New spending programmes were coming up for decision – timing of the raising of the school-leaving age, Channel Tunnel, decimalisation of currency, university building in excess of what was obviously needed to carry out the Robbins report; and the usual flow of decisions (some involving tens of millions of pounds, such as BOAC's choice between Boeing 707s and VC 10s), were taken against this background.

228. In his Budget speech, Mr Maudling continued the campaign started

by the December White Paper:

It is, I believe, generally accepted that this programme is the most ambitious that can reasonably be attempted, and that any attempt to carry out a greater expansion of publicly-financed services would be economically unsound and indeed self-defeating.

He continued to link this expansion strongly with incomes policy, as in his 1963 Budget; and indeed this combination of expansion and incomes policy would go on recurring, to the Labour Government's 'social contract' in 1974.[5]

229. The Chancellor raised indirect taxes by around £100 million, which cannot seriously be said to have affected the situation to any substantial extent. It might fairly be said that if considerations of the short-term situation of the national economy had been paramount, with a serious overload threatening and a balance-of-payments deficit building up, a spring Election would have been a natural choice, to give the new Government (Conservative or Labour) as much elbow-room as possible. With a decision to continue until September, political life was bound to be in something of a limbo, so that the 'if's and 'but's' of this situation are not very repaying.

NOTES

1. A peculiarity was that the benefits were always fixed in 'half-crowns' [units of 12½p.]. So on that occasion, with the current benefit 57s 6d single [£2.87½], the only 'feasible' increases were 5s [25p.], 7s 6d [37½p.] 10s [50p.], i.e. 8.7 per cent, 13 per cent, 17.4 per cent. With prices having risen by about 8½ per cent, it was necessary to choose between a figure that some might think 'low' (i.e. up to the national average of real consumption increase) and another which was clearly 'generous', and raised the expenditure permanently on to a new level.
2. Mr Macmillan commented, *At the End of the Day*, p. 399: 'When the final decisions were taken, the relief in taxation amounted to £269 million: to this had to be added certain Government expenditures such as £30m. for the shipping industry, and some other similar grants. Since the highest figure that I had dared suggest was some £400m., I was not disappointed at the result.'
3. Sir Alec Douglas-Home had succeeded Mr Macmillan on 18 October.
4. 1952, 40.7 per cent; 1957 and 1958, 36.0 per cent; 1959, 36.7 per cent; 1960, 36.9 per cent; 1961, 38.4 per cent; 1962, 39.3 per cent.
5. In his 1963 Budget speech, Mr Maudling's phrase was a 'compact' between 'the three major parties in our economic life'.

9 State of Play: Summer 1964

230. *Four Budgets.* The four-year period from 1961 to 1964 is of great interest as showing the beginning of the impact of the growth of public expenditure in relation to resources from the low point reached in the second half of the 1950s. Public sector expenditure (including debt interest) was going up at about 7½ per cent a year (in money): public sector receipts by about 7 per cent a year. There were, so to speak, four-and-a-half Budgets – Mr Selwyn Lloyd's of 1961 and 1962, Mr Maudling's 'mini-budgets' of end-1962, and his Budgets of 1963 and 1964: they occupied one modern-style trade cycle, with unemployment at the beginning the same as at the end:

- *Registered unemployment* *October**	*in Britain* *('ooo)*
1960	329
1961	366
1962	501
1963	474
1964	348

* Mid-point of the financial year, and political end of the period

231. In these four-and-a-half Budgets, the Chancellors' actions on tax rates cancelled each other out:[1] this includes both direct and indirect taxation, but not national insurance contributions, and excludes Mr Maudling's major structural changes in capital allowances in 1962 and 1963, which cannot readily be aggregated with changes in personal taxes (and were anyway replaced later by investment grants). In very broad terms, there were increases in indirect taxes of about £300 million a year; and the 1963 reductions of income tax personal allowances and of Schedule A were about the same. In the period 1961 to 1964, revenue from direct taxes increased by about £500 million, and revenue from indirect taxes by about £550 million.

232. Looking back over these Budgets, the striking fact is the immense

number of changes, particularly in indirect taxation. This was inevitable in a system in which every tax was in principle open for change and new decision every year, with the attendant political pressures and the need for every Chancellor to make an acceptable political package every April; but if one compares the list of duties as they stood before Mr Selwyn Lloyd's 1961 Budget with that after Mr Maudling's 1964 Budget; and if one then considers how an increase of something over 10 per cent in the average of these duties (i.e. the £300 million figure above) could have been achieved best, from an economic, industrial and social point of view, is it likely that one would arrive at anything like the same result? The value-added tax (VAT) has its defects, but it has done a great deal to simplify this regular annual reassessment. In direct taxation, the changes in substance (i.e. excluding those with an administrative purpose) are less frequent; but the same point applies there, especially where taxes on industry are involved, for these are crucial to their investment decisions, and if these are changed repeatedly there is great confusion: in this particular period, the Chancellors could not be criticised on this score.

233. In the counter-cyclical use of taxation, also, this period is of interest. Unemployment had reached a low point in 1960–61. Mr Selwyn Lloyd's 1961 Budget (plus the 'regulator' plus the full-year effect of the 1960 tax increases) increased tax rates by an amount yielding about £225 million in the year 1961–62 (compared with 1960–61), and there was virtually no change on balance in the year 1962–63. Mr Maudling's 1963 Budget (plus again the full-year effect of previous moves) reduced taxes (other than capital allowances) by an amount equivalent to about £300 million in the year 1963–64, and again there were virtually no changes on balance in 'Mr Maudling's part' of the year 1964–65 (for the tax increases in the 1964 Budget were offset by the extra full-year cost of the 1963 tax reductions).

234. In effect there were two two-year periods – 1961–62 and 1962–63 (in which the various tax measures were steadily taking rather less than 1 per cent out of the GNP); and 1963–64 and 1964–65 (in which a little more than 1 per cent was being steadily put in). In the latter period, also, there was the large growing effect of the reform of capital allowances – private investment in 1964 over £500 million (nearly 20 per cent) above 1963, after having been stable in the two previous years. The impression that I get, looking back at the actual experience – and it must always be remembered when appraising in retrospect that the Chancellor of the Exchequer is always like a general guessing what is on the other side of the hill – is that both in 1961 and in 1963 too much was done, in one case up and the other case down. To the extent that the scale of both decisions was necessitated by political considerations – the sterling crisis in 1961 and the winter unemployment experience in 1963 – it would seem that they should have been reversed earlier.

235. *Inflexibilities.* The difficulty that appears most clearly from the arithmetic is that it is in practical terms impossible to raise or lower taxes for the short periods which are relevant for demand management within the very narrow constraints that have become politically required. It has been known since the late 1950s that public expenditure is much too blunt an instrument for these purposes; and the experience of these four years (in which the various Budgetary changes were taking at least as much out of the economy in 1962 - 63 as in 1961 - 62; and - with the effect of the capital allowance reforms - putting in more in 1964 - 65 than in 1963 - 64) gives rise to the question whether taxation changes are not too blunt an instrument too.

236. It must be noted that in the previous cycle, which may be regarded as five years (in Octobers) with unemployment running from 215,000 in 1955 to 514,000 (very like 1962) in 1958 and then down again to 329,000 in 1960, the low point from which the next cycle started, the scale of the tax variations was much less. This was a period of large tax reductions (an average of about £100 million a year). But the change from year to year in the impact of the various tax changes, which we put at a little less and more than 1 per cent of GNP in the periods discussed above, was about ½ per cent of GNP in 1956 - 57 (taxes up, resulting from Mr Butler's second Budget of 1955), about ½ per cent (taxes down) in 1957 - 58, small in 1958 - 59. The only large move of the period was in 1959 - 60, resulting from Mr Heathcoat Amory's 1959 Budget, in which the impact of changes exceeded that of 1958 - 59 by 1½ per cent of GNP. In the following year, Mr Amory raised some taxes again (and incurred some criticism, having reduced the taxes before the 1959 Election); but once again (the same phenomenon as later) the full-year effect of the 1959 tax reductions outweighed the effect of the new taxes, so more was being put into the economy in 1960 - 61 by the two years' Budgetary actions than in 1959 - 60. Hence the overload in 1960 - 61, which was the reason for the severe (and probably excessive) 1961 Budgetary action . . . and so *ad infinitum.*

237. In short, my impression is that where Chancellors have changed the taxes on a large scale - by which I mean for this purpose an impact of more than about ½ per cent of GNP - it has tended to turn out badly; not necessarily because they are wrong to want to act on this scale, but because such a momentum is set up that they cannot politically reverse it quickly enough - and so at the next round too large an action is again required, this time in the opposite direction.

238. This leads again to another difficult dilemma. If the inflexibility (administrative and political) of the tax system is such that the effect of big changes will always last too long for the counter-cyclical purpose and will therefore set up forces for equally big changes the other way . . . and if

therefore changes equivalent to about $\frac{1}{2}$ per cent of GNP are about the most that is tolerable . . . is the operation worth doing at all? Is it possible to predict the future accurately enough to diagnose the need for a move of such size? We are talking here about numbers like 125,000 unemployed. Might it not be better for the health of the economy and for the stability of employment to abandon the idea of using taxation and public expenditure for counter-cyclical purposes; and instead concentrate the thought and work of the central core of Ministers and officials (whose time and energy are the scarcest resources of all) on getting the best structure of taxation and of public expenditure, and of course the right relationship between them, for the health of the economy?

239. Does not the experience of this period suggest that *from the point of view of stability of employment* it would be better to concentrate on getting the long-term structure both of taxation and of public expenditure right than to engage in a frenzied chase for short-term forecasts of the future (in a country whose economy depends increasingly on forces – European and world – outside its own control) and a succession of changes in Budgets, 'mini-budgets' and the like, the effectiveness of which to carry out the counter-cyclical purpose is at the very best dubious, and certainly does not improve with experience from decade to decade, and is certainly damaging to the long-term decision-taking of industry and thus to the quality of industrial investment and therefore to the competitive power of industry and the prospects of employment and the improvement of the standard of living? It is arguable indeed that the disappointing performance of the British economy over the decades has one of its chief roots in this endless search for Government action to bring about short-term stability. Certainly this is one of the areas in which the behaviour and practice of our chief industrial competitors has differed greatly from ours.

240. *PESC Technique.* The problem of how to turn the PESC system into an effective instrument of control was still in the foreground throughout 1964, especially with the possibility of a new Government ahead. The Plowden Committee's proposal for regular surveys of public expenditure and resources for a period of years ahead was in being. There were two major difficulties:

    (i)   The tendency for departments to underestimate the future cost of maintaining existing policies: it was taking a long time to establish realism in this. The 1963 Survey had, however, been a good advance in this respect, and when the 1964 Survey came out in June it showed some further increase in the further years ahead; and it was reasonable to suppose that departments were becoming adapted to the new problems of long-term estimation.

    (ii)   The introduction of overoptimistic figures for future resources because of the Government's commitment to the 4 per cent objective. This too was moderated in the 1964 Survey by having two growth rates, one based on 3 per cent and the other on 4 per cent a year, and showing the implications of both.

241. Both of these difficulties went the wrong way, making the prospective situation look more favourable than it in fact was; and so the Treasury was always vulnerable, giving the impression of crying 'Wolf'. The pressure by the Treasury on departments to produce more realistic (and thus higher) estimates of the future cost of existing policy led the departments also to raise their short-term estimates, thus causing underspending, a difficult state of affairs for effective expenditure control. This 'anomaly' of the Treasury pressing short-term estimates down and levering their long-term estimates up had been fully expected from the start; but it called for more sophistication than was easily communicable throughout the departments.

242. *Public Expenditure/Resources.* By 1964 it was clear that the country was facing a steady increase in the proportion of public expenditure to GNP.[2] Much thought was devoted to the implications of this; and how these could be explained to successive Governments all under pressure from public opinion to go on increasing this ratio. The following notes were made early in 1964:

The effect of an increase in public expenditure/GNP ratio is in the last analysis political, and the public becomes accustomed to one level of taxes. In the decade before World War I, it would have been universally believed that economic disaster would follow if the public sector were to grow to the level it reached in the 1930s; and so again to the present time. Nevertheless, in our present mixed economy there must be an upper limit somewhere, if only because the private sector provides the export trade, the industrial and commercial investment (other than nationalised industry) and the private consumption which is most closely related to the general concept of the standard of living.

Perhaps at some stage in the process of rising taxes there would be a reaction of public opinion against public expenditure. But this is slow to happen. The spending decisions are taken years before the consequential tax decisions; and because the latter are taken for reasons of short-term economic policy, the connection with expenditure is rarely immediate and obvious. The public cannot be said to be 'prepared to accept' rising taxes in order to get improved public services, for no deliberate choice can ever be made. The only moment at which the tax implications of rising public expenditure would publicly appear would be when it is necessary to raise the taxes to restrain the economy; and the odium of this tends to fall on the management of the economy rather than on the growth of expenditure.

It is not easy to detect any general public discontent with the level of central government taxes. But this may be because the impact of rising public expenditure (pensions, health, education) has been reflected in increased national insurance contributions (and health stamp) and in local rates rather than in central government taxes.

The immediate question of the effect of tax changes on the economy (and indeed on economic growth) is political. But in economic terms, increases in direct taxation beyond a certain point are certainly in the long term damaging to incentives and to the mainsprings of risk-taking: and increases in indirect taxation attract criticism in relation to incomes policy; and may become increasingly difficult if the Government become committed to a policy of stable prices. Rationally, increases in indirect taxes should be abstracted from incomes-and-prices policy, as in Sweden, but we are far from this.

The political and economic difficulty of raising taxes emphasises perhaps the most important danger, viz. that the effects of an increase in the PE/GNP ratio may well be inflationary; for the possible damage to economic growth policy on one hand and incomes policy on the other may lead Ministers (entirely reasonably) to run heavier risks of having inflationary Budgets. Our system has an inflationary bias now: as the X PE/GNP ratio grows the bias may increase.

It would seem unlikely, on the face of it, that the present tax structure is so burdensome on incentives and risk-bearing that any increase of tax rates would weaken the driving-force in the economy. Yet the behaviour of industry is not inconsistent with a view that incentives and readiness to run risks are inadequate; and the preoccupation with tax avoidance at all levels of society may not be insignificant. However this may be, the Y next cycle of tax increases could have considerable effect.

The composition of public expenditure is of great importance, because of different expenditures' different effect on the economy. Over a medium period, the public sector may pre-empt too much of scarce specific resources – leaving e.g. too little room for private construction work, or, by taking too much of the best manpower for universities, teaching and Government science, starving industry of its requirements. This should only rarely be damaging in the long run, for it should be possible over ten years or so to expand the scarce resources to the extent necessary. But it is important over, say, a five-year period.

Again, some expenditure policies, by ossifying a distortion of economic resources, or indeed intensifying it, can be very damaging to economic growth. Only in rare cases can subventions to particular industries be regarded as economically beneficial. On the other hand, the policy for nationalised industries which introduces economic criteria for new investment, could bring about a marked improvement in the direction of resources. The expansion of public services can be very damaging (apart altogether from effects via taxation) if it results in the excessive pre-emption of resources as above. On their own merits, some (e.g. roads) have potentially favourable effects upon economic growth;

others (e.g. education) may be regarded as providing economic benefits, but over periods of decades; others again (e.g. defence) pre-empt valuable resources from the private sector. The growth of pensions and related benefits does not distort the production structure (except to the extent that the aged, children, etc., consume different things from the working population); but the transfer of purchasing power from the working population to the non-working population through the national insurance apparatus is a large element in the tax structure.

Finally, the steady expansion of the share of the public sector would seem bound to extend the area of policy determination on non-economic grounds; and this may well lead to a change in emphasis in our whole economic and social structure in which the problems of private business and the relevance of competitiveness and economic criteria may get less
Z and less attention.

243. Eleven years later, I would not add to or subtract from this. The PE/ GNP ratio is now much higher than it was at that time (or was then expected to reach in the late 1960s) with no significant adverse reaction from any important section of public opinion. So it was right not to cry 'disaster' then and there: people outside government can always enjoy the luxury of being Cassandras, for sooner or later Cassandra usually turns out to be right; but people whose duty it is to advise Ministers and Governments lose their credibility if they are continuously prophesying disaster, and it does not happen. Nevertheless, subsequent experience has shown that the points at X, Y and Z in this 1964 piece had some relevance, and may be recognised in what has happened since.

244. *Expenditure Control.* The next step was to translate the Survey system into long-term expenditure control. In the autumn, Ministers had approved 'for planning purposes' the beginning of a system of 'block allocation'. The implementation in detail required some redefinition of the 1961 system of blocks in order to get the best compromise in classification between function – in essence, setting up blocks that Ministers and senior officials could discuss as coherent subjects with a common content of policy – and the administrative requirement of being within the re- sponsibility of one Minister.

245. It was decided to abandon the annual review by Ministers of public sector investment. In the Public Expenditure White Paper, nationalised industries' investment had been put into a separate block, entirely different from public service investment, and one which could be included or excluded from total public expenditure according to choice. The problem was to encourage these undertakings to develop on commercial lines following the 1961 Nationalised Industries White Paper. The year 1963 – 64 was very actively engaged in developing the sophisticated systems of

investment appraisal which were beginning to be introduced in the most advanced private companies; in improving the initial concepts of earning targets in the original White Paper; and the concept of Exchequer Risk Capital appeared on the Treasury scene. It would have been possible to publish a successor to the 1961 White Paper immediately after the Election; but this was reasonably delayed for very full consideration by the Labour Government, and the new White Paper did not appear until 1967.

246. Public service investment had been brought within the individual blocks of education, health, etc.; and the key relationship now emerging was the dynamic one between capital and current expenditure in each block instead of the relation between the various investment programmes and the aggregate. The impact on the load on the construction industry is of course important, but for this purpose all public sector demands on the construction industry needed to be brought together, including e.g. defence construction (classified as 'current expenditure', not 'investment' in the National Accounts and therefore not included in the investment review). A regular review of the prospective public sector load on the construction industry was set up accordingly, with decisions by Ministers in case of serious prospective imbalance.

247. Another relevant point in the abolition of the separate investment review was that the whole of public expenditure became within the scope of consideration for short-term variations in accordance with the short-term needs of the economy (formerly thought of for historical reasons almost entirely in terms of investment). Again, this emphasised that the 'economic classification' of the various expenditures was irrelevant to the purposes of expenditure control. There is a relevant point, as we have seen, in the timing of the impact of different expenditures on demand, and the economic categories are used as an approximate guide for this purpose; but this is a matter of calculation and not control.

248. The significance of the abandonment of the investment review was to ensure that all public expenditure was treated as one entity, and not treated differently according as it was classified in the National Accounts as 'public authorities' current expenditure on goods and services', the public sector element of 'gross domestic fixed capital formation', or 'transfer payments from the public sector'. This was a highly practical consideration for the control system, for it helped to eradicate fallacious views (sometimes ignorance but more often injected deliberately to create confusion in the decision-making process) such as:

> This country invests too little compared with other countries, so we should build more schools, roads, hospitals . . . [according to choice]

or

Transfer payments are not a charge on resources, and therefore don't count.

249. Of course, this kind of argument kept on recurring; and the fact that we had to use a National Accounts classification for the 'resources' side of the PESC work and for demonstrating the implications (e.g. for private consumption) of the scale of prospective total public expenditure, was a continuing source of confusion and difficulty in presentation.[3] But we were nevertheless moving step by step towards a comprehensive classification of public expenditure suitable for a clear and understandable system of control.

250. *Block Allocations.* The system that had been approved by Ministers was not strictly one of control; for the figures decided for each of the six civil blocks (plus defence) were not themselves control figures, but were laid down 'for planning purposes'. The departments proceeded as usual with their work, seeking Treasury approval for particular projects and indeed annual Estimates (for their activity financed by Votes) in the ordinary way. The allocations would bite if the department wanted to do something not previously provided for and could not convincingly find room for its long-term cost in its allocation: on the other hand, if it could find room, the Treasury's resistance was greatly reduced. Where there was an issue of overstepping the allocation, moreover, the matter had to be specifically referred to the Cabinet. So this was gently edging towards a new kind of system, quite distant from the 1961 concepts, but also still a long way from the later concepts (extended over all expenditure) of block allocations which were binding control figures, specified year by year through the five-year period.

251. The intention was that the permitted annual percentage increase for each block should be revised every year by Ministerial decisions in the light of the annual PESC report. Initially they had been fixed in accordance with the departments' own estimates in the 1963 PESC report, but this was only to get a starting-point; and although there might well be adjustments from year to year – indeed, there were bound to be, for the percentage increases started from a new base year each time round – there was no reason whatever why these should follow what the departments had put forward. In the ordinary course of business and in the absence of an Election, this process of adjustment would have followed the 1964 PESC report in June.

252. *Departments' Programmes.* Much the most difficult problem, however, regarded in the Plowden Committee discussion as equally important to this overall relationship between expenditure and resources, was the problem of construction and content and execution of the departments'

programmes. To my mind, this was always the nub of the control problem. The merit of the five-year planning system was that it gave the departments a sound basis on which to plan ahead (subject of course to marginal flexibility for reasons of short-term economic needs); and if it was possible for the department and the Treasury to get a real meeting of minds on the programme – the Plowden Committee concept of 'joint working together in a common enterprise' – the entire nature of 'Treasury control' would be changed beyond recognition.

253. There would be an annual review of the department's long-term programme (not just figures but the real policies and projects and performance behind the figures); and further approvals would then be needed only when new and unprovided-for developments took place. This was of course the genesis of the idea of a 'concordat' between the department and the Treasury which I made with Sir David Serpell (who after an interval succeeded me in the Treasury) when I was Permanent Secretary of the Ministry of Technology (not in fact a very favourable case for this concept, because of the sporadic nature of the department's activities, mostly unplannable five years ahead); but which I expounded further as a general system later.[4]

254. For the defence budget, there has been a system of this kind since the late 1950s, as I have previously explained; and I think it is fair to say that throughout the period of revolution in the nation's defence policy and commitments throughout the 1960s, the decision-making system stood up well under intensities of pressure to which no other part of government was subjected.

255. For roads, a rising five-year programme was fixed in 1961; and a Road Programme Committee was set up, of the Ministry of Transport (and the Scots) and the Treasury, to review its progress year by year. For the national health service, a five-year expansion rate had been fixed in 1961, but there was no formal continuing machinery as there had been for roads: I now think this would in the long run have been advantageous, not in the narrow interest of Treasury control, but because the occasion of an annual review of progress (and a report agreed with the Treasury) on a long-term programme is a valuable aid to management, and helps to establish and develop the central programming and financial apparatus that great public business organisations of this kind require: looking back from the NHS crisis of 1974, it would have been valuable also if such a review body could have included the people concerned with personnel in the Health departments and in the Treasury (later the Civil Service Department) who could have thought of these problems of the development of the NHS simultaneously in terms of their implications for manpower and pay.

256. For education, virtually no progress in creating a long-term programme was made in the whole period, and this was much the biggest gap in the system. There were institutional reasons for this. Education (up to university) is carried out by the local authorities, with an autonomy that was (very rightly) defended zealously, so much so that the Government, though providing most of the money (two-thirds of which was required for teacher's pay) had no participation in the salary levels negotiated by the Burnham Committees (hence the shocked outcry when Mr Selwyn Lloyd used his veto power in the 1961 'pay pause'). The Ministry did control their capital expenditure programmes (a factor of decisive long-term importance for their level of current expenditure, determining as it did the supply of teachers, schools, technical colleges). The exhortations (or lack of them) by the Minister, and the standards which he is seeking to impose are of first-class importance in determining the attitude to spending throughout the local government system. This tends to be reflected further in the Government's stance in the negotiations with the local authorities on the level of grant: the domination of educational spending in local authorities' expenditure means that it makes less difference than might be thought whether the grant is specifically for education or in support of local authorities' expenditure generally (the latter being of course preferable). Nevertheless, if one is talking of a block allocation for education, it could readily be argued by the Ministry – 'so sorry, we have no control over the local authorities' current expenditure.' The Ministry had no tradition, moreover, for the measurement and planning of its resources within its own field.[5]

257. In a block allocation for education, moreover, the universities must be included – and so they were – but their programmes and expenditures were completely outside the Ministry of Education's field of responsibility until April 1964, and then kept as a separate enclave until October 1964. Before this, the University Grants Committee, which provides nearly all the universities' money, had been responsible to the Treasury; but the breakneck expansion of the size and expenditure of the universities since the early 1950s had led to a situation by early 1962 in which this responsibility was unacceptable to the Treasury, who notified the Robbins Committee accordingly: but it took two years after this to make the consequential change in the machinery of government.

258. It was not possible to think of education as a whole in practical terms of policy and allocation of resources until the universities (which were expanding much faster than any other part of the educational system with the possible exception of technical colleges) were brought within the same control as all the rest of education. However, it must be stated that the Treasury, as the department responsible for university development, were completely unsuccessful in introducing the concept of the future demand

for university-trained manpower into the deliberations either of the UGC or the Robbins Committee about the size of expansion required. The Treasury's evidence to the Robbins Committee in mid-1962[6] is familiar enough ground in the mid-1970s, but this particular part was neither mentioned when we gave oral evidence, nor mentioned in the Report. Whether or not the expansion of higher education was taken too far and too fast (in itself, or in relation to other education, or in relation to other public services) is a matter for reasonable controversy; but in my opinion, the fact that Treasury Ministers (and the normal critical analysis by the department) were neutralised by their departmental responsibility for the university expansion, and that Education Ministers were freed from the need to allocate resources between universities and other education, reduced the likelihood of well-balanced decisions.

259. Of course there were powerful political interests involved. The education lobby – local authority education committees (which had a certain independence of status within their authorities), universities (increasingly powerful as expansion became more 'political'), teachers' trade unions and other educational organisations – was much the most powerful lobby in the country at the time. Institutional and political obstacles of this kind can sometimes be overcome, but not in this case up to 1964.

260. For housing and miscellaneous local authority expenditure, it was decided to include only investment in the 'block allocation'. This investment is mostly under the departments' control, through the requirement to get the relevant department's sanction for loans. The outstanding current expenditure is that on housing subsidies (from the Exchequer and from the local rates) which (rather like agricultural subsidies used to be) could be altered so much by single changes of policy (e.g. on rents) that such a change would transform the whole block. And much of the miscellaneous local government current expenditure (e.g. refuse disposal, or cost of administration) is far removed from even indirect control by departments. Up to 1964, however, it was never possible to get a real long-term programme even for the investment, in the sense described earlier (as distinct from a set of figures). This is a field, moreover, which is very vulnerable to 'stop-go', for housing is always a good candidate for 'go', and 'miscellaneous local authority investment' (i.e. the projects outside the politically sensitive national programmes) always tend to be regarded as 'non-essential' in times of 'stop'. So this is a difficult area for planning and control, but nevertheless a most important one. The creation of the Department of the Environment, which brings more of this together; and the creation of bigger and fewer local government units could make a change here.

261. Police and prisons were included in the block allocation partly to bring in another big department, the Home Office (with police another important local authority service), which had been handled in the Treasury outside the normal expenditure stream before the 1962 re-organisation; and partly because, although then a low figure, it was expected to rise considerably.

262. Benefits and assistance had always been planned in close co-operation between the Department of Pensions and National Insurance and the Treasury, so no new problems were involved in PESC at the time except in deciding how to interpret in the projections the all-party political undertaking that the pensioners should participate in the improvement in the national standard of living. I have explained earlier that more money is involved in the benefit and pension decisions that in any other single public expenditure decision that Ministers have to take.[7]

263. Next, the introduction of graduated pensions in 1961 (and in 1966 earnings-related unemployment and sickness and widows benefit) was a major departure from the flat-rate benefit/contribution systems introduced in the National Health Insurance Act of 1911, the Unemployment Insurance Acts of 1911 and 1920, the Widows and Old Age Contributory Pensions Act of 1925, endorsed by the wartime Beveridge Report and subsequent Acts. This was the essential principle of British national insurance,[8] basically agreed for fifty years with the major legislation enacted by Liberal, Conservative and Labour Governments. The opening of the floodgates (probably inevitable following the great expansion of occupational pension schemes) destroyed this fifty-year consensus, and has led into the typical governmental pattern of the 1960s and 1970s, in which each new Government begins either by repealing its predecessor's legislation or by announcing its intention to do so and then thinking what it would like to do itself. It must be said that the huge time-scales and the millions of people affected in one of the most intimate details of their lives (their security in old age) make this the worst of all subjects for this peripatetic treatment.

264. In terms of the needs of long-term expenditure control, it seems unlikely (and here I am looking entirely from the outside) that the absorption of the department into a much larger Ministry of Social Security under a senior Cabinet Minister, although good in machinery-of-government terms and for civil service management, is helpful; for it must weaken the link with the Treasury in this crucial financial subject (and one cannot help noting that this 'stop-go' handling of fundamental pensions policy dates from the first steps to this merger in 1968). Here again, I believe that some kind of regular programme review between the insurance part of DHSS and the Treasury would now be advantageous in

getting a stable long-term (in fact, very long-term indeed) policy: twenty years is the right time-scale for fundamental reforms in pension policy, not twenty months.

265. In the 'unprogrammable' areas, the same need existed for a regular programme review between the departments and the Treasury. In agriculture, such an arrangement existed early in the 1960s and attracted the Plowden Committee's attention as a useful prototype: in this case, the structure was laid down by law; and the value of the operation was to get a meeting of minds on how to use the statutory system in the best way in the national interest (quite separate from the hard negotiation of the annual price review). It was later that the computer analysis of the subsidy cheques revealed that the small farmers, whose interests the support policy was designed to protect, actually fared much worse proportionately than the large farmers who could plan their production to maximise their benefit from the price supports. For assistance to industry, which began to become large in the late 1950s as the 'interventionist' policies of the Macmillan Government came into being, a major PESC paper was agreed in 1962 by all the industrial departments, setting out procedures and criteria and checklists for the examination of proposals for assistance to industry. For civil aircraft projects, under the 'launching aid' policy initiated by Mr Sandys in 1960, proper analytical criteria did not begin to appear until the middle of the 1960s.

266. These brief notes on the individual blocks illustrate what was at the time (and still is) my opinion that it is the quality and articulation and phasing of the departments' programmes that presents the difficult and indeed intractable problem; and that the merit of the five-year programme was to enable them to do it better. The alignment of prospective expenditure with prospective resources was tremendously important, but the content and efficiency and coherence of the expenditure programmes was not less so; just as the second half of the Plowden Report – 'joint working in a common enterprise' – was not less important than the first half. The concept of a regular programme review for each main block, consisting of the department concerned and the Treasury, and when the programme has been reviewed and a Ministerial PESC decision taken, an agreement reached about the procedures for monitoring, new projects, etc., in the next year still seems to me to be the right way to develop the mix between the departments' initiative and responsibility for their own programmes and the Treasury's wider responsibility for public expenditure as a whole and its relation to the national economy.

267. We did not get as far with it by 1964 as I had hoped. This was partly because some Ministers refused to allow their departments to co-operate with the Treasury (preferring a back-door approach to the Prime

Minister); partly because of some Permanent Secretaries' ambivalence; even more often, perhaps, the Treasury's failure (from Second Permanent Secretary downward) to show on all occasions the lucidity, originality, conviction, insistence, helpfulness needed to get a new concept under way on a very wide front. However, when Mr Heath and his Government re-invented the wheel[9] in 1970, calling it PAR, and after some months' deliberation decided that it had some relationship with PESC, and that the hub should therefore be at the Treasury, it would have been valuable to have had in being some kind of apparatus for regular programme discussion between each of the main departments and the Treasury.

268. The 1964 PESC Report came out as usual in June but there was no governmental action to be taken on this report. Its main value was to provide the material for the submissions to be made to the new Government, whether it was to be Conservative or Labour. In either case, and quite irrespective of whether there was an autumn sterling crisis, the problem would be most formidable. Fortunately, in respect of the complex of public expenditure, taxation and resources, the December 1963 White Paper had set the prospective situation out in considerable, though somewhat optimistic, detail; which saved us from many of the difficulties involved in briefing new Ministers, that the rules forbid giving them the previous Government's papers. So if it turned out to be a Labour Government, and if the Ministers and non-civil-service advisers had done their preparatory work with any care and application to the published documents, they would in this area have no grounds for surprise or shock.

NOTES

1. This is calculated from the full year's cost of the changes in each Budget, as shown in the Financial Statement, plus tax changes made at other times (Customs 'regulator', July 1961; lower purchase tax, end-1962).

2. Excluding for this purpose the investment of the nationalised industries, which was like private investment, provided that the criteria were correct – and of course the implications for public expenditure of any further nationalisations.

3. There were also remarkable anomalies in the treatment of items in the economic classification; such as treating the universities (almost entirely State-financed) as 'private sector', so that when the colleges of advanced technology became universities they were transferred from 'public sector' to 'private sector' and the grants reclassified accordingly: and the cost of school meals and school milk, provided by public authorities on part-payment by parents, was classed as 'current grants to persons', whilst the cost of false teeth and spectacles, on exactly the same basis, was classed as 'current expenditure by public authorities'. Some of these anomalies still survive; but in practice they do not matter much, for they are small figures in the huge national aggregates in the main economic categories (and particularly in the changes in these aggregates which are the relevant points in the reviews).

4. *New Trends in Government* (HMSO, 1971) pp. 48 - 52.
5. But such traditions and situations change. In the 1960s the Ministry became one of the leading departments in its statistical work; and when PAR came along in 1971, the Department of Education and Science was one of the first civil departments to apply it. [Although the major Departments have been 'applying PAR' since 1971, DES and SED can claim that their respective White Papers of December 1972, *Education: A Framework for Expansion* (Cmnd 5174) and *Education in Scotland: A Statement of Policy* (Cmd 5175) were the first major outward manifestations of the PAR procedure. PAR reports themselves, however, remain unpublished. Ed.]
6. *Report of the Committee on Higher Education*, Cmnd 2154 (Nov 1963), Evidence - Part One, Volume F, pp. 1956 - 2000, especially paras 21 - 46 of Memorandum A. (Reprinted below at pp. 191-7 as Appendix C.)
7. Any Chancellor of the Exchequer going to the decisive Cabinet meeting on pensions always reminded me of Sir Winston Churchill's note about Admiral Jellicoe, then Commander-in-Chief of the Grand Fleet: 'the only commander on either side, whose orders in the space of *two or three hours* might nakedly decide who won the war' *The World Crisis* (Macmillan) Vol. III, p. 214.
8. Essentially, the State provision of a safety net as of right in a contributory scheme, leaving people to provide more if they wished by private insurance. The schemes of other advanced countries (except Eire and New Zealand) followed Bismarck's original scheme of 1883 relating benefits and contributions in various ways to income.
9. Cf. Mr Antrobus, in *The Skin of our Teeth*, by Thornton Wilder, first produced 1942.

10 Stamp Memorial Lecture

269. In February 1964, I was invited to give the Stamp Memorial Lecture, then as now a signal honour. Lord Stamp (1880 - 1941) was one of the truly outstanding men of his time. His death so early by enemy action makes it impossible to compare him with his contemporaries, such as Lord Waverley (still better known as Sir John Anderson, 1882 - 1958) or Lord Beveridge (1879 - 1963). But his career showed the immense opportunities offered to young men of ability by the civil service before the First World War: he entered the Inland Revenue as a clerk at the age of sixteen: by 1916 (aged 36) he was assistant secretary to the Board of Inland Revenue, and already perhaps the greatest expert on taxation in the country. He left the Inland Revenue in 1919 to be a director and secretary of Nobel Industries (future constituent of ICI); and was at once put on the 1919 Royal Commission on income tax and on the 1924 Colwyn Royal Commission on taxation and national debt.[1]

270. In 1926 he became what we would now call chairman and chief executive of the LMS railway. To readers to whom a nationalised railway system is as axiomatic as a nationalised post office, the London Midland & Scottish was one of the four groups formed in the 1921 Railways Act to merge 123 companies. The creation of a unified system - the LMS - which Lord Stamp accomplished with his three brilliant executive vice-presidents, Sir William Wood, Sir Ernest Lemon and Sir Harold Hartley, was one of the first great achievements of what would now be called modern management techniques - a small management executive with no great central bureaucracy, asset utilisation, budgetary control, effective research development, endless war on paper and forms, etc. One illustration of the complexity of the task was that the LMS found itself with the carriage and wagon workshops of nine separate companies: another was the nine different freight depots and marshalling yards of seven companies (not all LMS) at Carlisle etc.[2]

271. Stamp had many other interests - business (including being on the Court of the Bank of England, and the Abbey Road Building Society); economic and statistical (including being President of the Royal Statistical Society 1930 - 32), and a stream of writings and lectures.[3] When war broke out in 1939, he was commissioned by the Government to do what came to be called the 'Stamp Survey' of the economic situation and prospects, and

collected a team which ultimately became the Economic Section of the Cabinet Office and the Central Statistical Office. It is difficult for anyone now to match this breadth of contributions to the public service, to industry and to the academic world. The annual memorial lecture is organised by a trust constituted in London University in 1942 on the initiative of these institutions. It is required to have as its subject 'the application of economics or statistics to a practical problem of general interest', and to treat it 'from a scientific and not from a party-political standpoint'.

272. I accepted the invitation with alacrity. This was the nineteenth lecture: only two had been by professional civil servants. In 1950, Lord (then Sir Edward) Bridges, Permanent Secretary of the Treasury, gave what still looks (for its time) a very forward-looking lecture on Treasury Control.[4] He did me the great kindness of taking the chair at my lecture – one of many kindnesses that I remember in my Treasury days, notably a harsh but true kindness, unquestionably right in my own interests, in refusing to promote me to a job which I was deeply convinced I had earned, and moving me sideways into a completely new and different field – public expenditure (and I lost only two years before promotion anyway). Then in 1958, Sir Frank Lee, then Permanent Secretary of the Board of Trade, had given the Lecture on his department. So I reckoned I was in good company.

273. The date was fixed for 1 December; and I had to submit my manuscript for printing by mid-October. The practical problem was that I would not know, when submitting the text, whether there would be a Conservative or a Labour Government on the day I gave the lecture; and there would obviously be publicity in which I could not risk offending the Chancellor of the Exchequer (whoever he might be) or prejudicing my own relationship with him. I was debarred by the Trust Deed from being 'party-political', and it naturally would not occur to me to be so; but practically all 'practical problems of general interest' in fact have political implications and some Ministers will read very different messages from others into the most anodyne utterances by their officials.

274. So I chose 'The Management of the Public Sector of the National Economy', on the grounds that the public sector, and the annual spending of £11,000 million a year (as it then was) and to get the best possible contribution to the nation from these resources, were the hard facts at the root of every Chancellor's life and work; and it would give a good opportunity too to set out in public and place on permanent record what was now becoming the post-Plowden orthodoxy of Treasury thinking on the handling of public expenditure. It is worth recording that although public expenditure is the most 'political' subject of all, the lecture did avoid

the political pitfalls that I had feared, and the press comment was entirely non-political, and I never had any reason to suppose that Mr Wilson or Mr Callaghan (who of course were in the saddle on 1 December) were in the slightest degree embarrassed.

275. The Lecture is republished with this book and some of its thinking has emerged in the earlier chapters. Nevertheless, there were points in it which were new at the time, and may still not be fully appreciated, even by well-informed people. I will take one point from each of the four sections of the lecture.

276. First, the actual size and importance of the public sector. Public expenditure's proportion (excluding debt interest) of 40 per cent of GNP, as shown in Mr Maudling's first 'Plowden' White Paper of December 1963, is familiar enough; and we are now familiar with much larger figures. But the lecture went on to spell this out in less familiar terms:

> The public sector [which then excluded the steel industry; and many individual undertakings, such as Rolls Royce (1971) and the Government-owned shipbuilders] employs directly nearly 25 per cent of the nation's manpower, and probably about 60 per cent of those with full-time higher education. These authorities own about 40 per cent of the nation's capital assets, and are responsible for nearly 45 per cent of the nation's annual fixed investments. About 60 per cent of the nation's scientific and technological research and development is financed by Government agencies. The size and structure of important private industries, such as agriculture and aircraft production, are in effect determined by the decisions of Government; and the purchases of the public sector provide a large and in some cases dominant part of the demand for the products of other industries, notably construction, pharmaceuticals, electronics, electrical engineering, telecommunications equipment, and so on.

The point is still not taken: with four million employees in the public services and two million in the nationalised industries, successive Governments and commentators still talk about national concepts of 'incomes policy', when their obvious first task, as direct employers and in effect paymasters of subsidiary public authorities, is to find criteria to determine the pay relativities of their own staffs and to negotiate with the unions accordingly.[5]

277. Second, economic and administrative efficiency of the public services. The lecture analysed 135 cases brought before Parliament over five years by the Comptroller and Auditor-General; the links between departments to get a continuous interchange of experience between specialists in such functions as building, land transactions, purchase of goods, accounting, etc. (with over fifty subjects of common interest having

been under review in this set of committees in the previous eighteen months). this was interesting material but the essential point (exactly following Lord Bridges's Stamp Lecture) was the Treasury's responsibility for management as laid down by the Plowden Committee. As the lecture said:

> The Treasury's job is not to act as a censor, or as a back-seat driver, for the Departments. It must satisfy itself that every Department's management is as adequate as the resources of the Service permit; and that the techniques of management are being steadily improved and extended. Instead of being a back-seat driver, the Treasury's job is to ensure that every Department has the best possible cars and drivers and is properly equipped with maps.

278. In so writing, as in the Plowden report, I never dreamed that the responsibility for financial control of departments would be separated from that for management control, as was done when the Treasury was split in 1968 and the Civil Service Department set up. I discussed this at length in *New Trends in Government* (1971), and elsewhere in this book. All I will say now is that if I was still responsible for public expenditure I would insist on my staff carrying out control of management too, and if this duplicated the Civil Service Department's work, so much the worse for that. I say this because the non-responsibility for management control drives the Treasury back to the worst kinds of financial control of departments, which not only loses the sight of the woods for the trees, but also loses the sight of the forests. Still unfinished business.

279. Third, appraisal of expenditure projects. I was optimistic that we could be on the verge of important technical advances 'during the next few years'. For example, starting with defence I said:

> In the last five years the annual cost per serviceman, at 1964 value of money, has risen from £3,325 to £5,075, i.e. by over 50 per cent; and the defence services are probably the most highly capitalized part of the economy – in the sense of having most equipment per man, on a scale not unlike oil refineries or electric-power stations. For some years the defence budget has absorbed about 7 per cent of the gross national product. The manpower employed for military purposes, in the forces and in industry, is somewhat above 1½ million. If it becomes possible by new techniques of analysis to make more effective use of this valuable block of resources, this will be highly significant. . . .

> Teaching in universities and schools and technical colleges employs 350,000 out of the 750,000 people in this country who have had full-time higher education. These are very scarce and important resources of people, and their deployment between the various levels of education, from primary to university, and between education and the rest of the national economy, may be of considerable economic significance. We do

not yet know where the strengths and weaknesses of the educational system are from the point of view of the nation's economic potential; and it will be many years before there is a body of knowledge which could permit a more purposeful allocation of resources within the educational programme. But a light of one candle-power would illuminate the darkness; and we may be at a beginning. . . .

The techniques which are being developed for the comparative examination of road projects are still at an early stage; but looking ahead one can see the possibility of analysis leading to better choice and better value for money. Whether this will reach the point at which railway investment and road investment can in practical terms be examined side by side is for the future – but a very crucial element in public sector policy. . . .

The quality of [the nationalised industries] business decisions, and particularly those determining the size and nature of investment, is fundamental; for with the scale of operation of these industries, with annual investment of over £1,000m., the misdirection of resources of labour and capital resulting from wrong decisions can be very large, and devastating to economic growth. This is the relevance of the system of financial objectives for nationalized industries, which has been introduced in recent years. . . . To enable these industries to make their proper contribution to the national economy, it would seem essential that they should have clearly defined financial objectives which give a practical basis for energetic management and provide lucid and economically valid criteria for their investment and commercial policy decisions.

280. I would not deprecate the work that has been done, both in departments and in universities. But we have not got far in ten years. The fate of the immensely elaborate and expensive cost-benefit operation by the Roskill Commission on the Third London Airport has thrown doubt on (i) whether one can ask the right questions; (ii) whether the genuine uncertainties of the future do not greatly outweigh the considerations that are subject to analysis, so that the latter is literally not worth while; (iii) whether the human and political problems created by these decisions would not in any case become overriding. In the nationalised industries, the processes outlined above, continued by the Labour Government, were destroyed in the early 1970s in pursuit of incomes and prices policy, leaving these huge and vital industries rudderless. On the other hand, I think that more is known of the results and cost-effectiveness of regional policy; certainly more is known of the appraisal of civil aircraft projects; and there is much more scepticism (which I believe to be a good thing) about the return to the national economy on Government-financed industrial and scientific research. So there have been some gains, but not, I fear, the beginning of the fundamental gains that I had hoped to see.

281. Fourth, the lecture described the basic concepts of the relation of long-term aggregates of public expenditure to future resources on familiar lines. Indeed, the 'macro' side of the 'Plowden' philosophy has been much more successfully understood and applied than the 'micro'. The interest of the lecture in this field was that it was the first public presentation of the concept of a long-term programme for public sector receipts to drive home the implications of the long-term programme for public expenditure:

To sum up . . . it is necessary to base expenditure decisions upon a long-term review of expenditure, because this is the time-scale of the technology and management needs of the public services. But it is impracticable in this process to match expenditure decisions with taxation decisions, because the time-scales are different: today's expenditure decisions mostly affect expenditure in years ahead; today's taxation decisions affect revenue very quickly, and have the purpose of bringing about short-term balance in the economy as well as raising the money to pay for the public expenditure. The long-term expenditure has to be considered in relation to the long-term resources and thence to the long-term claims of private consumption and private investment; and thus to the consideration of what changes of taxation will in the long-term be likely to be needed in order to enable the economy to accommodate the growing public expenditure.

It may not perhaps be unduly fanciful to see in this kind of approach the beginnings of an idea of long-term budgeting the consideration of public sector expenditure and receipts, over a period of years, in relation to the prospective course of the national economy and the claims of private consumption, investment, and exports; with on the one hand long-term plans for the development of each of the major public services, and on the other hand corresponding long-term plans for the development of the various kinds of public sector receipts; the structure on both sides geared as far as possible to support economic growth.

This would over a period of years build up a system for the long-term balancing of the development of the economy, operating side by side with the existing system for the use of taxation measures, together with monetary and other measures, for the short-term balancing of the economy.

282. Looking at it all ten years later, with I hope a reasonable objectivity, the lecture does seem to me to have brought together more clearly than any public statement (by me or anybody else) has done before or since the three dominating aspects (macro and micro) of the management of the public sector and its control from the centre of government:

    (i)   the size of the aggregate of public expenditure – i.e. the total use of resources by the public sector;

    (ii)   the evaluation of expenditure proposals, and hence the allocation of resources, or authorisation of expenditure, to each of the public services;

(iii)   the value that these services in the event provide for the money.

283. The lecture concluded:

Each [of these three aspects] is worth a lecture to itself; but perhaps the most relevant point is the interdependence of the three. One cannot argue the first *a priori* without a detailed knowledge of the second; or form judgements on the second without knowing what is actually happening to the third. One single central task of government is embodied in all three – that of deciding how the Government should use the power of the purse and direct the outlay of public funds in order to further the nation's social and economic objectives. Historically, the need to carry out this task was one of the great formative influences in the development of our political and administrative institutions and machinery of government; and with the importance of the public sector growing all the time, it is most unlikely that this task will recede into the background.

284. For a civil servant, it is unusual to get the opportunity to describe in public one's concepts about the work in which one was engaged, and in this case, the political twilight in which it had to be completed turned out to be an advantage; and I would stand by every word ten years later – my own concepts, not tailored in any respect to suit the views of my Chancellor of the Exchequer (for I had no idea who he would be) nor, as all practical administrators must, to carry the necessary agreement to get a project off the ground.

285. The press comment was extensive (by the standards of this kind of occasion) and without exception well-informed and going for the right points (particularly the "value for money"). But I will quote *The Banker*:[6]

Sir Richard's paper is clothed in the measured discretion of the experienced administrator. But between the lines one can read the reality that Ministers – whether Tory or Labour – have yet to grapple with the thorny political problems of genuinely planning these huge outlays in due relation to national resources and to a realistic view of 'growth'. Planning, one is entitled to say to the Government when it reaches out to regulate the private sector, begins at home.

286. Finally, I hope I may be excused for quoting a charming letter from Lord Stamp's son Max:

'My father would have been pleased'.

NOTES

1. To present-day civil servants (and perhaps politicians and journalists too) the ease of movement from civil service to industry even as little as fifty years ago is very striking.
2. There is much about this management epic in A. J. Pearson's *Man of the Rail* (Allen and Unwin, 1967).
3. My most vivid personal recollection is of quite a different character, deriving from my *Financial News* days. One day in the mid-1930s, Keynes wrote one of his seminal articles on unemployment. Stamp wrote a reply: we put out the poster

STAMP

ON

KEYNES

Keynes replied, and our poster was naturally

KEYNES

KEYNES

STAMP

4. Such is the perversity of some people, that when in my lecture I was at pains to point out the continuity between his thought in the 1950 Lecture and mine, it was said to be a formal politeness on my part. But to anyone who takes the trouble to read the two texts, the strands of continuity are there clearly to be seen. I had not then read Bridges's Pollak lecture at Harvard at end-1961, which lucidly expounded the concepts in the Plowden Report as the natural next stage in the development of his own thought on the historical development of Treasury Control.
5. See for example my research report of June 1973, *Incomes Policy in Phase IV*, op. cit.
6. January 1965.

11 PESC and the 1964–66 Labour Government

287. The Labour Party was voted into office on Friday 16 October, and Mr Harold Wilson took charge immediately. The first issue was machinery of government, and the long-expected break-up of the Treasury and the creation of the Department of Economic Affairs (DEA); and Mr Wilson has described in his memoirs[1] the background of his thinking, and how he reached agreement with Mr George Brown and Mr Callaghan on that first evening. For the control of public expenditure, the division of responsibilities and the ability of the two Ministers and their departments to work effectively together was of crucial importance.

288. *Treasury and DEA.* Mr Wilson says how when he became Leader of the Opposition in February 1963 he decided that:

while the Chancellor of the Exchequer should be responsible for all actions necessary in the monetary field, foreign exchange, internal monetary management, Government expenditure and taxation, Britain could hope to win economic security only by a fundamental reconstruction and modernisation of industry under the direction of a department at least as powerful as the Treasury. This new department would be concerned with real resources, with economic planning, with strengthening our ability to export and to save imports, with increasing productivity and our competitiveness in domestic and export markets.

289. Mr Wilson had followed up the theme of industrial modernisation in his Swansea speech in January 1964. This was the starting-point for a lot of thought and discussion; for the machinery of government naturally depends upon the policy, and not vice versa. To create and carry out, in combination with industry, a massive plan for industrial development and modernisation and competitive power – something like what the Monnet Plan had achieved in France – would obviously require a new Government department like the *Commissariat du Plan* in France, with one of the most powerful Ministers in the Government, and a mixed staff who were capable of working closely both with industry and with the Whitehall machine. But this would never have made sense unless such a plan had been the Government's top priority.

290. If, however, the intention was to continue to develop the lines of industrial policy which had been begun under Mr Macmillan's Government – 'Neddy' and 'little Neddies' type of 'planning', incomes and prices policy, regional incentives, etc. – it was unlikely that a new department would suceed, for it would not be performing a clearly indispensable major role. The most promising course would then be to jump straight to the solution which Mr Wilson reached in October 1969 when he abolished DEA, and which Mr Heath improved upon in forming the Department of Trade and Industry in October 1970; and make a powerful industrial department containing within itself the responsibility for all the important private sector and public sector industry and trade (and doing its own co-ordination). Possibly in October 1964 this could have brought in the Ministry of Labour too, for there was then more room to manoeuvre in terms of workable departmental loads than there was five or six years later. This creation of a powerful industrial department was the only way to meet Mr Wilson's specification of 'a department at least as powerful as the Treasury': there would have been a duumvirate, with the Treasury responsible for economic and financial policy and the Department of Industry for industrial policy in the widest sense.

291. These were the alternatives of policy (and consequentially of machinery-of-government) as they struck me earlier in the year; but the policy turned out to be the second and not the first, and machinery-of-government the opposite. Mr Wilson describes the agreement reached on:

the fundamental distinction between monetary responsibilities on the one hand, which must come under the Treasury, and, on the other, the co-ordinating responsibilities for industry and everything to do with the mobilisation of real resources for productivity and exports. . . .

George Brown quickly and rightly added to his departmental duties responsibilities for prices and incomes, though there were moments in succeeding years when I felt that the DEA had become so overborne by prices and incomes questions that it was not driving ahead sufficiently fast with industrial planning and productivity questions. . . . He also added – I now think I was wrong to agree – responsibility for the main issues of overseas economic policy. . . .

It took some time to sort this all out into agreements between the Ministers concerned; and a great deal longer to build up even an embryo staff for the DEA – creating a new department (especially when four more are being created at the same time) is the most forbidding of all tasks.[2]

292. *Public Expenditure in the New Regime.* The Treasury's responsibility for public expenditure was clearly established by the agreement reached between the Ministers. There were some minor difficulties, which might have been major. It was argued, for example, that 'public investment' – power stations, houses, schools, roads – was 'physical', or 'real resources',

and therefore should be controlled by DEA: but it was bound to be accepted that this was an integral part of public expenditure, on the grounds expounded in earlier chapters. Throughout the field of public expenditure there were aspects of great relevance to DEA's responsibilities; and it was agreed that for each area of public sector expenditure, a working arrangement would be made between the two departments.[3]

293. Once the arrangements had become clarified, they worked very smoothly (much eased by Sir Eric Roll, Douglas Allen, Douglas Henley in DEA). This was an area, moreover, in which Mr Brown and Mr Callaghan usually found little difficulty in agreeing; and their combined action in many areas of expenditure proved very effective. On the resources side, the transfer of the economic and statistical analytical staffs from NEDO to DEA at once permitted integration of the work of all the departmental staffs concerned with these problems, and this was of course advantageo .s.[4]

294. Taking all these considerations together in retrospect it seems to me reasonable to say that the machinery-of-government decisions of 16 October 1964 had no significant effect on the control of public expenditure or the management of the public sector. The Government's decisions had a great impact on public expenditure; but I do not believe that on balance these would have been significantly different if the machinery at the centre had been left unchanged, at any rate in the period with which I am dealing. Although much was talked at the time about the virtues of 'creative tension' between the 'expansionist' DEA and the 'restrictionist' Treasury, these cannot be said to have left any mark on public expenditure.[5]

295. '*The First Hundred Days*'. Mr Wilson reports in his memoirs (p. 5) that:
    The pattern our first hundred days would have to take was set in the first hundred minutes.
The precedents for 'first hundred days' are not propitious. The original ran from Elba to Waterloo: the last, President Kennedy's, finished at the Bay of Pigs.

296. Mr Wilson's first few weeks were dominated by the sterling crisis. On 26 October, the 'Statement on the Economic Situation' was issued (it could not be a White Paper for Parliament had not yet met); including a sharp attack on the Conservatives' public expenditure programmes as one of the critical problems in the situation, some needing to be increased and others reduced. A series of specific policy points,[6] included:
    The Government will carry out a strict review of all Government expenditure. Their object will be to relieve the strain on the balance of

payments and release resources for more productive purposes by cutting out expenditure on items of low economic priority, such as 'prestige projects'. The Government have already communicated to the French Government their wish to re-examine urgently the Concorde project. The social programmes of the Government will be unfolded in the Queen's Speech. The country realises that these will have to be paid for, and the Government will state what is involved and how the cost will be met.

297. Public expenditure was therefore right at the top of the agenda for 'the first hundred days'; and I cannot recall any other new Government within my experience which devoted so much time and effort to it in the critical first months. Mr Callaghan had clearly taken the PESC concepts on board, following the debates in the previous year on Mr Maudling's White Paper, and laid down from the start that expenditure decisions must be taken together, that new proposals must be matched with new revenue: he wanted to have a 1964 - 65/1968 - 69 PESC with his colleagues' new proposals in it so that strategic decisions could be taken quickly; and he wanted to get at the 'stern review' and the elimination of waste of resources.

298. The sorting out of the new Ministers' bids was done quickly; and the two selected items, announced in Mr Callaghan's autumn Budget, were increases of national insurance and associated benefits (including an immediate increase in national assistance rates) and the removal of prescription charges on medicines. These were regarded as having been firm pledges for immediate action made in the election campaign. For the national insurance, as always, the Government chose the biggest increase that was plausible, 18 per cent, in relation to the concept of keeping the pensioners in step with the growth of earnings in the two years since the previous increase: and the total cost was put at about £300 millon a year, of which about two-thirds was covered by additional contributions. Taking the whole package together, the Exchequer cost was about £130 million in 1965 - 66. Increases of 6*d* [2½ p.] in the income tax and 6*d* a gallon in the oil duty were to produce £215 million in a full year; and there were also highly uncertain receipts from the import surcharge and cost of a tax rebate for exports. There was so much new in the Budget, including the intention to produce in 1965 the new Capital Gains and Corporation taxes, that it was a difficult operation to sum up; but it triggered off a sterling crisis of great intensity.

299. *The Re-shaping of Public Expenditure.* It is fair to say that once the Government had decided that they must increase pensions (to the maximum extent) and to remove prescription charges, there was nothing to be done on public expenditure at this stage. But the Government's

strategy for the longer term was developed fast.

300. First a *fundamental review of defence*, initiated by a weekend conference at Chequers on 21/22 November. There were many detailed problems to decide, but the fundamental issue was the future size of the defence budget, for this was the only way to establish a limit within which a consistent strategy could be built and the nature of the choices made clear. The Ministry of Defence now had the systems of building-blocks described in para 90, which made it possible to cost the alternatives. The 'inherited' defence budget was £2400 million (at 1964 prices) for the year 1969-70. Mr Callaghan and Mr George Brown drove hard from the start to establish the limit at £2000 million (at 1964 prices), which was the level of the 'inherited' 1964-65 Estimates; and this was in effect decided in January 1965, so that there was a long-term year-by-year ceiling on the defence budget into which the strategy had to be accommodated.

301. To live within the present level of defence expenditure at constant value of money was formidably difficult, with the cost per man rising at about 10 per cent a year as equipment (and the men to operate it) became more expensive; and with the additional problems of the big chunk of direct overseas expenditure, and the call on the resources of the most advanced industries and most skilled researchers and engineers. Our defence was already spread dangerously thin; and it had been clear for years that we could not afford, either consistently with our own needs or in comparison with our European competitors, to keep up these commitments.

302. So the great debate was initiated, with its first outcome in the cancellation of the three new aircraft under development, the TSR2 (announced in the Budget on 6 April) the P 1154 and the HS 681; and its final conclusion in the Prime Minister's statement of 16 January 1968, saying that withdrawal of forces from the Far East (including Malaysia and Singapore) and from the Persian Gulf would be completed by end-1971; so that by then (apart from Hong Kong and other dependencies) we would no longer maintain military bases outside Europe and the Mediterranean.

303. This process took three years, and went through many phases, and aroused deep emotions: the abandonment of 'East of Suez' was the final abdication from being a 'world Power'. The decision-taking was bound to take a long time, for it was conducted against the continuous changes in the overseas situation, notably the confrontation with Indonesia. In my opinion, it would have happened sooner or later under any Government, for the economic load was unsupportable. Moreover, the Commonwealth countries East of Suez were ambivalent,[7] some looking towards USA and

some to neutrality, and few seeing any tangible defence threat: all could see Britain's interests moving towards Europe.

304. It had become clearly established that Britain's economic interests in the Far East were not of a size and nature to enter significantly into the defence and foreign policy decisions; and there was considerable argument whether even our oil interests in the Middle East could be defended effectively by forces within our capability, and whether this was not an altogether too expensive premium. Looked at in 1974, indeed, it is difficult to imagine that the presence of what could only be token British forces could have been any restraint on the actions of the OPEC countries of December 1973. These considerations would certainly have come to look the same to any Government.

305. However, from the technical point of view of government, this review was well conducted. The establishment at the start of the £2000 million limit was important: the development of the block-building techniques that the Ministry of Defence (under Sir Henry Hardman) had been so quick to acquire from Mr McNamara's team of Rhodes Scholars (Hitch, Enthoven and Rowan) were even more important in enabling Ministers to carry out their discussions with the costs of the choices clearly in mind. These considerations go wider than defence.

306. I cannot refrain from quoting the following minute by Dr Dalton to the Prime Minister on 20 January 1947:
    . . . What shall it profit Britain to have even 1,500,000 men in the Forces and Supply, and to be spending nearly £1,000 millions a year on them, if we come an economic and financial cropper two years hence? . . . And I am told in Cabinet that to have only 1,400,000 Service and Supply personnel, and to spend only £750 millions on them is 'unilateral disarmament'. . . .
    In 1964 we were still employing 1½ million people in the Forces and supplying them, and they cost over £2000 million a year.

307. The pressures under which the Chancellor lives do not change much.

308. Second, the strict review of '*items of low economic priority, such as "prestige projects"*'. The most important of these was Concorde; for which there had never been a convincing economic case; and the Government had announced their intention to seek to re-examine this urgently with the French Government. The French, however, were entirely unwilling to do this; and the Government faced a difficult dilemma. The 1962 treaty embarking on the project had no review clause: this had been deliberate British policy at the time. A straight cancellation would have led to a confrontation with General de Gaulle at the beginning of the life of the new

Government, at a moment of major sterling crisis, and at a time when we were in great difficulties on other fronts of overseas commercial policy.

309. Moreover, it was argued by the lawyers that the French could take the dispute to the International Court, and we could be liable for heavy damages. Some argued, indeed, that we might be required to pay half the total cost if the French went ahead alone (this half then estimated at around £200 million); and whilst this was never a very realistic argument, for the French did not have the technological capability, particularly on the engine, to 'go it alone', the possible implications injected a strong element of financial caution to support the wider political considerations. Until a positive decision to cancel was taken, the project would automatically continue; and as the weeks passed the determination to cancel gradually faded; and on the aircraft side the Government's attention became concentrated on the cancellation of the three new military projects.

310. In retrospect, this was in my opinion nevertheless the best opportunity to extricate ourselves from the project and at the minimum of cost, for as time passed, and more and more resources were committed by the French and ourselves, the only practical breaking-point was an agreement with the French that the project would fail, either technologically or commercially; and such a point never arose, for to the French as well as ourselves this had become a 'prestige project'; and at the end of 1974, the whole story is not yet determined. There is little doubt in my mind, however, that the true long-term cost may well have been to the development and international successes of the British aircraft industry, for the Concorde project had pre-empted such a large proportion both of the physical and manpower resources of the industry, as well as the available Government money, that different lines of development were inevitably ignored or underdeveloped.

311. For the *strict review* a strong group of two officials, an economist and a very distinguished scientist was set up to review a long list of projects of 'low economic priority', ranging from the project of a nuclear ship to civil space research and the Channel Tunnel. There were some useful things done; but, as chairman of this operation, my opinion is that it did not get results as good as the quality of the members and the amount of time spent. The big projects (like Concorde itself, the AEA reactor programme and the Channel Tunnel) already had a life and tremendous time-scale of their own, backed up by years of international, Ministerial and departmental discussion; and were in essence too firmly established to be shaken by the weight of any group of officials, however strong. In other courses of policy, such as the British Railways Board subsidy, or the provision of agricultural

advisory services, the notion of 'low economic priority' was difficult to define in a way that carried conviction.

312. Looking back over the years, one cannot fail to reach the conclusion that large amounts of Government money and manpower have been expended for 'economic' purposes which have failed to achieve a commensurate return to the economy. It had been believed from the mid-1950s onwards that more resources should be made available to Government-financed civil research establishments and Research Councils: but as soon as this belief was examined by the Ministry of Technology in the mid-1960s[8] and later by Lord Rothschild in the areas outside Mintech's scope, it was very difficult to find such economic justification, and the belief was continuously challenged by industry. The failure of the nuclear power programme of 1957 (and its successors) has lost us a leading position in the reactor world. The relation between nationalised industries' R & D and design work and that of their suppliers has (whatever the advantages for the nationalised industries may be) left the latter in a much weaker position than their United States and German competitors, who do the R & D and design themselves. The evaluation of civil aircraft and other advanced technology projects was another. On a smaller but not less important scale, the cost-effectiveness of providing advisory services for small firms in agriculture (done on a huge scale since the war), manufacturing (some done in Mintech and continued in DTI) and construction has never been fully explored.

313. These illustrations are not mentioned to criticise either Government or nationalised industry or private industry – far from it. But they all relate to the area in which Britain is unquestionably weaker in structure and interrelations than any other advanced country, i.e. the relationship between Government and governmental institutions, nationalised industries and private industry. In terms of waste of resources for the national economy, this is where the big figures have been; and the most effective way to tackle the strict review of 'projects of low economic priority' would have been to identify these areas, many of twenty years' standing, and to devise some technique for making a substantial contribution towards each of them within, say, five years. In the ten years, some progress was made with some of these. But in 1964 (and maybe still in 1974), the importance in a country with as big a public sector as Britain's, of being aware of the existence of such problems, and the need to concentrate effort on solving them, were not yet widely understood.

314. Third, there was a review of *non-economic civil expenditure* by the Chief Secretary, Mr Diamond. This was a formidable task, partly carried out through the normal review of the Estimates, applied very strictly for the first figures were looking very high; partly by initiating reviews of difficult

subjects, such as civil defence; partly by consideration of 'value for money' points in the social services; and partly by giving a push on relatively small subjects which needed a Minister's initiative to get them moving. This method of operation is set out more systematically than it actually happened – it ranged right across the business on expenditure at December/January.

315. It is always difficult to measure the success of this kind of operation, for the problem of expenditure control is continuous. The Estimates for 1965–66 finally represented an increase of 8.9 per cent over those for the previous year; compared with 6.7 per cent, 9.4 per cent and 8.2 per cent in the three years before that. Much was made by the Government, fairly enough, of the 'inherited' increases, but about 2 per cent (or nearly one-quarter) of the 8.9 per cent did represent the increases in Exchequer expenditure for national insurance and assistance and the removal of prescription charges announced in the autumn Budget.

316. The most important single issues in these first weeks were those of nationalised industries' price increases, beginning with Post Office charges. These confronted the Government with exactly the same problems as Mr Macmillan's 'price plateau' in 1956 and Mr Heath in 1970; but Mr Callaghan and Mr Brown were absolutely firm on continuing and developing the financial objective and target system, subject to their being satisfied that the price increases were justified; and this policy (announced in the House of Commons on 22 December and 4 February) was broadly sustained.

317. *The Long-term Public Expenditure Programme.* The next urgent step, once the autumn budget and the sterling crisis were resolved, and the 'strict review' set in motion, was to establish the basis for the first long-term public sector expenditure budget. This was urgent for three immediate practical reasons:

    (*a*) It was thought essential for the Chancellor to be able to make a specific statement on the Government's long-term expenditure plans when he announced the rise in the 1965–66 Estimates on 22 February.

    (*b*) It was necessary to decide what would be the public sector content of the National Plan, due to be published in September.

    (*c*) The Government had to establish a framework for departmental Ministers' work. Only two of the Government's new proposals (national insurance/assistance and prescription charges) had been announced in the autumn budget; and all the Ministers were full of new proposals.

318. So to provide any sort of orderly government, a framework had to be

settled by end-January at latest, providing the basis for the PESC operation in July, which would establish the allocations for the period from 1964 – 65 to 1969 – 70. This meant that the first crucial decisions had to be taken by Christmas.

319. The technical problem was difficult but manageable. In the course of November, we had been bringing up to date the expenditure projections for 1964 – 65 to 1968 – 69, which had been in the PESC 1964 Report in July, making such amendments as had occurred in the ordinary course of time, including the changes announced in the autumn Budget but no other policy changes. This gave as it were a 'state of play' on present announced decisions and at 1964 prices. It was clear beyond any conceivable doubt that on any rational estimate of the growth of GNP, and given the need both to put the balance of payments right and to allow room for more private investment, acceptance of this level of public expenditure would imply intolerable annual increases in taxation and intolerable reduction in the rate of improvement of private consumption per head (except for pensioners and others on social security benefits).

320. Two consequences flowed from this:
  (a) the need to decide and publicly announce a medium-term rate of increase of public sector expenditure that would be viable on reasonable assumptions of the rate of growth of GNP;
  (b) preliminary decisions on the most important programmes, to guide the preparation of the PESC programmes so that the Government would not, later in the year, be confronted with an unmanageable gap between the departments' requirements as then stated and the aggregate resources available.

321. This situation was faced with great determination by Mr Callaghan and Mr Brown, whose interests marched totally in unison, for failure to deal effectively with this problem would wreck both the future Budgets for the whole period of the Administration and the possibility of producing a credible and acceptable National Plan. They carried the Prime Minister with them in the days before Christmas. In essence, the provisional decisions were:
  (a) The growth of public sector expenditure (excluding investment of nationalised industries) should be limited to an average annual rate of 4¼ per cent (i.e. 23 per cent) from 1964 – 65 to 1969 – 70. This was subsequently announced by the Chancellor on 22 February:
  (b) The defence budget to be kept at the 1964 – 65 level of £2000 million a year at constant prices;
  (c) For the main 'programmable' civil programmes (roads, public sector housing investment – and ultimately housing subsidies – education, health and welfare, police and prisons, benefits and

assistance, overseas aid) 'basic' limits for programmes for 1964–65
to 1969–70 were laid down broadly speaking on the basis of existing
decisions; and specific treatment was laid down for the 'non-
programmable' programmes, e.g. agricultural subsidies, British
Railways Board deficit, etc.

(*d*) Departments were allowed to submit 'additional' programmes.

(*e*) Allocation decisions would be taken in July.

322. The difficulties which had arisen hitherto about having a different
growth rate for the National Plan from that for public expenditure (25 per
cent and 22½ per cent from 1964 to 1970) caused no problem. It was
thought reasonable that if output did rise at the planned rate (3¾ per cent a
year) it would always be possible to adjust taxation, or indeed the
expenditure programmes; and that it was reasonable to be more cautious
in public expenditure commitments. For nationalised industries' planning,
the 25 per cent figure was taken.

323. The plan of campaign was agreed at the end of January, after
inevitably keen argument about the 'basic' figures (for nobody expected
there would be much room for the 'additional' programmes). To get to this
point, however, virtually within 'the first hundred days' must be regarded
as a remarkable achievement. Of course this was only the first stage, with
something for each Minister to play for; but nevertheless it must have
become clear to many Ministers that after the thirteen years of being in
Opposition, their prospects of making the reforms they had planned were
beginning to look very thin. If they had appreciated, what nobody had yet
really faced, that the rate of growth over the period would be less than 2½
per cent instead of 3¾ per cent, and that the truly wise public expenditure
growth figure would have been more like 3 per cent than 4¾ per cent a year,
it is indeed difficult to imagine what their reaction could have been. But
the fact remains that the acceptance of this course of action (apart from one
or two mavericks) within 100 days of coming into office for the first time,
showed good statesmanship.[9]

324. Then followed a period of four months, while the PESC report was
being prepared on the lines agreed, to which we shall return later.

325. *Fiscal Incentives.* In these first weeks also, an immense range of activity
opened on the public sector income side. The Chancellor announced his
intentions to introduce the Capital Gains and Corporation Taxes in the
1965 Budget, and Customs were heavily engaged on the import surcharge
and export rebates. These were clearly within the normal scope of the
Revenue Departments' work. What was different was the call for a
strategic policy – concentration on the use of taxation as an instrument of
long-term policy, the widening of the basis of taxation, the inter-

relationship of taxes, local rates and national insurance contributions, and the relation of all this to the distribution of income and wealth. Previous chapters show that the Treasury had been thinking a lot about these problems in 1963 and 1964; but now they were presented in much more urgent form, and a committee was set up accordingly early in December.

326. The priority task was to consider fiscal measures, compatible with our obligations under GATT, to encourage exports. The problem here was to sort out the possibilities. Most of the obvious moves were ruled out by GATT; and the use of indirect routes could never be confined to the encouragement of exports alone, but were inevitably related to industrial investment, regional and other objectives. Moreover, any plan would require legislation, and must be one that could be expected to become part of our permanent structure. Ideas of introducing value-added tax to replace purchase tax or other public sector income or to finance subsidies were rejected, both as lacking effectiveness and as involving new legislation by the Revenue Departments, obviously impracticable for a considerable time ahead.

327. Gradually three lines of thought sorted themselves out. One, which became the genesis of the future Selective Employment Tax (SET) and Regional Employment Premium (REP) involved taxing payrolls in congested and over-employed areas and subsidising them in under-employed areas. This idea was coupled with a proposal to tax non-manufacturing employment and subsidise manufacturing employment, partly in the interests of providing a stimulus to exports.

328. A second idea was to replace investment allowances by investment grants on purchases of plant and equipment. It was argued that investment allowances were not an effective stimulus to investment, and that investment grants would be more so, and would in particular be available to firms not making profits and would thus help new enterprises. Others thought that the grants system would call for much greater public accountability than the allowances system, which had merit in itself though unlikely to please industry. There would be substantial administrative costs and problems, especially if there were regional and industrial discriminations between the eligibility of different purchasers for grant.

329. A third idea was to concentrate the benefits of the removal of investment allowances on grants to the engineering industry. This was thought to be difficult to defend internally and impossible to defend internationally, but it was favourable to exports and to investment, and retained some support throughout.

330. It would be improper for me to describe the long process of

Ministerial discussion,[10] which was devoted to the balance of advantage between the plans, and interminable calculations of costs and benefits (on varying assumptions about Corporation tax). Nevertheless, it is an important case, and an official history of the full proceedings from December 1964 to the January 1966 White Paper on Investment Incentives would be instructive.

331. Ten years later, I am sure that the decision to substitute investment grants for investment allowances was wrong. When Mr Heath's Government reversed it in 1970, nobody was sorry except those who were caught by the injustice of the transitional arrangements that were chosen. Such changes in Government policy towards industry are useless unless they can last at any rate for ten years and preferably for much longer. It was therefore in my opinion wrong for Mr Wilson's Government to make this important change unless they were certain that the case was so strong that it would survive in a future Government.[11] The case was at best marginal.[12]

332. When one looks at the subject more widely, definite conclusions emerge:

(a) None of the cases for any of the Plans was even nearly strong enough to justify the disturbance cost.

(b) It was known very early (certainly by February 1965) that there was no practicable scheme consistent with our international obligations to provide fiscal incentives for exports.

(c) It may have been desirable to provide new systems of regional or investment incentives. But these should have been defined and. organised, not as a by-product of work on 'export incentives' but as projects in their own right. (Indeed, SET could have had very full study instead of being rushed into the 1966 Budget at the last moment; and REP could have been weighed much earlier as part of the package of regional incentives.)

(d) About a year's time of the scarcest resources of all — Ministers and senior administrators and economists – was wasted, in the most critical year of the Government, in which that time could have been used by these people to much better advantage. If the return on time spent is compared, for example, with that involved in creating the Industrial Reorganisation Corporation, the dimensions are entirely different. I can only blame myself, as chairman of the committee, for not having advised the Chancellor strongly on the lines of (a), (b) and (c) above when we had finished the first round of thought in February 1965.

333. *Preparation for the July Allocation.* At the end of January, the Government had decided the ground-rules for the allocation from 1964

65 to 1969 – 70 which was to take place in July; and the relevant part (the 4¼ per cent a year) had been announced by the Chancellor on 22 February, was repeated in the Budget speech on 6 April, and by the Prime Minister in his address to the Economic Club of New York on 14 April. I had of course warned the Permanent Secretaries of the departments of what was likely to be afoot, so that the departmental machine would be able to get ahead speedily with its work, and the operation went forward.

334. Early in February Mr Crossman, Minister for Housing and Local Government, asked his colleagues for a greater programme of housing authorisations to 150,000 (England and Wales), an approach which was accepted and added about £50 million to his 'basic' programme. It had been provided in the original decision that Ministers could seek Cabinet approval for additions between then and July, for life can never stand still. But this was the only case as far as I know; and it would be interesting to know whether he had already decided to seek agreement to this extra approach at the time when he had accepted his basic programme when it was decided a few days earlier. In May, moreover, Mr Crossman came forward with a further programme increasing public sector housing subsidies and for the provision of funds for local authorities at a reduced rate of interest and for a reduced rate of interest on a part of new mortgages taken out by owner-occupiers. Thus, subsidies came into the allocation operation.

335. This was the first time the PESC operation had been carried out subject to the constraints laid down by Ministers - the 4¼ per cent average increase from 1964 – 65 to 1969 – 70; the concentration first on the eight main programmes (which, plus defence) were about 80 per cent of the whole public sector expenditure (excluding nationalised industries); the division between 'basic' and 'additional'; the need to leave enough room for the remaining 20 per cent of the total. These eight main programmes, called Category A, were overseas aid, roads, public sector housing investment, housing subsidies, police and prisons, education (with school meals and milk), health and welfare (with welfare foods), benefits and assistance (with family allowances). Category B was a mixture, some of smaller 'programmable' items, like research councils, for which allocations would later be made in the same 'tone' as the decisions on Category A, and some large ones like agricultural support which depended on the course of the market and could not be reasonably predicted five years ahead.

336. The operation was carried out jointly by the Treasury and DEA (with the inter-departmental PESC committee as usual doing the analysis and producing the factual report, a printed document of 48 foolscap pages, setting out and describing all the programmes through to 1969 – 70. All this work had to be done by a day-to-day timetable: the deadline for

presentation to Ministers was fixed in March for 18 June, and it was actually circulated on 17 June. Of course it all had to be done in 1965 prices (translating Minister's guidelines accordingly); and it was found that Category A had gone up by 7.4 per cent from 1964 - 65 to 1965 - 66; leaving only an average of 3.3 per cent a year for 1965–66 to 1969–70. This was no new phenomenon, but it brought its problems with it!

337. The Treasury/DEA steering group, besides pressing the PESC work timetable, had to look after the interaction with other reviews in progress (defence and civil defence on the one hand, and a large number of reviews of particular subjects, e.g. coal, agriculture, ports, which were a necessary part of the National Plan). It so happened that these did not present great difficulty. There were two serious limitations on the public programmes as a whole - construction capacity, which looked like being very tight indeed if Mr Crossman was allowed to press forward with the public sector housing and also stimulate the private sector housing; and manpower, in which the estimates which were being made for the National Plan were showing a large deficiency, roughly equal to the increasing requirements of education, health and other public services and public administration generally. It was not easy to inject either of these general limitations into the process of allocation; but they were part of the relevant considerations.

338. The most difficult question was that of the 'path' to 1970. The 25 per cent growth of GNP in 1964 - 1970 called for a rapid increase towards the end of the period. To keep within the $22\frac{1}{2}$ per cent growth, the public expenditure figures pointed to a reducing of growth - for Category A 'basic', 7.4 per cent in 1965 - 66, 4.1 per cent in 1966 - 67, 3.6 per cent in 1967 - 68, 2.9 per cent in 1968 - 69, 2.6 per cent in 1969 - 70. It was already clear that in balance of payments and every other way 1966 - 67 would be a very difficult year. It was obviously impracticable, therefore, to conduct the operation solely in terms of 1969 - 70, for this would have allowed departments to start whatever 'additional' programmes were allocated straight away. Ministers eventually decided to conduct it with separate allocations for 1966 - 67 and 1969 - 70, with the minimum possible 'additionals' for 1966 - 67.

339. In the simplest possible form, the arithmetical constraints on the operation were as shown in the following pages.

340. The total 'bids' for 'additionals' were £762 million, so at the most only one-third could be accepted. On the other hand, the eight main civil programmes showed a 'basic' increase of 29 per cent over five years, and the margin for 'additionals' would raise this to 33 per cent, which was an impressive increase on any reckoning and at least double the past and prospective rate of growth of private consumption.

	£ million at 1965 prices
Permissible increase 1964 - 65 to 1969 - 70 on '4½ per cent' formula	2435
Increase in Category A 'basic':	
Defence	Nil
Eight main programmes	1860 (i.e. 29%)
Increase in Category B	225 (say 10%)
Contingency allowance (very small; Mr Maudling had allowed 250)	100 - 150
	2185 - 2235
Possibly available for Category A 'additionals' in 1969 - 70	200 - 250

341. The Prime Minister and Mr Callaghan and Mr Brown arranged that the operation should be conducted, for decision by the Cabinet, by a special Ministerial group of Mr Callaghan, Mr Brown, Mr Diamond and five 'non-spending' Ministers. At the time, it was thought inevitable that only 'non-spending' Ministers should be included, but in retrospect the inclusion of spending Ministers not concerned with the eight main programmes (such as the Minister for Defence Mr Healey) might have been useful.

342. *The Allocation.* The technique adopted by the Ministerial Group was to have an all-day meeting (on Sunday, 4 July) in which they interrogated in turn the six Ministers (Mr Crossman had two of the programmes and Sir Frank Soskice, the Home Secretary, could not attend). Great care was taken to protect all these Ministers' rights with the Cabinet, and the papers put to the Group were appended to the Group's report.

343. The Ministerial Group carried out the examination vigorously, and finished with £25m. 'additionals' for 1966 - 67 and £240m. for 1969 - 70; and this was subsequently endorsed with minor modifications. According to the score-sheet, it must be regarded as having been a successful operation. Indeed, the Group was reconstituted as a permanent standing committee early in August. The quotations from Heclo and Wildavsky (p. 187) show how effective the process was both in bringing pressure on Ministers to defend their programmes in detail (which they had probably never previously had to do) and of course in the support for Mr Callaghan and Mr Brown when the report came to Cabinet.

344. Three aspects appear to have been fundamental:
   (a) With only eight main programmes to deal with (and enough time to

deal with them), it was possible for Mr Callaghan and Mr Brown to be properly briefed (identically), for the other Members of the Ministerial Group to weigh the alternatives, and for the spending Minister to say his say; and at the end of the day, when the subject-matter was still fresh in the Group's minds, they could decide the general lines on which they would report. This process of deliberation is rare in government. In my opinion, it could have been done with ten programmes, and conceivably even twelve, but certainly not more.

(*b*) There was no difficulty in handling 1966–67 and 1969–70 simultaneously, but probably impossible to do more years simultaneously. The essential question in administration is the amount of numbers and data that the decision-makers, whether Ministers or boards of directors, are expected to absorb and judge upon. Some individuals have a wider span than others, but in all committee work it is the collectivity that counts.

(*c*) There was no tendency whatever to take the simple route of 'fair shares'. The Group decided at the outset to choose its priorities; and in the end housing got about half, benefits and assistance came next, and the rest very little (except that Mrs Castle found an ingenious device to justify a slightly bigger figure on overseas aid, which could not be fairly resisted).

345. In the autumn, the 'programmable' items in Category B were decided. Most of them were settled directly between the departments concerned and the Treasury. A few raised difficult questions which had to be decided by the Ministerial group: the pressure was not as great as on that Sunday in July, but the amounts of money were comparatively trivial – some hundreds of thousands and a small number of millions compared with tens of millions and hundreds of millions; the balance was reasonable. For the 'non-programmable' Category B (agricultural, industrial, regional and transport subsidies the main ones), there could be trimming for 1966–67 in the Estimates, but the long term turned on difficult long-term policy which the Government did not tackle at this stage.

346. *The Sterling 'Package' of July 1965.* Following the bad trade figures for May and the gold reserve figures for June, there was a run on sterling, and in the latter part of the allocation operation considerable thought was being given to the 'package' of measures which the Chancellor could announce at the end of July. There was an ominous whiff of the disaster of July 1961, in which Mr Selwyn Lloyd was persuaded 'in defence of sterling' to make an unwise undertaking about public expenditure, which not only weakened his own position sadly, but also lost the best opportunity we ever had to get PESC off to an effective start (see para 178). However,

these hazards were kept within reasonable bounds. In the end Mr Callaghan secured decisions from his colleagues which endorsed the Category A allocations; enabled him to announce some of the politically difficult consequences of these allocations (justified, of course, as part of the sterling 'package'); got some genuine savings in Category B (which helped to keep within the amount we had allowed for that); restrained the nationalised industries from proceeding with investment programmes designed to keep up with the 25 per cent growth implied in the National Plan; and was able to announce a firm intention on the 1966 – 67 Estimates.

347. It therefore did not turn out badly in substance; although it has never been good to submerge PESC decisions, which should be taken by Governments in the interests of good housekeeping and living within what the economy and the tax potential can afford, in the excuse of a short-term sterling crisis. Fortunately however from this point of view there were repeated sterling crises, and there was no moment for a long time at which 'stop' could legitimately be turned to 'go'.

348. In his statement on 27 July, the Chancellor featured the expenditure side:

(a) Government non-industrial capital projects' starting dates (except housing, schools, hospitals, development districts) to be postponed for six months; deferment of purchases of goods.

(b) Nationalised industries and local authorities (Category B) to follow suit.

(c) Loan sanctions and grants for local authorities (Category B) for 'miscellaneous projects' only on grounds of urgency; big reduction in lending by local authorities on mortgage for house purchase.

(a) Government and local authorities to review staff.

(e) Reshaping public expenditure within the limits laid down (particular reference to 1966 – 67 Estimates and to defence).

(f) Postponement of income guarantee and removal of remaining NHS charges and scheme of specially favourable interest rates for owner-occupiers (all implications of Category A decisions).

349. This was matched with introduction of building licences (except for housing and industry); sharpening of controls of development in the South and Midlands; tighter hire purchase; changes in exchange control, etc.

350. These postponements of 'starts' could not last long, and on 8 February the Chancellor announced the incorporation of these into the normal procedure of expenditure limits, both for departments and their control over local authorities, with loan sanctions for 'miscellaneous' local authority projects still very tight. This whole operation was strengthening the strands of control over local government spending, which was a

fundamental weakness in the implementation of PESC allocations, in which one had to edge towards a solution which in some way reconciles the need for central control of local authorities' current and capital expenditure with the need for local authorities' autonomy. (A lot of thought was devoted to this in 1965.)

351. *Implementation*. Once the allocation had been made for the first time how was it controlled? Even in the days of 'simple' control of supply expenditure, in the 1950s, the control could never be absolute within the levels of the Estimates determined in January. There was always room for Supplementary Estimates, and it would not be easy to recall cases (though no doubt there were some) in which the Treasury (or then Parliament) refused to assent. The Plowden Committee urged that underspend (which meant that the Estimates had been put too high) was as reprehensible as overspend; and everyone in Whitehall (and most people outside) knew about the operations by departments in March either to spend more so that they would not 'waste' their allocation (and worse, be debited by being given a lower Estimate for the following year), or postpone their maintenance or anything else manipulable to avoid the sin of an 'Excess Vote'. Even as late as 1965 I was approached by a Permanent Secretary because his department's contractors were prepared to give discounts if they could be guaranteed against these annual interruptions of work.

352. The introduction of local authority and other public expenditure made this much more complicated. Their current and capital expenditure were much influenced by departments, both through general grants and through specific authority for capital expenditures and loan sanctions. But these influences could not be relied upon to be reflected in their actual expenditure in specific years (whether immediate or future).

353. Moreover, every year's PESC programme was stated at that year's price level; so that it was never possible to confront Ministers squarely with overspending except in cases which were clearly outrageous and agreed with their departments to be so. With inevitably changing difficulties of definition, even to get a clear picture of the way in which the total had moved was a formidable task. In preparing this chapter ten years later, with the relevant White Papers, and with some familiarity with the business, I cannot satisfy myself about what really happened. There was a big total increase from 1964-65 to 1965-66, and then a much lower increase from 1965-66 to 1966-67, and then big increases in the following two years until the effect of Mr Jenkins's emergency post-devaluation operation of January 1968, a series of very severe cuts indeed; but I must leave the measurements to the experts. Moreover I am here talking only about totals, not the individual programmes.

354. I drew the conclusion that trying to police allocations by statistical measurements, if taken beyond the most elementary level, would not be effective. My thought went back to the old concept of the defence budget, which had played such a role in the Plowden Committee's work; which was that the only effective system was to set up machinery to get co-operation between each main department and the Treasury and DEA to ensure that their medium-term policies were aligned to the allocated resources. For several years, we had had a successful Road Programme Committee with the Transport Departments; and if we could get Education and Health and above all (if politically possible) Housing (bringing in private sector housing and miscellaneous local government too), and National Insurance, we would have the big fields covered (and particularly the big local authority fields – other Category B was mainly direct Government expenditure).

355. We found the Education and Health Departments receptive. The concept in education, for example, was for the committee to consider in particular the development and control of the educational services within the financial limits laid down, the relation between capital and current expenditure and the relation between the different services e.g. primary, secondary, further and higher education; the needs for manpower and how to use it most efficiently; the requirements for capital expenditure; the use of statistics and analysis as a basis for decision-making, including the development of measurement of cost effectiveness and of activity costings. This got under way in February 1966, with the Education Department, Treasury and DEA[13]–the essential was for the Education Department to be in the chair, for the whole idea was to get the departments to create their own machinery for deciding their priorities, and developing their work constructively within their resources; and for the Treasury and DEA not to act as censors but to make the relevant points about the national economy and to help with management services, etc. – while also keeping very close to what was going on and being informed as they should be for work on the next PESC return.

356. All the Treasury/DEA team, and indeed all who had worked on PESC from the start, had become much impressed by the inflexibility of departments' programmes, which might in fact be accentuated by the requirements of PESC and PESC decisions; and by the fact that the alternatives over a five-year period might well be greater than appeared; and we hoped that this kind of machinery could begin to unfreeze 'current policy'.

357. The Treasury's real difficulty, in tackling work of this character, is that it called for a different kind of man from the traditional work a man who could both constructively help a department to build up its central

planning and programming machinery, yet never take this eye off the ball of getting policies that would enable the department to live within its prospective resources without continuous alarums and excursions. We never got enough experience in my time: but I would still say that this was the right plan – indeed, to get something of a mix between the two Plowden doctrines of getting better programmes and getting them in line with resources.

358. *1966 PESC.* Then we had to consider how to shape the work for the 1966 operation, rolling forward to 1970–71, and concentrating at the near end on 1967–68, which showed no signs of being any better than 1966–67. DEA had decided not to roll the National Plan forward for another year, so we started a special exercise on 1967–68, like the previous Long-term Economic Reviews. It was decided not to repeat the Ministerial operation of January 1965, nor to seek Ministerial instructions fixing 'basic' and 'additional' programmes. It was decided again to fix allocations for Category A, and where possible for Category B.

359. *Definitions.* Finally there was a valuable but time-consuming discussion with Dr Balogh about some of our definitions. Mr Crossman had attacked these in the 1965 operation because they limited his freedom of manoeuvre on housing subsidies (and this of course happened again when he became responsible for social security later, and claimed that 'transfers didn't count'). He did not get far. Dr Balogh's criticisms, however, were much more sophisticated, mainly related to those cases where the Government had a choice between tax relief (or increase) and expenditure (e.g. investment grants versus investment allowances); and we felt that we needed to bring his concepts into our system, for although at the moment we saw no practical difficulty, there could be future trouble.

360. *Individual Cases.* This chapter, concentrating on great macro questions of total public expenditure and fiscal incentives may give a wrong impression of the balance of activity; so I have listed some individual cases between October 1965 and March 1966.

361. (a) First step towards the English Electric/ICT alliance which ultimately led to the creation of International Computers Ltd, which after vicissitudes did establish a viable British-owned computer industry.

    (b) Choice between Rolls – Royce Spey engine and American J79.

    (c) Choice between Dounreay and Winfrith Heath as site for the prototype fast reactor: the AEA case was definitely for Winfrith Heath (where they had the SGHW prototype already, and, more particularly, which is highly accessible to overseas and industrial visitors); whilst for Dounreay it could only be a short-term

employment project anyway. However, as always, the Scottish
site won.[14]

(*d*) Family allowances versus income tax relief for children.

(*e*) Possibility of 'ceilings' on overseas defence and other expenditure.

(*f*) Problems of how the State exercises influence over wholly or
partly-owned companies.

(*g*) Effect of France leaving NATO.

(*h*) The continuing series of nationalised industry price increases.

362. *White Paper.* The Chancellor had intended to publish a White Paper
in the autumn to set out the 1966 - 67 and 1969 - 70 decisions. For a variety
of reasons the White Paper[15] was delayed, in the end to appear
concurrently with the Estimates statement in February. The Estimates
operation (which covered the 'unprogrammable' subsidies etc. in Category
B) had been successful, with an increase on a comparable classification of
7.3 per cent over the previous year, or 1.8 per cent at constant prices. The
White Paper reckoned that the total public sector expenditure for 1966 -
67 would be within 4½ per cent of 1965 -- 66; but it is difficult to say certainly
the actual outcome.

363. The White Paper was a much more advanced document than Mr
Maudling's of end-1963, and it does describe in considerable detail the
basis of PESC and of the PESC operation. It was a political document, as a
Government's White Paper on public expenditure should be, setting out
the Government's hopes of what they intended and would be able to do
over the coming years. I cannot personally see how a White Paper on
public expenditure, which is intended to set out the Government's
decisions on some of the major issues of public policy for the life of the
Parliament can be anything but a strongly party political document.[16]

364. I can still remember the satisfaction that the Treasury felt (and I
particularly for I was due to leave on 31 March) that Mr Callaghan had
succeeded in persuading his colleagues to publish, probably on the eve of
an election: with both parties having published a PESC White Paper, I felt
that the system was established: of course it would change over time, but it
would not disappear. Now that the system is well established, it may be
difficult to recall that it was often nip and tuck; and we were fortunate that
in December 1963 Mr Maudling took the opportunity to accept Mr
Callaghan's challenge, and that a year later both Mr Callaghan and Mr
Brown stood firmly for it.

365. The Paper showed the prospect of expansion of social and environmental services very favourably. But it was all sticking to the
Conservative plans: and the July operation in fact scrapped over two-
thirds of the additional things the Ministers wanted and had expected to

do. As one said plaintively, 'I didn't become a Minister to carry out the Conservatives' plans – I want to carry out my own' – but there were none of the Conservatives' plans that he was politically able to scrap to make room for his own.

366. Again, of course the 4¼ per cent growth rate was too high, especially as the 1964 – 65 'actual' (obviously unknown in December 1964) turned out lower than expected, so that the first year took too much. The National Plan growth figures were also too high. But after the all-party acceptance of 'Neddy' in 1963, Mr Wilson, Mr Callaghan and Mr Brown could not in practical terms have worked on lower figures. It had to be sweated out in 1967–68. For my part, I never thought that a lower figure than 4¼ per cent could be acceptable, and I cannot recall that there were others in responsible positions who disagreed.

367. Lastly, the White Paper was very weak (as we were) on implementation. I have given my views earlier: the implementation has to be done by departments. As Sir Warren Fisher said, to the 1929 - 31 Tomlin Commission:

> Economy was not something to be imposed on other departments by a Treasury acting as the 'single-handed champions of solvency keeping ceaseless vigil on the buccaneering proclivities of Permanent Heads of Departments' but rather that 'the Heads of Departments should work together as a team in the pursuit of economy in every branch and every detail of the public service'.[17]

The problems of PESC, both in time-scales and in the extension to the whole public sector, required completely new apparatus of expenditure control in every one of the departments heavily concerned (just as it had in the reconstructed Ministry of Defence in 1963). But this could not be worked out by the Permanent Secretaries until they (and their Ministers) knew there was a permanent new structure to be created. The system of committees described in paras 354 - 7, which I tried to develop later, was in my opinion the way to move, in these new circumstances, towards new structures within departments and between them and the Treasury (and Civil Service Department) which would create the apparatus for implementation; and I believe that this would have fitted in very well with Fisher's and Bridges's thoughts (though not necessarily with those of their more conventional No. 2s and No. 3s).

368. But the Treasury/DEA team were only setting out on this road; and we had only one real PESC operation behind us. I could certainly not claim that I knew where the road was leading, or that my colleagues in the team saw it as I did. I was and remain convinced that there was no answer to the all-public-sector implementation problem by a formula of Treasury statistical control, and that the answer must be in joint operations between

a properly equipped Treasury and properly equipped Category A departments. But it is hardly surprising that the White Paper was very weak here!

369. *Longer-term Thinking.* In the early 1960s, Sir Norman Brook, who had been much impressed by the foreign policy and defence paper on 1960–70 described in Chapter 2, asked whether this kind of thought could be applied to the home economy. It was really like drawing a medieval map of the world, with some parts very well known twenty years ahead (e.g. population), some rather less known (e.g. amount of manufacture), some totally unknown ('Here are Dragons'). We recruited Dr Holmans, who went round to departments, and produced a large and interesting report on '1980'. The main advantage of this had been to make departments think explicitly about the situation in 1980; for many of the decisions being made in the early 1960s (e.g. about infrastructure, higher education, civil aviation) were creating the economic and social conditions of 1980. The subject 'VLT' – Very Long-term – passed to DEA, who continued the work.

370. In the winter of 1965–66 we came back to the subject: we were beginning to find that we needed to look ahead seven or eight years in quite a number of fields – well beyond the PESC limits. We thought that the areas which were important from this point of view were education, health, urban redevelopment, cash benefits, subsidies, tax structure–in all of which the fundamental choices had a longer time-scale than five years. We saw no purpose in trying to create an economic model so far ahead – it would confuse, not enlighten; for the problems were a mixture of policies and numbers, and the best plan was to take each subject by itself.

371. We thought the new Education – and when we got it, Health – Committees would be excellent for this; and we began to work up methods of doing the others. In cash benefits, for example, should we be moving towards universal benefits or to using the money to deal with the real poverty problems? What were the criteria for agricultural, industrial or transport subsidies? Could we get a better and more broadly-based tax structure? These could not be considered within the PESC time-scale, so we aimed at about 1973–74, to give Ministers a clearer set of choices (including choices between taxation and expenditure) than was now open. This need to go to seven or eight years in some fields tends to confirm my view in Chapter 4 that we should have had a shorter period for PESC.

372. *Management and Organisation.* Lastly, the immense activities of 1965/66 had revealed deficiences, both in the Treasury and in departments generally. The annual Permanent Secretaries' conference at Sunningdale in autumn 1965 had discussed this, and I tried to work it into proposals.

373. First, were the Public Sector and Management Groups in the Treasury working closely enough together to ensure that the big spending departments had the right kind of 'Programme and Budget' apparatus to allocate resources, improve cost-effectiveness, and better value for money, and what quantitative aids did they have, or was it just the old Finance Division? Sir Philip Allen (head of the Management Group) and I had been having a series of meetings with our staffs to exchange views on departments' capability and organisation; and this was to tie it down to a specific area for a period.

374. Second, following the disclosures in the National Plan about the future manpower gap, caused mainly, it was thought, by the rapidly increasing requirements of education, health, etc., there was considerable apprehension, especially as the public sector is much the largest employer of well-educated people, say, people with a respectable number of 'O' levels, people with at least one 'A' level, and the rapidly increasing numbers with full-time higher education. The suggestion here was that we should get a top-class statistician to draw up prospective balance-sheets for each of these categories.

375. Third, there were the various management services:
   (a) classical O & M;
   (b) comparison of performance of small units (e.g. local authorities, hospital management committees);
   (c) operational research;
   (d) appraisal of economic investments (nationalised industries, South Wales ore ports, advanced technological projects, etc.);
   (e) cost-effectiveness of non-economic services (choice of deployment of resources in defence, in education, in the Health Service, in science, etc.).

376. In each of (a) to (e), much had been done, particularly where there was a clear division of responsibility – Management Group for (a) and Public Sector group for (d) and part of (e). The proposal was to set up a unit within the Treasury, with a strong professional core of economist, statistician, accountant, operational researcher, to do specific jobs for departments (and the Treasury) and to help departments to do them for themselves. Also, see how strong the departments were in these fields.

377. There was tremendous potential money in all this (the return on the cost of work done in classical O & M is about 250 per cent); and getting the correct choices in (d) and (e) is worth millions of £s a time. But the separation of the Treasury from Civil Service Department must have made more difficult the creation of joint initiative, and joint approach to

departments. The marginal areas, which can be very important, may always slip between the interstices.

378. *Treasury Finale.* We had a system in the Public Sector Group that when the Head of a Division left his job, he had to write a report on it. So I wrote one. It was a long report, but mostly about staff and related matters. However, the final conclusions had some significance:

(*a*) The structure, size and staffing of the Public Sector divisions did not call for any radical change. [But the need for a different kind of junior was approaching].

(*b*) The worst weakness, and one which was damaging our work, was the rapid turnover of staff; and I hoped that it would be possible to devise a specific plan of campaign to overcome this.

(*c*) The need to do all we could to improve the interlocking within the Group [in the PESC world, divisions are no longer independent empires, each with 'its own' set of departments: they have to do both the general and the particular: likewise, each Deputy Secretary should be in charge of some divisions and some general expenditure work].

(*d*) We should try to develop a detailed course of action to improve the joint working of the Public Sector Group and the relevant parts of the Management side for the control of expenditure.

(*e*) We needed to devote continuous attention to the Permanent Secretaries of all the departments, apart altogether from the day-to-day contacts on specific points [e.g. I had meetings with them before the crunches were reached in the January and July PESC operations; we should have regular informal meetings with them to discuss both allocation operations and value for money; we should produce an annual report on progress in the control of public expenditure (as in December 1963) and discuss it with them – a valuable process in itself for Treasury Ministers and ourselves; always have an item on the agenda of the Permanent Secretaries' Conference at Sunningdale that enables us to give our message, and also to get feedback].

NOTES

1. W. Beckerman (ed.) *The Labour Government's Economic Record 1964–70* (Duckworth, 1972) pp. 3–5.
2. See inter alia my description of the problems of creating the new Ministry of Technology in 'Mintech in Retrospect', *Omega*, Vol. 1 (1973), pp. 28, 29. The experience of that time is to my mind a very powerful warning against trying in future to create new departments (as distinct from renaming or regrouping parts or all of existing departments). One can always get Ministers, Permanent

Secretaries, Deputy Secretaries, etc. - the problem is to get Principals, executives, above all clerical workers and typists; and these are the people on whom the department's work depends entirely. The more junior the staff, the greater the scarcity.

3. For example, DEA would obviously be responsible for saying whether public construction should be cut back because of overload on the construction industry; and for saying what future demand for electricity the electricity authorities should provide, etc.: but it was always the Treasury's responsibility to authorise both the expenditure of departments and their authorisations to other bodies (e.g. local authorities and nationalised industries).

4. It would be interesting, however, to know who was the first individual (and when) to say that on the best objective assessment that he could make, the Government should plan for five years on the basis of a 2 per cent a year growth rate (1966 - 71 was 2.1 per cent) and abandon not only the 4 per cent but also the 3 per cent a year that seemed to have become established. The PESC system depends both upon the ability and foresight of the appraisers and upon their courage to give unwelcome advice to their official chiefs and thence to Ministers.

5. There was no equivalent, as far as I can recall, to the 'creative tension' among Mr Roosevelt's advisers in the early days of the New Deal, cf. the preparation of his keynote speech on tariff policy in the 1932 campaign when he asked his high-tariff advisers and his low-tariff advisers both to prepare drafts, and then according to his chief brains-truster Raymond Moley, 'read both with seeming care, and then left me speechless by announcing that I had better "weave the two together"' Arthur M. Schlesinger Jr., *The Crisis of the Old Order*, (Heinemann, 1957) p. 442.

6. Paradoxically, perhaps, but not really surprisingly, the reaction of many of our best friends abroad to one of these was much more unfavourable because the Government had decided upon a 'liberal' method of reducing imports, the tariff surcharge, which was held to be against our international obligations rather than the introduction of import quotas which was much more restrictive, but would have been unquestionably justified (and accepted) in our balance-of-payments situation.

7. For example, if Australia had ordered the TSR2 instead of the American F111A (which we bought instead of the TSR2 and cancelled in 1968), it might well have turned the scale for the TSR2, about which there had been violent controversy in the Cabinet, described by Mr Wilson (op. cit., p. 90). What had made the cancellation of the highly sophisticated TSR2 inevitable was that the future development cost was far greater than could be justified for the number of production aircraft needed by the RAF; and tangible evidence of export orders could have improved this arithmetic.

8. *Mintech in Retrospect*, pp. 40 *et seq.*

9. [It is not clear why, after the lengthy discussion of the previous government's commitment in 1963 to the objective of 4 per cent growth and the risks that this entailed in the planning of public expenditure, no comment is made on the still greater risks entailed in the commitment in 1965 to an even faster rate of growth in public expenditure. The force of the previous commitment was a powerful factor in deciding the basis for public expenditure in the National Plan.

It should also be noted that, as in 1963, the expenditure guidelines took no account of Clarke's Law (or the relative price factor). Ed.]

10. Mr Wilson's memoirs give no guidance at all.

11. It has become conventional for Governments to reverse their predecessors' actions and legislation in matters which are regarded as politically controversial fundamentally; and I personally believe that in the 1970s this has been done more often than is sensible or indeed tolerable for continuous democratic government; but this action by Mr Heath's Government could not in my opinion be reasonably put into this category.

12. I had personal experience of some relevance. In October 1969, the investment grants distribution machinery was transferred from the Board of Trade to my department. It so happened that a few weeks later, I had to attend four sessions of the Public Accounts Committee to be examined on the first report made on the working of the system by the Comptroller and Auditor-General. The department came out reasonably well, and for me it was a good opportunity to satisfy myself about its administration. But it was clear to me that the complexity (and to some extent arbitrariness) of the administrative decisions were the opposite of what was required in a system designed to induce industry to invest. At the same time, the department had a continuous flow of cases from the Ombudsman criticising us for not having taken decisions which would have been contrary to what had been laid down by the PAC. So we (and thus the firms) were between Scylla and Charybdis.

13. We then moved to set up a similar committee with the Health Departments.

14. Although this decision was wrong, and may well have lost time and increased cost and isolated the knowledge of and interest in this crucial project from the rest of the nuclear/industrial world, one must pay tribute to the remarkable success of AEA in turning farm-workers and fisherman into workers with complex and dangerous apparatus.

15. *Public Expenditure: Planning and Control*, Cmnd 2915.

16. Indeed, my only objection to the subsequent series of Public Expenditure White Papers from 1969 onward is that they have been statistical documents of extraordinary quality, but with the politics so dessicated out of them that the only people who can interpret them are less than a handful of first-class economic journalists like Peter Jay and Sam Brittan and the professional economists who advise or appear before the Select Committee on Expenditure.

17. Quoted by Lord Bridges, *Treasury Control* (Stamp Memorial Lecture, 1950).

12 Public Sector Control at the Top

379. Most of this book has been about concepts and systems and the harsh realities of every Government's public expenditure decisions. But the subject is really about people, and how they spend their time, and what they actually do. This is nowhere more important than in the Treasury; for the job is to supervise and authorise, by direct or indirect means, the expenditure of some £30,000 million a year. This function is carried out by a very small number of high-quality people – rightly very small, and rightly of high-quality, for the only way to begin to deal with a task of this kind is to find the crucial points on which to press,[1] and to enlist the help and support of hundreds of other people, in departments, local authorities, nationalised industries, etc. The whole purpose of PESC is to do precisely this; and for my part I would sooner tackle it with a hand-picked staff of 100 than with a great bureaucratic empire of 10,000.

380. Mr Gladstone talked of 'the saving of candle-ends'; but must also be regarded as the founder and honorary[2] president of PESC, as is shown in his great Budget speech of 1860 – a hundred years ahead of his time, passages from which are printed here as Appendix A; and there is no doubt whatever that Mr Gladstone, confronted with the task of managing a public sector of our size and complexity, would have insisted on action by the Treasury of a breadth commensurate with the scale of his problem which again is what PESC is all about.

381. In truth, none of us is up to this stupendous task; but it may be useful if I try to set out how the problems looked in my time, and how this time was spent. I take the year 1963, for the 1962 Treasury reorganisation had come into operation in November, and I had become Second Permanent Secretary in charge of the Public Sector Group; so there was an element of 'glad, confident morning': 1964 was a twilight year, dominated by the impending election: and of course in 1965 the new Treasury had gone. An organisation chart at January 1963 is appended at pp. 144–5, with some explanatory notes about the people (for fifty-year-old beliefs about the composition of the top echelons of the Treasury die hard).[3] To few matters in my experience has so much high-powered work been devoted to create

such a short-lived entity as the 1962 Treasury turned out to be; but what comes below might be unintelligible without the chart.

382. Mr Maudling was Chancellor of the Exchequer; Mr Boyd-Carpenter was Chief Secretary (in the Cabinet and responsible for public expenditure); and Mr Barber and Mr du Cann were Financial and Economic Secretaries respectively. It was a strong Ministerial team.

383. Much of my time was of course spent in discussion with our Ministers, and at their meetings with other Ministers; with my immediate chief Sir William Armstrong and other senior colleagues; in the regular work of the Budget Committee, which organised the material and set out the alternatives for the Chancellor's consideration on budgetary and related matters; in giving decisions, advice and indoctrination to the staff in my Group (going well off to the right of the chart, with the Assistant Secretaries and Principals and of course the economists and statisticians); in inter-departmental meetings of Permanent Secretaries, but more importantly in visits from Permanent Secretaries of other departments, to get advice, or to get a reaction to a project that their Minister had in mind, or sometimes to tell me that my own staff were behaving unreasonably with theirs; or I might similarly have some problem to discuss with them. All this is what might be called the 'day-to-day' business of the Second Secretary. Without my appointments diary of the time, or indeed any diary whatever, I cannot estimate how much this would usually take out of a day's work - it varied considerably.

384. As soon as I reached a sufficiently senior position (i.e. when I became a Deputy-Secretary in 1955), I began to form a judgement that I should not spend more than half my time (counting both day-time at the office and evening work at home) on the formal 'day-to-day' work of the job. I should spend half my time initiating and carrying out new constructive developments in the task - concepts that I was putting in, rather than running the machine. Where the new developments were successful, they would become incorporated into the 'day-to-day' work; and some of the activities described above as 'day-to-day' work were in fact very actively concerned with the constructive developments that I was trying to introduce. The dividing line could never be absolutely clear; but the distinction was always in my mind between work in which the constructive initiative came from and depended upon me, and work which was coming on to my desk in the normal course of events.

385. To digress, I continued to do this throughout my four-and-a-half years in Aviation and Technology: I believe it is the right course for people at the top in any activity; and in my years in industry after leaving the civil service, I have noticed that the great successful industrialists whose

working methods I have been able to see at close quarters all follow a principle of this kind – that you must not get bogged down with 'day-to-day' work, but must keep a large proportion of your intellectual resources and nervous energy free to be taking initiatives, driving new ideas through, and thinking about the future development of your business and organisation. So whenever anyone in the upper reaches of a department or a business says that he 'has no time to think', my conclusion is that he is in a job above his ceiling, and should be given short shrift.

386. Another relevant point, fortunate for my immediate purpose, is that my natural working habit is to write: my six years as a professional financial journalist left this permanent mark. So I always wrote a flood of notes, minutes, memoranda. This has some advantage in that you can make your concepts and decisions clear and avoid woolliness: it has the disadvantage that it requires readers – and if the ideas are unfamiliar and the problems difficult, it calls for careful readers; and they are rare at the top. There is no universal rule in this. Some pick up and develop their ideas in discussion: others just listen: one of the best administrators I ever knew never seemed to be doing anything – if you went to see him, there would never be any papers on his desk, and he would either be sitting cogitating or sometimes reading a newspaper;[4] but his width of knowledge and clarity of opinion were devastating.

387. But I did it by writing, keeping a chronological set of carbon copies.[5] For the year 1963, I wrote or dictated something like 1250 pieces of paper.

388. Virtually nothing of what I wrote was about individual personnel questions: these were usually handled by talk. Specific expenditure questions calling for decision also gave rise to little written record: these were always handled directly with the Chief Secretary by the expenditure divisions, with a copy to me, and if he wanted my advice, I would walk along and talk to him. In terms of what I committed to paper in a typical year such as 1963, about two-thirds of the weight of my work was in five main areas.

389. First, management within the Treasury, and what would now be called 'communication'. Both joint Permanent Secretaries attached more importance to this than had been previous Treasury (and indeed civil service) practice; and got the balance about right between 'under-management' and 'over-management' (which is just as bad).

390. Second, we were much occupied in 1963 with what became known as 'Plowdenry'. It was a year, starting with reflation and ending with a menacing threat of inflation, in which concepts of long-term management of expenditure had to move forward inch by inch. But there were two

major advances. Mr Maudling and Mr Boyd-Carpenter were successful in getting some reversal of engines in July, and the first rudimentary 'block' system was introduced in September (with a significant effect on the decisions on the Robbins Report and the raising of the school-leaving age); and Mr Maudling's decision to publish the first 'PESC White Paper' in December was one of the major landmarks in the history. We also began to get to grips with the analogous development in public sector receipts, but this did not appear until later.

391. Third, nationalised industries, the efficient and profitable management and operation of which seemed then, as it does to me now, to be near the core of British industry's success or failure. The target earnings system of the 1961 White Paper was getting under way, with great support from the nationalised industries' chairmen, who for the first time felt that they had coherent management objectives; but it was not entirely easy, for if one was allowed to resile, there was always the danger of a 'domino' process. We were working out the next refinements, due to be introduced at end-1964, but then much delayed.

392. Fourth, and perhaps most difficult, were the new large subjects coming forward, such as the distribution of population and employment (a better phrase than 'regional policy', which has become identified with only one part of the national problem, the development areas), Buchanan, the Robbins Report, the Channel Tunnel, decimalisation and so on. These were difficult to grasp, partly because their substance was inchoate and it was difficult to find a way into it that would lead to effective action, and partly because the departmental responsibilities were confused. Often I found myself having to take the lead until the initial stages were sorted out and responsibilities established; and this process was often painfully long. At end-1974, of the items listed, decimalisation was certainly the most successfully accomplished.

393. Fifth were some very important subjects like defence reorganisation, nominally problems of machinery-of-government, but actually dominated by the need to get an effective system of policy formation and (the same thing) of allocation of resources and finance. So, in the Treasury, we found that the specification was properly written by the public sector group, which was at the sharp end in the actual business. This reorganisation was one of the great successes of 1963, and a major achievement by Mr Macmillan.

394. To sum up 1963 as I recall it, there were definite successes and there were failures; and there were dismal cases of good progress being made, in essentially long-term activity, which within ten years had been destroyed; and perhaps most depressing of all, problems arriving in 1963 and worked

on since by successive Governments, and still no nearer a solution, or even a route to a solution, by the end of 1974. It is a wise Government that refuses to spend time (the most precious asset of all) on wrestling with a problem, however urgent and pressing it may look, when it cannot see its way clearly to a solution in less than ten years; and a wise Opposition that refrains from harrying such a Government and claiming that it has a solution when it has nothing of the kind.

NOTES

1. In my files of correspondence, I found a reference to 'Otto's garotte', the discovery that the long-term level of educational expenditure depended on the numbers entering the teacher training colleges, and therefore, behind that again, on the building programme for teacher training colleges.
2. Of course we couldn't afford to pay him! For the discovery of this relevant Budget speech, the original Public Expenditure Survey Committee of 1961 was indebted to Peter Vinter.
3. The creation of DEA in November 1964 bore most heavily, naturally enough, on the National Economy Group (especially as Mr Douglas Allen, as he then was, went to DEA): the second split of the Treasury in 1968, setting up the Civil Service Department, broadly speaking divided the chart into two, the top half becoming the CSD and the bottom half remaining as the Treasury (reinforced a little again in 1969, when the DEA was abolished). But this is all history, and not very profitable.
4. A very distinguished Second Secretary in my early days in the Treasury would likewise have his desk clear, but would be reading a detective story which he surreptitiously slipped into his drawer as one came in.
5. I learnt the value of having such a chronological list, as a tool of management, from [now Sir] Hugh Weeks in the Ministry of Supply in the war. Everything typed was numbered consecutively, so there was a fool-proof reference system, and you (or your secretary) could leaf it through quickly to see whether the recipients had duly replied (and if not to chase them). I have done this now for over thirty years.

NOTES TO ORGANISATION CHART

These give (*a*) age in January 1963; (*b*) subsequent style; (*c*) subsequent appointments of Permanent Secretary (and 2nd Permanent Secretary) rank; (*d*) time of entry into service (when not direct from university).

(1) (*a*) 54 (*b*) Lord Helsby (*d*) during war; age 32; university lecturer in economics
(2) (*a*) 47 (*b*) Lord Armstrong (*c*) Head of Civil Service Department and Head of Civil Service
(3) (*a*) 50 (*b*) Lord Allen (*c*) Head of Home Office
(4) (*a*) 52 (*b*) Sir Richard Clarke (*c*) Head of Ministries of Aviation and Technology (*d*) during war; age 29; financial journalist
(5) (*a*) 55 (*d*) joined staff of Economic Advisory Council in 1931; age 24; Fellow of All Souls, Oxford
(6) (*a*) 51 (*b*) Sir Alec Cairncross (*c*) Head of Economic Service (*d*) alternating Government and academic service
(7) (*a*) 55 (*b*) Dame Elsie Abbot
(8) (*a*) 56 (*b*) Sir Wilfred Morton (*c*) Head of Customs and Excise
(9) (*a*) 45 (*b*) Sir Douglas Allen (*c*) Head of Department of Economic Affairs; then of Treasury; then of Civil Service Department and Head of Civil Service
(10) (*a*) 49 (*b*) Sir Louis Petch (*c*) Head of Customs and Excise
(11) (*a*) 49
(12) (*a*) 51 (*b*) Sir Arnold France (*c*) Head of Ministry of Health and then Inland Revenue (*d*) during war; aged 32; District Bank
(13) (*a*) 50 (*b*) Sir Samuel Goldman (*c*) 2nd Permanent Secretary, Treasury (*d*) post-war; aged 34; statistician in City firms and then Bank of England
(14) (*a*) 62 (*d*) Treasury Medical Adviser from 1954
(15) (*a*) 50 (*d*) post-war
(16) (*a*) 46
(17) (*a*) 45
(18) (*a*) 51
(19) (*a*) 54 (*d*) Entered Government Information Service in war
(20) (*a*) 48 (*b*) Sir Bryan Hopkin (*c*) Economic Adviser and Head of Economic Service
(21) (*a*) 43
(22) (*a*) 45
(23) (*a*) 48 (*d*) during war
(24) (*a*) 45
(25) (*a*) 56 (*d*) during war
(26) (*a*) 48 (*d*) post-war
(27) (*a*) 56 (*b*) Sir Stuart Milner-Barry (*d*) during war
(28) (*a*) 53
(29) (*a*) 50 (*d*) during war
(30) (*a*) 48
(31) (*a*) 51 (*d*) post-war
(32) (*a*) 46
(33) All the twelve administrator Permanent and Deputy Secretaries at January 1963, except Sir Douglas Allen, had retired by July 1974. Their average age at January 1963 was 51. Eight of them had academic qualifications in economics or banking experience. Eight were educated at Oxbridge, two at LSE, one at Glasgow, and one at no university: few at expensive schools; just over one-half entered the service by the traditional pre-war route.
(34) The seventeen Under-Secretaries (omitting the Medical Adviser and the Chief Information Officer) had an average of age 49. The economist, Sir Bryan Hopkin, is the only one to have reached the top rank: by September 1974, seven had become Deputy-

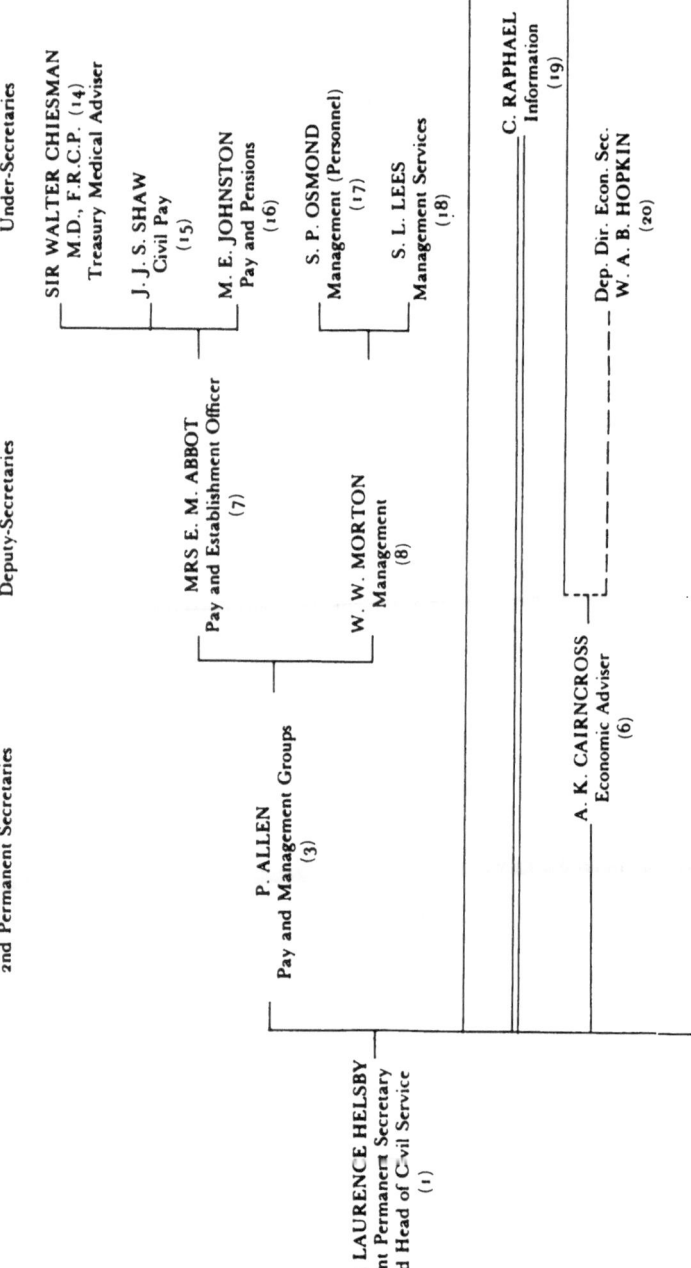

Organisation Chart, January 1963

2nd Permanent Secretaries   Deputy-Secretaries   Under-Secretaries

SIR LAURENCE HELSBY
Joint Permanent Secretary
and Head of Civil Service
(1)

P. ALLEN
Pay and Management Groups
(3)

MRS E. M. ABBOT
Pay and Establishment Officer
(7)

W. W. MORTON
Management
(8)

SIR WALTER CHIESMAN
M.D., F.R.C.P. (14)
Treasury Medical Adviser

J. J. S. SHAW
Civil Pay
(15)

M. E. JOHNSTON
Pay and Pensions
(16)

S. P. OSMOND
Management (Personnel)
(17)

S. L. LEES
Management Services
(18)

A. K. CAIRNCROSS
Economic Adviser
(6)

C. RAPHAEL
Information
(19)

Dep. Dir. Econ. Sec.
W. A. B. HOPKIN
(20)

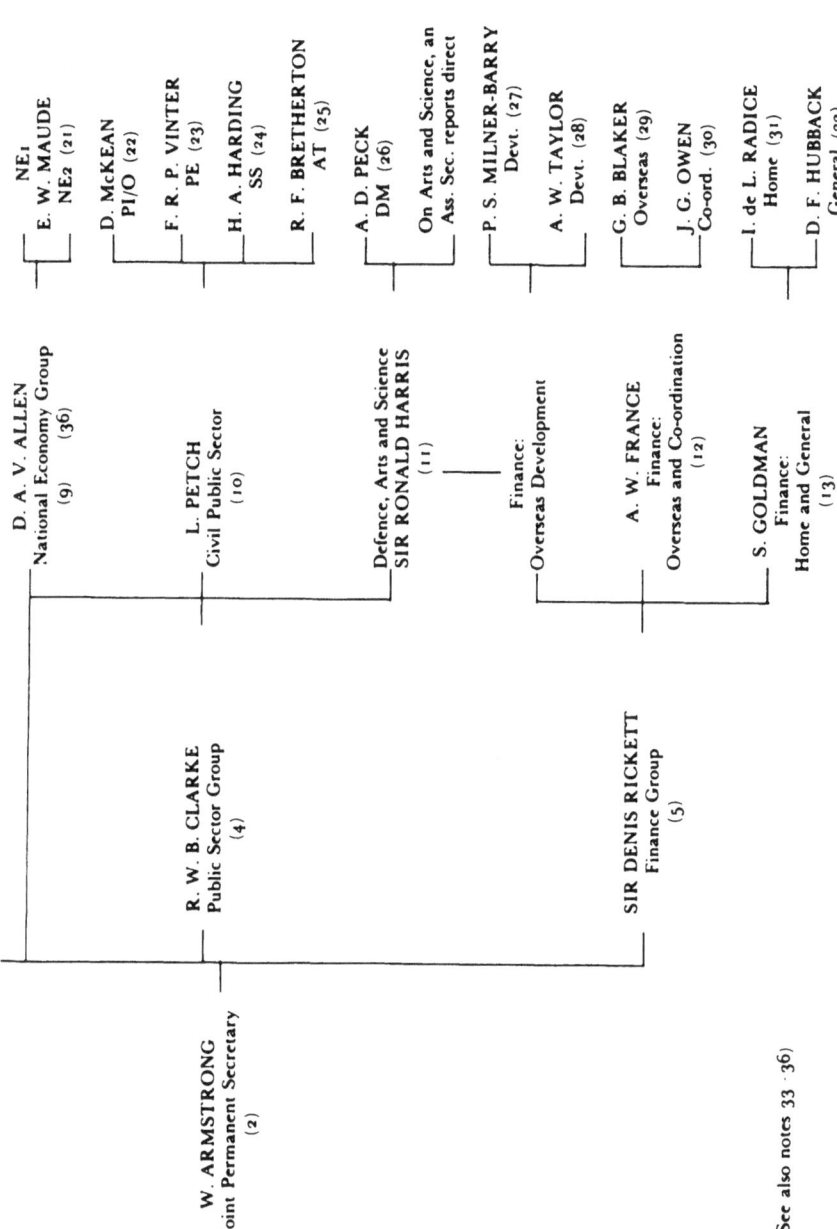

W. ARMSTRONG
Joint Permanent Secretary
(2)

R. W. B. CLARKE
Public Sector Group
(4)

SIR DENIS RICKETT
Finance Group
(5)

D. A. V. ALLEN
National Economy Group
(9)   (36)

L. PETCH
Civil Public Sector
(10)

Defence, Arts and Science
SIR RONALD HARRIS
(11)

Finance:
Overseas Development

A. W. FRANCE
Finance:
Overseas and Co-ordination
(12)

S. GOLDMAN
Finance:
Home and General
(13)

NE1
E. W. MAUDE
NE2 (21)

D. McKEAN
PI/O (22)

F. R. P. VINTER
PE (23)

H. A. HARDING
SS (24)

R. F. BRETHERTON
AT (25)

A. D. PECK
DM (26)

On Arts and Science, an
Ass. Sec. reports direct

P. S. MILNER-BARRY
Devt. (27)

A. W. TAYLOR
Devt. (28)

G. B. BLAKER
Overseas (29)

J. G. OWEN
Co-ord. (30)

I. de L. RADICE
Home (31)

D. F. HUBBACK
General (32)

(See also notes 33–36)

Secretaries. Oxbridge and boarding school education predominated more than in the higher group; and a slightly larger proportion entered just before the war by the conventional route.

(35) Ten of the 40 Assistant Secretaries at January 1963 are now (1977) of Permanent Secretary rank: Sir John Hunt (then 43, now Secretary of the Cabinet); D. W. G. Wass (then 39, now Sir Douglas Wass, Head of the Treasury); J. L. Rampton (then 42, now Sir Jack Rampton, Head of the Energy Department); D. O. Henley (then 43, now Sir Douglas Henley, Comptroller and Auditor-General); I. P. Bancroft (then 40, now Sir Ian Bancroft and Head of the Civil Service); D. J. Mitchell (then 40, now Sir Derek Mitchell, lately 2nd Permanent Secretary, Treasury); L. Pliatzky (then 44, now Permanent Secretary, Department of Prices and Consumer Protection); and L. Airey, K. Couzens, and A. K. Rawlinson (then 37/38 and all now Permanent Secretaries, Treasury).

(36) The National Economy Group discharged a common service function; so Mr D. A. V. Allen worked under the direction of Mr Armstrong but might also report to Sir Denis Rickett, Mr Clarke and Mr Cairncross. The initials of the Under-Secretaries' divisions are: NE - National Economy; PI/O – Public Income and Outlay (i.e. PESC etc); PE - Public Enterprises; SS - Social Services; AT - Agriculture, Towns, Transport; DM - Defence Materiel.

13 PESC: Past and Future

395. In the course of this narrative from the beginnings of 'Plowdenry' to early 1966, I have interspersed a great many comments, both those of the time and in retrospect. I shall not repeat them; and in this last chapter I shall try to look at PESC in historical and critical perspective. If the years of effort devoted to it since 1960 have been justified, the future will recognise it as one of the great historical reforms in the control and management of public expenditure, in the same line as the Exchequer and Audit Department Act of 1866, which brought together into one system the procedures of Estimate, Appropriation, Expenditure and Audit, and Sir Warren Fisher's reform of 1920, that the Permanent Secretary of each department should be Accounting Officer, ensuring that responsibility for policy and responsibility for finance were inextricably linked together, and that control of finance was no longer an 'outpost' of the Treasury. If what (for the sake of convenient abbreviation) one may call the PESC system succeeds and survives, this will be seen as the point at which control was established over the public sector of the second half of the twentieth century – double the old 'Supply' and involving scores of institutions, from nationalised industries to local authorities to a great miscellany of public bodies. It is this survival power that is examined in this chapter.

396. *The Results So Far.* One must start by setting out what has actually happened. The following table, for which I am indebted to HM Treasury, shows a simple comparison between public expenditure (as defined for PESC purposes) and the gross domestic product (GDP). The ratio between the two is a rough-and-ready indicator of whether public expenditure is outstripping resources. It is well known that there are traps and inconsistencies for the unwary. Yet it is the simplest measure that anybody has invented.[1] If you try to remove some defects you are likely to introduce others; and you can rapidly run into endless philosophical discussion of what is the meaning of the concept at all, and the defeat of the attempt to draw any practical conclusions from experience. So we must do our best with what we have.

397. The table is divided, with a slight disregard for historical exactitude, into the 'Butler' period, the 'Macmillan' period, the 'Wilson' period and the 'Heath' period. In the 'Butler' period (1952 – 7) came big savings on defence (and on housing after Lord Woolton's 300,000 target had been

PUBLIC EXPENDITURE AND GROSS DOMESTIC PRODUCT, 1952 – 71
(£'ooo million)

Year	Public Sector Expenditure (1)	GDP at factor cost (2)	'Ratio' of (1) to (2) %
1952	6.4	13.8	46.6
1953	6.7	14.9	45.1
1954	6.7	15.7	42.4
1955	7.1	16.9	42.0
1956	7.5	18.3	41.2
1957	7.9	19.4	41.0
1958	8.3	20.2	41.2
1959	8.8	21.2	41.3
1960	9.4	22.6	41.5
1961	10.3	24.2	42.6
1962	11.0	25.3	43.5
1963	11.7	26.9	43.3
1964	12.7	29.1	43.8
1965	14.1	31.2	45.4
1966	15.3	33.0	46.3
1967	17.5	34.8	50.3
1968	19.1	37.3	51.2
1969	19.8	39.2	50.5
1970	21.9	43.0	50.8
1971	24.4	48.4	50.3
1972	27.4	54.4	50.3
1973	32.0	62.2	51.4

achieved), lively economic growth backed by Mr Butler's expansive policies, and a big reduction in taxes. I have begun the 'Macmillan' period (1958 – 64) with the resignation of Mr Thorneycroft and the two junior Treasury Ministers and then the acceleration of expenditure (no more declining programmes): there were tax reductions in 1959 and 1963, but this was the very significant period in which Conservative opinion was beginning to regard the expansion of social and environmental services as more important than tax reductions; and the risks of inflation more acceptable than risks of deflation. The spending programmes of the early 1960s were rapidly eating up the gains in the 'ratio' of the Butler period, and it was certain that unless the economy expanded much faster than could reasonably be expected, there would be difficulties in the mid-1960s. So this happened in the 'Wilson' period (1964 – 70), with the growth of expenditure continuing to exceed the growth of resources, and the 'ratio' topping 50 per cent for the first time in 1967. After the November 1967 devaluation, Mr Jenkins took the most determined grip yet on expenditure, and succeeded in stabilising the situation in the late 1960s, this extending into the 'Heath' period (1970 – 3). However, after Mr Heath's 'U-turn' in 1972, the ratio began to move upward again, reaching a new record in 1973, exceeded again in 1974.

398. So from the date of the appointment of the Plowden Committee to 1973, 10 per cent of the gross domestic product was switched to public sector expenditure; and nobody at the end of 1974 could see forces in motion to change this course. In the discussion recorded ten years before in para. 242 (p. 91 above) I expressed the view that there was great doubt whether there was a 'right' figure, but that a steady rapid increase would certainly lead to great trouble. The private sector has to provide for the investment in manufacturing industry, which is the basis on which everything rests; and for the private consumption of everyone (except those on social security benefits and other grants); and the exports for buying our overseas needs. The present margin is not nearly enough to fill these requirements, and we survive only by borrowing from abroad about 7 per cent of GNP: this obviously cannot continue for very long. So over a comparatively short period of years, the most favourable post-war public expenditure/resources situation has been transformed to the worst.

399. *Lessons from experience.* The major conclusion that I draw from the experience is that the years since 1960 have confirmed over and over again the Plowden Committee's central point, with which it opened its confidential report, that the forces of public opinion, political parties, Parliament, and generally speaking Ministers were increasingly committed to a rapid growth of public expenditure, and that there was now no significant body of opinion opposing this. So the Chancellor was standing virtually alone to resist the tide; and that much the most important need was to give him powerful reinforcement. This was the Plowden Committee's main recommendation on the basis of the relatively modest experience of the 1950s.

400. Various attempts were made with Ministerial Committees, second Cabinet Ministers in the Treasury, etc., to meet this point, but in my opinion this effective strengthening happened only twice – when Mr Callaghan and Mr Brown stood together to make the July 1965 allocation, and when Mr Jenkins as the new post-devaluation Chancellor in January 1968 could in no circumstances be allowed to resign. Both of these were accidentally favourable situations.

401. I do not believe that for the period now facing the country, the

Plowden Committee's recommendation for a Ministerial Committee is adequate. Nor do I think that any change of machinery-of-government would solve this situation. I believe that the only possible combination to grasp the control of the public sector is the Prime Minister and the Chancellor, and for them to be seen publicly to be grasping it together. Just as in the 'normal times' of the 1950s and the 1960s (at any rate judging from their memoirs) Prime Ministers spent most of their time acting as super-Foreign and Commonwealth Secretaries, now I want to have them as deeply and continuously involved in public sector management, with same expertise and commitment and attack, as they were previously on, say, Rhodesia, the bomb, or Suez – working as super-Chancellors. Of course sometimes the Chancellor is an inflationist; and some Prime Ministers are too. But if the parties choose such men in the 1970s there is nothing to be done.[2]

402. *PESC as an Instrument.* Suppose that the weight of the Plowden Committee's recommendation for the reinforcement of the Chancellor had been expressed with knowledge of the scale of the next fifteen years' events, and accepted, would the PESC innovations have provided an effective instrument? One Permanent Secretary to whom I happened to be talking during the latter stages of this book said that to him PESC seemed like a theological and doctrinal system; in much the same way, I suppose, as I regarded the rituals of Parliamentary 'control' of expenditure when I first encountered the subject in the mid-1950s.

403. This opinion surprised and interested me, for readers of this book would, I hope, see the development in exactly the opposite light. The Plowden Committee proposed a number of innovations, and there then followed a long period of experiment and pragmatism and opportunism to find means of getting these accepted as practical administrative operations to help Ministers solve the expenditure problems. To me, the most significant points at the time were the publication of Mr Maudling's and Mr Callaghan's White Papers, for they got the innovations publicly accepted; and one of the most striking impressions that I have formed in writing this book is the continuous change of approach to find procedures that would both work and be acceptable.

404. When I left the Treasury, this task was far from complete. My successors made great developments in the late 1960s, as described in successive White Papers and by Sir Samuel Goldman,[3] particularly in creating a much more comprehensive statistical and monitoring apparatus. But I would be surprised if finality had yet been reached, or a 'doctrine' established (except, perhaps, an unintelligent one by someone who finds it easiest to have a rule-of-thumb and tell other departments that it is 'Treasury doctrine').

405. *The Basic Innovations.* The innovations are what create PESC, and not the scores of different possible methods of operation. In my opinion, four of these are, so to speak, the litmus paper that determines whether a system of public expenditure planning and control is or is not in the PESC family. These are:

 (a) Classification of all public sector expenditure as one entity, divided into programmes which both represent coherent subjects for Ministerial consideration and are each within the responsibility of one Minister (subject to Scotland, Wales, etc).

 (b) Collective decisions by Ministers on public expenditure and resource allocation.

 (c) Inclusion of time, beyond say two years ahead, in the arrangements for public expenditure planning and control.

 (d) Relationship of future expenditure to future resources.

406. These are the indispensable innovations; and it would be surprising if any failed to survive as part of the permanent apparatus. Indeed, they now appear so obvious that many people, inside and outside Whitehall, would find it difficult to believe that they did not exist in the 1950s. But the practice and procedure for handling these innovations has changed and certainly will continue to change.

407. The first innovation, (a), was the foundation: for it enables Ministers to discuss programmes, such as education, health, roads, which could not formerly be expressed as programmes at all, or be subjects for Ministerial choice and decision. This came from the start in 1961.

408. It was never as easy as it now looks, for the great 'panorama' had to be constructed to meet the needs of both administration and national income analysis. But it was done, and is now highly flexible. The programmes can be fitted in with any change in the machinery of government; and particular programmes can always be treated separately, as nationalised industries' investment was treated separately when it was governed by economic and financial criteria. If Scotland had more fiscal independence, there would presumably simply be a new main pro-gramme, 'Scotland', and the Scottish elements would be taken out of the relevant other programmes (like education and health). I now think we made a mistake in 1960 in not having a 'Northern Ireland' block, which the Home Secretary would have had to defend, instead of leaving this large and potentially controversial expenditure in 'miscellaneous'. But the point is that it is difficult to imagine changes in governmental structure that could not be accommodated readily.

409. In (b), it is surely certain that Ministers will insist on retaining the innovation of collective Ministerial decisions on public expenditure policy,

instead of allowing the pattern to emerge from scores of individual negotiations with the Chancellor and his officials. As I have said, it is essential for the Chancellor's position to be reinforced; but the more this is done, the more surely will Ministers insist upon collective discussion and final decision. I would expect indeed that the widening of Ministerial and public discussion of tax policy and structure will continue; and that the area of taxes in which the prospective changes in specific tax levels must be treated as being of top secrecy will tend to contract.

410. Again, (c) is self-evident, but there have been considerable changes over the years in the periods used and on where the emphasis was concentrated in the Ministerial decision-making. From the start, the PESC operations were conducted over a five-year period (or six, if one includes the previous completed year); but they began by thinking of the end of the period – where the five years were leading; then to the beginning and the end (July 1965 dealing with 1966 – 67 and 1969 – 70); then to the 'path' and the concentration on the third year; and so on.

411'. In my opinion, there will be further changes; for as I have said earlier, I think the original choice of five years has been shown by experience to have been wrong, because for some of the public sector's work a five-year programme is unnecessary (or indeed impossible), but for very important parts of it a five-year programme is too short. So the five-year operation is an uneasy compromise. I would sooner think of seven to eight-year individual programmes for the blocks of expenditure that need longer periods and for the fields which are not 'programmable' in any but the short periods but need long-term policy (e.g. industrial assistance); and a universal PESC operation covering, say, three years, which would decide the rate at which these long-term programmes could be implemented. Development on these lines would greatly reduce the scale of the annual PESC operation, and enable more effort to be put into getting better and more flexible long-term programmes and policies for those expenditures that need them. The abandonment of a universal five year PESC would be a very radical change; but it would fit in with the dual purpose of PESC–to get good long-term programmes and to keep total prospective expenditure in line with resources.

412. Although (d) was the most distinctive of the Plowden Committee's recommendations, and great efforts were devoted to it, it has been the least repaying, for nobody has succeeded in finding a technique of expressing effectively the long-term resources limitation on long-term expenditure. The PE/GDP ratio used in the table was good to begin with, and simple, but too easy to question. Some very good resources projections were made in the early years, but as soon as 'economic growth' and the 'Neddy 4 per cent' came on the scene, the whole concept became what I have called

'anti-PESC'. Even at best, however, the national income analysis could not give comprehensible and sharp enough results to lead to decisions: Ministers and top officials could not envisage the difference between 2 and $2\frac{1}{2}$ per cent in the future annual growth of personal consumption; yet this would be about equivalent to the amounts at stake in the choices before Ministers on social service programmes.

413. I have continuously argued in this narrative for the Chancellor to have a specific future tax programme with which to confront the expenditure programmes: but this was never gained many friends, partly because Chancellors rarely like talking about taxes but also because of the role of taxes for short-period economic management and for social policy. The simple remaining course, especially with a three-year PESC, is for the Chancellor, with the Prime Minister's support, to lay down the aggregate limits for three years as his determining judgement, like the Budget judgement.

414. So within each of these four main 1960 innovations, many changes have been rung already; and there are many possible changes for the future. Indeed, I would hope that the changes will be rung quite often, for the danger is that working will become standardised and ritualised; and a race of 'PESC experts' is bred, having unique arcane skills, and squeeze all life and thought and originality from the system. But given the continuing flexibility, I would rate highly the prospects of survival of the innovations, in one or other of these patterns, for a long period of time.

415. *Programmes and Implementation.* Whatever is the central PESC apparatus, the success of PESC as a whole (and thus of the management of the public sector) depends upon its ability to create sound and well-based programmes, making the most effective use of the resources allocated to each. There is the dual task of making each programme, and of making the apparatus to monitor and control its rate of progress. Both sides of this task are the responsibility of the department. Nobody else can do either; and if the Treasury tries to do either, it will assuredly fail – this was what led Sir Warren Fisher to the reforms of 1920, when the amount and complexity of expenditure was quite trivial by present standards.

416. The department must be properly organised and equipped to carry out this dual task; and the Treasury (and/or the Civil Service Department) have the responsibility of satisfying themselves that this is done. What is meant by 'properly organised and equipped' varies from department to department, for their size, width, homogeneity and time-scale of operations vary. Nevertheless, those that are important for PESC are all large and few in number; and I would not myself accept any of these as being 'properly organised and equipped' unless it had a central 'Programmes

and Resources' division (or some such name), responsible both for co-ordinating the making of the department's programmes and for keeping their progress within allocation (where there is one), and normally for the day-to-day finance.

417. This central combination of these responsibilities is the heart of the matter. In the PESC era, this division is the hub of the department, with its head responsible directly to the Permanent Secretary, just as in the Supply era, the Principal Finance Officer played the same kind of role (and until comparatively recently his appointment required the Prime Minister's approval – i.e. in practice that of the Head of the Civil Service). I do not know how many of the dozen or so departments that count are so organised now. The Permanent Secretaries of those which are not would no doubt call it interference from the centre. But in my opinion it is not only right but necessary for the Treasury/CSD to insist on this; for if they are not satisfied with a department's organisation for the PESC work, how can they rely upon either the validity and content of the programmes or on the department's ability to keep within its resources?

418. Assuming that the department's organisation is right, and the PESC apparatus is working effectively in one of the many possible variants, what is the right continuing relation between the Treasury/CSD and the department? In my opinion, the only course is to get back to the Plowden concept of 'joint working together in a common enterprise'. In practical terms, there are three big points to be covered.

419. First, there must be a regular and very full discussion of the department's long-term programmes with the Treasury and there is much for the Treasury to contribute positively. Originally this was intended to be the first stage of each PESC operation.[4] But it proved impossible to fit all these stages into an annual operational time-table; and the appearance of a demand for 'PAR' in 1970 as though this was something new showed that in practice this element of programme examination in depth did not exist, and PESC was concentrated on the figures submitted for the allocation operation. So there is a gap, filled only to the extent of PAR operations.[5]

420. Second, the Treasury clearly needs to keep in close touch with the department's monitoring, to retain its own running record, and to lay down the ground-rules.

421. Third, whilst the department should have the maximum freedom of manoeuvre in carrying out its programmes, there is a continuous flow of new questions arising which carry with them implications for future allocations. The development of departments' activities is a continuous process, not settled once-for-all every year. So regular contact between the

department and the Treasury is needed in any case, whether one calls the system 'department's independence' or 'Treasury control'.

422. In my opinion, probably it will be found that the only practical way to handle these three interdependent questions is to have a joint committee between each of these major departments (and the Scots and where relevant the Welsh) with the Treasury/CSD, so that a regular working agreement is developed between them. This may differ according to the development of the PESC apparatus and the machinery of government; and there is no reason why it should be of the same structure for, say, defence, education, health, environment, social security. The essential is an organised machinery for continuous collaboration in all three areas.

423. Some similar kind of apparatus may be appropriate for the development of *subsidy policies* for industry, energy, food and agriculture, aviation, transport, regional development, etc., and this is bound to bring in the revenue departments. This would be a difficult field to organise, but it is impossible to talk sensibly about assistance to industry (or consumer subsidies) without also talking about taxes. It might be most practical to start from the long-term end, for there is no area in which the *ad hoc* policies of recent years (and very expensive ones too) are so much in need of being sorted out; and the fact that these are 'unprogrammable' five years ahead tends to suppress their importance from the PESC operations.

424. I have written a lot about the dangers of 'stop-go' policies for short-term demand management, as being both ineffective in itself (unless confined to areas specified in advance) and damaging to long-term expenditure control. But 'stop-go' in long-term policies towards industry is even worse. The effect of repeated fundamental changes, e.g. for and against nationalised industries' financial objectives, from investment allowances to investment grants and back, endless change in regional incentives, is self-defeating, for industry develops a numbness and insensitivity towards these incentives, being unable to rely on their continuance. Of course successive Governments will wish to develop their own policies; but if they do not observe a reasonable degree of continuity, they frustrate the private sector without gaining any of their own objectives.

425. *Local Government.* This is another area which will perhaps require a closer association with the PESC apparatus. It is indirectly there already, in the co-operation of the local authority associations with the departments in the collection of the figures which provide the basis for departments' programmes and their monitoring. But with reformed structure of local government and a reconstruction of the financial arrangements between central and local government with probably some new system of control of

local government expenditure, some more fundamental form of association may be required. Increased central government financing of local government (and increased central government control of the main local government services) is difficult to reconcile with having 'stronger' and more 'independent' local government units, and some form of association in the PESC context, for discussion of public sector expenditure and receipts as a whole, so that the local government representatives see their problems, and the background of the central government's attitude to them in a wider perspective, and vice versa, could help.

426. The original Treasury papers to the Plowden Committee contained a germ of this idea (see para 79, p. 29). In building up long-term programmes, the first idea was to do the education and health five-year programmes in one year and the local authority five-year expenditure programmes in the next, and so on. There was a policy concept here, in that it seemed right, when the essence of PESC was to bring all public sector expenditure together, to get the local authorities on to the same wavelength, to explain what we were trying to do, and to explore their thought about five-year programmes for themselves.[6] The practical concept was that if central government could carry them with it, this would ease the task of co-operation on creating departmental programmes. It has always been an anomaly to me that local authorities have been required to prepare 'development plans' for their areas extending for decades ahead, without correspondingly having to consider their financial future too.

427. This concept (in my view, unfortunately) never happened, partly because PESC operations went faster than expected; and partly because of the illness and later tragic death of the man in charge of the relevant division. At the next of the periodical reviews of local government finance and sources of revenue (in which it was always hoped that someone would produce a miracle) we did work out five-year estimates of local government expenditure and receipts; but this showed that the problem would get worse, not better, for the most fast-moving national programmes were those in which the local authorities were most heavily engaged.

428. In my opinion, there would be advantage in exploring these lines of thought as the new structure of local government and its financial relations with central government began to take shape; the idea of some kind of association between the PESC apparatus and the local authorities could perhaps help to round a very difficult corner.

429. *Public Service Manpower*. There are about four million men and women engaged in the public services (another two million in the nationalised industries); and my impression is that this is a subject also that

would merit further examination, especially as the public services employ an altogether disproportionate proportion of the better-educated population (people with a substantial number of 'O' levels upwards). The growing needs arising from the expansion of the public services were pointed out as one of the great future problems in the 1965 National Plan. Ten years later it is difficult to say how important the problem is likely to be. The public services are probably more attractive to the better-educated than the private sector, partly because of better security and a preference for what is believed to be a less anxious and competitive life. But these preferences change. The slowing down of the growth of the education industry, for example, could affect this substantially. Nevertheless, it is worth keeping score.

430. Much the more important and difficult problem, however, is that of public service pay. It is indeed mysterious to understand why successive Governments have failed even to begin to tackle the problem of how to pay (and to establish the relativities between) these four million people, who are employed directly by the Government or by local authorities and other grant-dominated authorities, and how the pay should be related to the Government's demand for the growth of the various services. In the days (and in the grades) where the Government took only a small part of the output, 'comparability' with the private sector was a fair and reasonable formula. But when we are considering fields of manpower in which the public services are the predominant aggregate employer, the idea of 'comparability' is irrelevant, and the Government must think for itself.

431. This is nothing to do with 'incomes policy'. Admittedly a Government which favours incomes policy without trying to solve its problems for the sector for which it is responsible can hardly be aggrieved if others do not take it seriously; and the series of 'crises' with teachers (school and university), doctors, nurses, medical auxiliaries, hospital workers, police, dustmen, even civil servants have been a huge factor in the failure of incomes policy. But if the Government is hostile to incomes policy, and favours free collective bargaining (with or without the constraints of a 'social contract') it is even more important for the Government, as employer, to determine the pay and pay relativities for which it will negotiate. If it allows the different departments and local authority groups to set up separate 'impartial' enquiries, and to create their own objectives and to let the groups of the four million public service workers leapfrog over each other, chaos (and greatly increased public expenditure and higher taxes) must result. I have suggested elsewhere[7] a Public Services Pay Commission, for Government is by nature ill-equipped to handle pay negotiation.

432. There is the related problem of nationalised industry; but this is

much less complex, provided that the Government is standing firm to a 'commercial' nationalised industry policy, so that the Exchequer is clearly *not* standing behind the industry, and costs have a meaning in the market. Where the Government is prepared to provide subsidies to the industry, it is simply a power struggle between the Government and the union, with the nationalised industry management playing hardly any role; and it is wisest to recognise this; but the weakness of Government in all pay negotiations has been demonstrated up to the hilt.

433. *PESC and Inflation.* Looking ahead, however, the most critical problem for PESC may be that of working in conditions of inflation. From the start, it was decided that the only practical course was to set up the programmes and everything else in terms of 'constant prices', with the basis changed every year; and the recent White Papers show the extraordinary statistical virtuosity with which this has been done. But when the fall in the value of money exceeds 10 per cent a year, and when it reaches say 20 per cent a year, the credibility of the numbers in the programmes and their monitoring against 'actuals' raises immense problems: for example, if a department gives a pay increase far above the average, how should this excess be scored against its programme 'at constant prices'? Subsidies are normally scored as constant cash: should there be some indexation, and so on? The numbers agreed by Ministers for a five-year programme (or for a three-year programme) become unintelligible as constraints for the growth of programmes without new volumes of interpretative ground-rules. The Treasury is no doubt dealing with this as it goes along, but any procedure is bound to increase the complexity of the system and obscure the clarity of the decisions reached.

434. *Manpower control.* Referring back to 'public service manpower', it may be worth considering whether over some parts of public expenditure, the permissible rate of growth could in time of inflation be more lucidly expressed in 'physical' terms. Is it impossible to imagine a constraint on the growth of the education or health services being defined as an increase of X per cent or Y per cent in the numbers employed by these services, particularly where, as in both these cases, the administration is directly part of the service? The numbers in the armed forces are already limited in this way, though this constraint arises from different historical reasons, and the work of defence is so capital-intensive that one could not base a defence budget on the numbers. But for education and health, for all the obvious defects, a manpower limit might well be as lucid for those who are running the services as an allocation 'at constant prices' or an allocation 'at prices assumed to be rising at 20 per cent a year'.

435. Another possibility, which would appear as a separate operation to normal PESC, would be to limit the manpower of the various units in the

public services – central government departments, local authorities, the hospital service, etc. The belief is widely held that the reorganisation of local government, designed and justified as getting 'the economies of scale' has in fact resulted in substantial increases in manpower; but this is only one, though very important case. If each unit (or group of units) in the public services was given a definite limit, this could be a very effective constraint. For any service not subject to the pressures of the market, control of manpower numbers is much more tangible than control of money: this is equally true in controlling those parts of businesses that are not directly dependent on the market – when the board of a business decides that its overheads or HQ staff or whatever it may be are too high, it insists upon a reduction in numbers. This is what bites in management.

436. Again, if it was laid down that each of the new big local authorities should live within manpower ceilings equal to the sum of the manpower of the authorities that were merged into it, so getting the promised economies of scale, this would undoubtedly create much more fundamental thought within these authorities about the economical development of their functions than any conceivable change in their financial allocations. I am not directing attention to the local authorities as such; but to the point that in a non-market body, where the remote taxpayer or the ratepayer provides the money, manpower can be the most effective form of control, and if the value of money is falling so that financial allocations lose their coherence, manpower control may be the only effective instrument in forcing public bodies to think about value for money and how to restrain their 'natural' growth.

437. In the civil service, manpower control has a bad reputation, as exercised both by the old Treasury and (in my time) by the Civil Service Department. This was partly because of the inadequate delegation (by the standards of the expenditure control) to departments on their numbers of people in quite junior grades, in which no central department could possibly have the knowledge to 'control' the decisions of the departments responsible for doing the job. But also, when the attempt was made to control total departmental numbers (normally, it is fair to say, under pressure from Ministers to 'reduce the size of the civil service') it would be lacking in the sophistication of control procedures required: in pursuit of 'fair shares', situations would be created in which the revenue departments (and the social security examiners) were asked to reduce (or not increase) staffs which were earning several times more revenue (or saving expenditure) than their salaries; or would force departments into reducing their O & M activity, which was highly profitable in terms of manpower saving. Such nonsenses rarely in fact happened. But these were occasional operations, and the task of controlling anything over an organisation the size of the civil service requires great sophistication and long experience.

Moreover on most of these occasions the remit was intrinsically unreasonable, for Ministers could not reasonably expect simultaneously to pile increasing duties on to the civil service and to get them done by the fewer people.

438. Nevertheless, in the civil service, the very necessary task of manpower control requires continuous pressure, for the bureaucratic tendency is always there; and this can be constrained only by manpower control and not by control of finance. I have always taken some pride in the fact that when Mintech was disbanded in 1970 it had fewer staff than it had taken in during its eventful six-year career from DSIR, Board of Trade, Ministries of Aviation and Power, and DEA:[8] but this did involve a continuous and rather rough manpower control operation.

439. In local authorities and other public bodies, it can equally be argued that the pressure from central government to impose new tasks is highly relevant; but some limitation would be exercised on this if the growth of manpower for, say, the education programme was limited; and the comparison of manpower with that under former systems of organisation (e.g. Property Services Agency *vis-à-vis* the old Ministry of Works) always gives scope for thought.

440. One cannot reasonably press particular ideas without up-to-date knowledge. My point is that, in my opinion, provided that it is done in a practical and sophisticated way, manpower control may become much more important throughout the public sector, especially in conditions of continuing inflation, than it has been in recent decades.

441. *Concentration on Essentials.* If I had to draw one lesson from the experience since 1960 (except for the overriding need to strengthen the position of the Chancellor) it would be this. The real purpose, and indeed perhaps the only one, is to get the big things right, which means identifying which are the big things, and getting agreement and understanding that they are the big things which must be got right; and simplify everything to get them right.

442. To the Plowden Committee, the 'biggest thing to be got right' was the relationship of total prospective expenditure to prospective resources. This has not been 'got right'. I say this not because of the great increase in the PE/GDP ratio that has actually happened, but because the expenditure decisions that led to this were not taken, in general, with a realistic understanding of their implications. Admittedly, the 'Neddy' overestimation of the rate of economic growth in the middle 1960s, and the stagnation of economic growth in the late 1960s and early 1970s were factors injected, so to speak, from the outside.

443. But the fact remains that the reams of analysis of the future resources and the implications for expenditure decisions, brilliant and distinguished though much of this was, never looked like providing the navigation chart that would implant itself in Ministers' minds and govern their thought and action about the future. It was clear from the analysis that there were delicate judgements to be made and considerable uncertainties to be taken into account (which, as we have seen, were well judged in the early PESC Reports). So it did not provide the earthy background for critical political decisions about expenditure policies.

444. The alternative course would have been to abandon the 'resources' side of the annual operation; and for the Chancellor to have said from the start (winter 1960 - 61 or spring), with the Prime Minister's support:

We must keep the growth of public expenditure [as defined] at constant prices within 3 per cent a year. This is somewhat above the annual increase in resources in the last ten years [2¼ per cent], and seems to me a realistic but also confident basis on which to plan our future spending. I propose that we continue to plan at this rate until we have clear and decisive evidence that we can sustain a faster rate, or that we must satisfy ourselves with a slower.

To Ministers who wanted to go faster, even when 'Neddy' came along, 'wait until we have proved we can do it' would have always been a solid answer; and at no time would there have been a good case for revising the figure upward; and in the ten years the resources growth was about the same as in the 1950s.

445. The contention is that by having straightforward annual long-term public expenditure operations, based on this pragmatic but realistic 3 per cent a year average expenditure growth; and having quite separate and disconnected periodic Ministerial discussions of economic growth; the operations would have been much simpler (only expenditure, not expenditure and resources) and freer from many of the snags and misunderstandings that arose. Of course it would have created great difficulty to keep the long-term expenditure plan within a 3 per cent annual increase. But it can well be argued that the Chancellor would have had more tactical flexibility in handling the situation, as it was not being treated within a specified annually prepared statistical 'resources' framework. They are only contentions, but it does seem to me conceivable that this simpler operation would have improved the possibility of 'getting the biggest thing right'.

446. The other 'big things to get right' emerged from the 'panorama', which identified them immediately as defence, education, health, social security, nationalised industries' investment, social infrastructure, subsidies; although the departmental structure of the last two has changed

greatly. The fifteen-year history of each would be interesting to have; with improvements of programmes made and lost, sometimes retained, sometimes never made. My opinion is that to get a sound and valid programme for each of them, consistent in the aggregate with resources, and accepted and understood by the people engaged on it – departments, local authorities, professional bodies etc – needs an operation for each comparable with that on defence in the mid-1960s or nationalised industries in the early 1960s. Each starts from the aggregate allocation, to get the resource availability into the right area; but this is the starting-point for getting a lasting and efficient programme; and that is why I believe that in these 'big things' a special continuing organisation is needed.

447. The other 'big point' is tax structure, partly in its own right, partly because of its overlap with certain forms of expenditure, and partly because of its interrelation with the aggregate of public expenditure.

448. *Parliament and People.* It may perhaps be thought odd by some that I have mentioned Parliament so little in this narrative. The first reason is that the subject-matter is Whitehall business – how Ministers construct their policies – and not Westminster business at this stage. The second reason is that Parliament has an important and specialised role in this series of questions, which it handles through three Select Committees – Public Accounts, Expenditure, Nationalised Industries: I have written at length about these recently,[9] and I hope in a constructive way; and I have little to add, except to express some apprehension that the Expenditure Committee with its expert technical advisers may be moving towards the 'national economy' side rather than the expenditure side, the macro-macro rather than the micro, or even the micro-macro. At some stage, though not yet, opinions may be formed about how Select Committees work best – on very detailed questions, like the Public Accounts Committee, or on big single questions, like the original Nationalised Industries Committee, or on general questions, which tend to become the Expenditure Committee's central interest.

449. My third reason, however, is the really important role of Parliament as the sounding-board between Government and public opinion; and looking at it from outside, it is not easy to see this role being played at all in the field of public expenditure. This may be part of the diagnosis of the Plowden Committee in 1960 – that nobody in Parliament and no influential or vocal section of public opinion cares about public expenditure, except to see it increased in whichever direction suits whoever is speaking. It admittedly takes at least ten years to have any impact on public opinion; and economic matters are not often handled in a manner that makes them easier for public opinion to understand. But no matter how strongly the Chancellor's position is reinforced; and no matter what

administrative virtuosity is displayed by Ministers and their advisers, in the end – and a long way before the end – what happens in this field as well as any other will be determined by public opinion; and my last point is that if this or any other Government wants to make progress in making a coherent plan for the public sector, it is right for it to start talking about it now.

450. *Summing Up.* To sum up a chapter which is in essence a summary of my experience in this field may be redundant. However, the points that I wish to emphasise, and indeed on which I would like to see action taken are:

(a) The experience of the last fifteen years shows that the strength of the forces and interests in our society which favour increase of public expenditure, and the weakness of those who see this as contrary to their interests, are much greater than diagnosed by the Plowden Committee; and that a more powerful reinforcement of the Chancellor is needed than was then considered necessary.

(b) The basic PESC innovations – classification of expenditure, collective Ministerial decisions, bringing time in as a dimension in public expenditure policy, relationship of future resources to future expenditure – are likely to survive as the permanent foundation of public expenditure planning and policy.

(c) But there could, and probably should, be changes within the next several years in how these are developed.

(d) The dual task of creating the programmes and controlling their rate of progress is the departments' responsibility. It is the Treasury's and Civil Service Department's responsibility to satisfy themselves that the main spending departments are properly organised and equipped to do these tasks, normally centred in one 'Programmes and Resources' Division.

(e) There should be a continuously working and organised relationship between the Treasury and each main spending department to consider the long-term programmes, the monitoring, and the new points arising between programme settlements (joint working together in a common enterprise).

(f) A similar inter-departmental organisation is needed to consider long-term rationalisation of subsidy policy.

(g) It may be desirable to develop a direct relationship between PESC and local government.

(h) There is still the major outstanding problem of pay relativities of public service manpower.

(i) There may be scope, particularly in continuing inflation, for expressing public service programme limits in terms of manpower.

(j) In considering the future of PESC the objective should be to simplify operations, and to enable Ministers to concentrate on essentials.

(k) Too little has been done to acquaint public opinion with the problem.

NOTES

1. There are useful pointers in *Handbook on Methodology* (HM Treasury, 1972) paras 80 – 7.
2. [See para 76 above for a rather different view. Ed.]
3. *The Developing System of Public Expenditure Management and Control* (HMSO, 1973).
4. [This point is elaborated in a letter written in April 1974 to Aaron Wildavsky while Otto was undecided whether to write this book:

    'Only time-table difficulties stopped us from having "P.A.R.-like" programme examinations as the first stage in the regular P.E.S.C. operation in the early 1960s. Your chapters on P.A.R. and C.P.R.S. show very clearly that it was never possible to get P.A.R. accepted against bitter Ministerial hostility as a new and separate operation: it had to be an integral and inescapable part of the normal procedure for getting Departments their money. If the Treasury are ever to get the P.A.R. idea into play, they will have to abandon it and go back to Plowden position I and incorporate long-term programme examination of a much more searching character into the P.E.S.C. system.' Ed.]
5. [This may be taken to imply that 'programme examination' did not exist before PAR. But as is obvious from para 79 (p. 29 above), there were 'forward looking' long-term programmes for education, health and other big blocks of expenditure much earlier. There were also Treasury/Departmental programme committees for education, health and roads in the late sixties. Beginning in 1965, both Health and Education were set by Treasury action along a path towards the development and use of programme budgets, so that it is not correct to suggest that only PAR filled the gap. Ed.]
6. The corresponding problem of incorporating the nationalised industries within the new concepts was dealt with by the 'new deal' in the 1961 White Paper on economic and financial objectives, issued just before the Plowden Report.
7. *Incomes Policy in Phase IV* (Manchester Business School, 1973).
8. *New Trends in Government* (HMSO, 1971) p. 14.
9. 'Parliament and Public Expenditure', *Political Quarterly*, April 1973.

Appendix A
Mr Gladstone's Budget Speech, 1860

Sir, the period at which I address you is a period of so much interest and so much importance that, even at the risk of occupying a few minutes of your time, I wish to dwell a little on the subject of public expenditure, because I admit that my statement thus far, though true, and I hope clear, is an imperfect statement. It would not be fair to speak of the great increase in the expenditure of the country without considering the great extension of the means by which that increase is supported. The country is richer than it was in 1853 in a degree really astonishing. Permit me to lay before the Committee, as well as I can, a criterion by which we may arrive at some idea of the truth with respect to the increase in the wealth of the country; and then we can institute a just comparison between the rate of increase in this wealth and the rate of increase in the public expenditure. The best mode of making an estimate of the rate of increase in the wealth of the country is to resort to the income tax. No other criterion is comparable to it, for, though it may not be an exact index of the truth in this matter, in any one year, yet, as between any one period and another, I believe it is an index on which we may safely rely. . . .

But the test of the wealth of the country by comparison must be taken principally from Schedules A, B, and D. The profits derived from lands and tenements, from all real and moveable property, are included in Schedule A. Schedule B represents the tax levied upon the occupiers of land, and it varies mainly with the amount of rent paid. Schedule D includes the profits derived from trades and professions. I will take two periods; the period from 1842, when we commenced our great career of commercial legislation, to the year 1853, when we closed it – I hope to be renewed – under the pressure of war. I will also take the period from 1853 – 4 to 1857 – 8, because it is the last year in which the returns are made up; and I will carry it on for two years by estimate, assuming the same rate of increase to have continued to 1859 – 60. Now the net amount shown by these three schedules of the income tax conjointly is as follows: –

In 1842, £154,000,000; in 1853, £172,000,000; in 1857 – 8, £191,000,000; and in 1859 – 60, £200,000,000. The increase in the wealth of the country between the first period and the second was 12 per cent in eleven years; the increase between 1853 and 1860, as thus returned, was 16½ per cent in six years. That undoubtedly shows a very large increase in the wealth of the country. I think it will also be interesting to the Committee to know in what proportions that increase has been distributed between the classes represented by three of the Schedules to which I have referred; for I must say that the statement is one which throws a very considerable light upon the condition of the landed interests, and more especially upon that of our old friend the farmer. . . .

Having thus spoken of the increase of wealth in the country, the Committee will, perhaps, permit me very briefly to compare it with the rate of increase in our expenditure. I shall in the first instance compare the growth of wealth with the total expenditure – that is to say, with the whole State as well as the whole local expenditure, as far as the latter can be ascertained; for the local expenditure of the country is likewise beginning to form a very considerable item in our financial calculations, and it shows a disposition to grow to an extent which makes it well worthy of the serious attention of the Committee. . . .

It thus appears that in the eleven years from 1842 – 3 to 1853 – 4, the expenditure of the country under the two comprehensive heads which I have mentioned, increased at the rate of 4½ per cent, while in the six years which have elapsed between 1853 and 1859 it became much more mercurial, and increased at the rate of 22½ per cent. But in order to bring home to the Committee the real importance of the question which is raised, not so much by the gross amount of the Imperial expenditure as by that portion of it which is under the control of Parliament, and for which Parliament is responsible, let me take the increase which has occurred during the same period in the expenditure which has been voted by this House, or which is, for certain miscellaneous purposes, charged on the Consolidated Fund. The two items which come under this head I shall call optional expenditure, and I may briefly state that they amounted in 1842 – 3 to £21,487,000; in 1853 – 4 to £23,361,000. Thus the increase in this expenditure which, as I before said, is under the control of Parliament, and whose amount is in the main determined by public opinion, in eleven years amounted to no more than a sum of £1,874,000, or at the rate of 8¾ per cent; but during the period from 1853 to 1859, a period of six years, it increased from £23,361,000, at which it had stood in 1853 – 4, to £36,898,000, or at the rate of 58 per cent.

Now, therefore, you have at your command a tolerably complete comparison between the rate of growth in the wealth of the country and the increase in its expenditure. Between the years 1842 and 1853 the increase in her wealth was at the rate of 12, and that in her expenditure at the rate of 8¾ per cent; while between 1853 and 1859 the national wealth grew at the rate of 16½, the public expenditure, so far as it was optional and subject to the action of public opinion, at the rate of 58 per cent.

I have troubled the Committee with these particulars because I deemed it right to invite their attention to what is a subject of vital importance. The country may be right in the course which she is now taking, but, at all events that course ought not to be pursued blindfold. We ought, on the contrary, to have a clear knowledge of the proportion which our wealth bears to our expenditure, in order that we may be able to take a comprehensive view of our financial position, and have full means of measuring the policy which we ought to adopt. . . .

With what views, then, and upon what principles, are we to face this state of circumstances; I may at once venture to state frankly that I am not satisfied with the state of the public expenditure, and the rapid rate of its growth. I trust, therefore, that we mean in a great degree to retrace our steps. . . .

Hansard, 10 February 1860, cols 821 – 6

Appendix B
The Management of the
Public Sector of the
National Economy
Stamp Memorial Lecture,
1 December 1964

I

When in February the Stamp Memorial Lecture Board did me the honour of inviting me to speak on this occasion, and I was asked to select a subject within the limits laid down by the Trust Deed, my natural course as a prudent administrator was to look up the precedents. The previous occasion on which a Treasury official had been so invited was in 1950, when Sir Edward Bridges, as he then was, spoke on Treasury Control. He traced the development of the Treasury from the early years of the century through two world wars to 1950, showing the continuous broadening of the Department's function from what he described as the traditional duties of prudent housekeeping to develop the new function of general co-ordination in the economic field, and the way in which these older and newer functions supported each other.

My first thought was to continue this story, describing the next stages in this development, the events leading up to and following the Plowden Report[1] and the reorganisation of the Treasury in November 1962. As I re-read Bridges's lecture I was struck by the continuity of thought between his presentation and the concepts of the changes which have since taken place. It would have been agreeable to work this out, and would have given me a welcome opportunity to pay tribute to the work of a former chief to whom I have always felt much professional indebtedness as well as affection and respect.

I decided, however, that these questions of machinery of government might this year conceivably become the subject of political controversy; and I therefore chose a title of perhaps less parochial significance, viz. 'The Management of the Public Sector of the National Economy'. This seemed to meet equally well the first condition of the Trust Deed, 'the application of Economics and Statistics to a practical problem'; there can be few more practical problems than the spending of £11,000m. a year. It presented no difficulty under the second condition of the Deed, that it should 'be treated from a scientific and not from a party political standpoint'. Of course the size and shape and future development of the public sector are the very stuff of party political controversy; but my concern today is with the question how to ensure that the resources which are engaged in the public sector make the best possible contribution to the national well-being. This problem is always with us; and everything in this lecture, in my opinion, applies equally to whatever Government are in power. Indeed, I had to submit the lecture for printing early in October, when no one could say what Government would be in power today.

The public sector, in the sense in which I speak of it here, is that part of the national economy for which the Government have some direct executive responsibility. Within it, I include the local authorities and nationalised industries as well as the central Government. This is not meant to detract from their independence. Their financial affairs are so interlocked with those of the Exchequer, however, that it is not realistic to think in terms of the central Government separately. In considering the public sector, one has to think about the education service, not about the general grant; about electricity investment and not about the electricity industry's borrowings from the Exchequer. Besides this interlocking, the whole public sector shares the characteristic that the decisions which determine its use of economic resources are to a greater or less extent outside the criteria of the normal market economy, and are taken in accordance with political and social as well as economic considerations.

The size and weight of the public sector in the national economy may not be sufficiently widely appreciated among those whose duty it is to cogitate and comment upon economic affairs. With the help of a number of colleagues, I have put together some illustrative facts, to go in a Statistical Note to the published lecture. The dimensions are impressive. Public expenditure as defined in the White Paper[2] of last December, excluding debt interest, is 40 per cent of the gross national product. The public sector employs directly nearly 25 per cent of the nation's manpower, and probably about 60 per cent of those with full-time higher education: these authorities own about 40 per cent of the nation's capital assets, and are responsible for nearly 45 per cent of the nation's annual fixed investments. About 60 per cent of the nation's scientific and technological research and development is financed by Government agencies. The size and structure of important private industries, such as agriculture and aircraft production, are in effect determined by the decisions of Government; and the purchases of the public sector provide a large and in some cases dominant part of the demand for the products of other industries, notably construction, pharmaceuticals, electronics, electrical engineering, telecommunications equipment, and so on.

The public sector, besides being responsible for a substantial part of the nation's production of goods and services, either as supplier or as purchaser, predominates at many crucial points in the modern economy—construction, research, the use of highly educated people and the most advanced scientific and technological development. This emphasises the importance of the decisions which allocate resources of manpower and capital to the various parts of the public sector; and of the economic efficiency with which these resources are used. These decisions by Government can never be determined wholly by economic considerations: they must inevitably be taken with a wide variety of considerations of public interest in mind. But the economic quality of these decisions is one of the big factors, positive or negative, which determine the nation's economic growth.

There has been a welcome increase of interest in these subjects in recent years among professional economists; and it has been a fruitful period for reports by the Parliamentary Select Committees. I hope that this lecture will make some contribution from the administrator's point of view.

My plan is to discuss three interrelated aspects of the management of the public sector. I have to pack the argument tightly; and I may make the three aspects appear more separate than they really are. But this is the price of rapid exposition.

The first aspect is the efficiency of the administration and management of the public services to carry out the policy decisions when they have been made.

The second is the evaluation of an existing policy or a new proposal to judge whether it gives the community good value for the resources that it uses. Seen in terms of the public services as a whole, this leads to the question whether we are getting the best possible results in terms of achievement in public policy for the money devoted to the public services and the resources of manpower and capital employed in them.

The third aspect is the relationship of the aggregate of public expenditure to what the nation can afford. How can the Government find and maintain a viable balance between the size of the services that are publicly provided and the taxes that people are willing to pay; or, to put the matter in a different language, between the resources devoted to producing public services and those left available for producing goods and services for private consumption, or for private investment, or for exports?

Is the public sector of the right size? Is every part of it designed to give the best possible social value for the resources which are needed to provide it? Are these resources in the event efficiently used? In the early days of this century, when public expenditure was only about 10 per cent of the total gross national product (G.N.P.), the public services were marginal to the national economy. But now they are 40 per cent of the gross national product, and their share is growing; and it seems to me most important that these questions should be searchingly discussed.

II

My first question was the economic and administrative efficiency of the public services in carrying out policy. All public services could give much better results if more resources were employed in providing them. But the point here is whether the best possible results are being obtained, given the nature and shape of the service which has been laid down by Ministers and by Parliament, and given the resources which are allocated to it. This is the basic test of management and administration. It is difficult to generalise because of the immense variety of the operations which are carried out. But we can get a reasonably clear view of the strengths and weaknesses, and, one would hope, get them into fair perspective.

One approach, which can be carried out equally well inside or outside the governmental machine, is to analyse the reports to Parliament of the Comptroller and Auditor-General. In his reports in the last five years, Sir Edmund Compton has drawn Parliament's attention to 135 cases, of which about one-third were in defence and two-thirds in the civil field. The investigations of the C. & A.-G. are nowadays to an increasing extent directed to inadequacies of management. At one time his work was mainly focused on matters of financial impropriety, write-offs of losses, inclarities of accounting, and so on; for his traditional role was to act as the watchdog of Parliament in making sure that the money voted by Parliament was applied by the Departments to the purposes for which Parliament had voted it, and that a proper report had been made in the accounts of the way in which it had been used. The importance of this function is not to be underestimated even now. But only twenty-five of the 135 cases reported to Parliament in the last five years were of this kind. About eighty were directed to inadequacies of management—failure to get value for money, inefficiency and waste, or insufficient financial control. About a dozen were related to the problems arising from inability to place competitive contracts; and the rest were concerned with the use of grants and subsidies.

The cases which the C. & A.-G. reports to Parliament are, as it were, the part of the iceberg that shows above the surface. His officers examine a great deal more. We can assume that over a five-year period the reports give a conspectus of the whole field. It is unlikely that there is any area of Government spending within the scope of the C. & A.-G.'s investigations in which there is substantial inefficiency which he would not have brought to public notice in five years.

Taking these reports as a whole, the biggest and most intractable problem is certainly the control of the cost of research and development and production on the frontiers of aircraft and electronics technology. There are similar problems, though not nearly as acute, in the somewhat less sophisticated technological areas; and on a smaller scale in the scientific research establishments. More is at stake here than the avoidance of nugatory waste of public funds, important though this is. The Government are here using scarce skilled scientific and technological manpower, and industrial resources of high quality, which could potentially be contributing strongly to the national economy. Wrong decisions here are exceedingly costly from every point of view; and great efforts are made, by the Departments and by the Treasury, to improve them. But the problems are most difficult to overcome; and the United States also finds them so.

The C. & A.-G. mentioned thirteen cases dealing with building and construction—hospitals, roads, universities, Downing Street, and so on. These range from building standards and contract methods to financial control techniques and errors in the original estimation of cost. This again has a wider importance than the purely financial one. The public sector as a whole, including local authorities and nationalised industry, takes half the output of the construction industry; so that improvements in the way in which it places its orders and in the encouragement which it gives to better practices may lead not only to savings in themselves but also to better productivity for the whole industry. This is another field of great importance, and near the top of the Whitehall agenda.

There was a series of reports on drugs, prescriptions, and chemists' remuneration; and on a variety of agricultural subsidies; several on land purchase and disposal; two important tax-relief cases; and a few cases in which a thorough reorganisation of a block of Departmental work was recommended. There were over twenty cases, some of which were admittedly small, of failures by Departments to charge, or to charge enough, for services provided: this brings out an important point, for our system of voting and handling public money may put excessive emphasis on expenditure and too little on increasing receipts.

Only two cases were noted from the Departments with large nation-wide branch organisations, such as the Ministry of Pensions and National Insurance and the Inland Revenue. These Departments employ about 150,000 people, and carry out the biggest tasks of pure executive work; an area of Government operation which earned a favourable report from the Plowden Committee.

In the dispersed services, such as education and hospitals, which are managed in England and Wales by 146 local educational authorities and 383 hospital management committees respectively, the units of administration are small, and their performance must be uneven. It is difficult to form a judgement about how efficient these relatively small and independent units are, and how much scope there may be for saving, and by what management techniques and services this potential saving can be realised—without of course endangering the quality of local responsibility and flexibility to local circumstances which is fundamental to these services. They certainly spend very large sums: local education authorities spend, current and capital, over £1,000m. a year, and hospitals nearly £650m.

Altogether, there is clearly no room for complacency. But it would seem difficult to argue that there is a widespread inadequacy; or to point to substantial improvements which could be made readily. To improve performance is a long slogging job.

In order to carry this out effectively there must be a definite division of responsibility between the Departments and the Treasury. Ever since the reforms of the early 1920s, which are associated with the name of Warren Fisher, it has been basic to our system of public administration that the Department is responsible for both management and finance. The Minister is responsible to Parliament for the policy and running of his Department. The Permanent Secretary is the Accounting Officer; and in all matters of administration, management, and finance, the notice is there, either on his desk in clear black type or in his conscience, saying, in President Truman's phrase, 'The buck stops here.'

We believe that this system is sound. The Public Sector group of divisions in the Treasury, which deals with the control of Departmental expenditure, has 101 officers. Their salary bill this year is £233,000. Keynes used to say that any Treasury official who was worth his salt should be able to save £1m. a month. The 101 are a very able group of men and women. But, nevertheless, I do not believe that either they or a force double the size could supervise in any meaningful sense the detailed spending from the Exchequer of £9,000m. a year or the management of a civil service of 423,000 non-industrial staff [3]—and hundreds of thousands more. We are sometimes criticised in the Treasury for concentrating on the sprats and failing to catch the mackerel. If we divided the Departments' responsibility for·management from that for finance, and tried to control the finance in detail ourselves, I suspect that we should be missing the sprats in order to catch the minnows.

But the fact that responsibility for finance must be firmly settled on the Departments does not leave the Treasury in a happy oasis of disengagement. We have our own responsibility as custodian of the Exchequer, and for allocating the amount of money and economic resources to be made available for each purpose to each Department. We are responsible for advising the Departments on economic and financial matters, and for assisting them to maintain proper practice in the expenditure of public money. The essence of the Treasury's responsibility for management was laid down by the Plowden Committee,[4] which said that the Treasury had the responsibility, *inter alia*, for:

The overall efficiency of the public service, and thus for seeing that the Departments are staffed, particularly at the top levels, with the best available officers drawn from the Service as a whole;

the development of management services throughout the public service; for taking the initiative in the introduction of new management techniques; and for keeping an oversight over the management practice of all the Departments;

the settlement of pay and conditions of service, and grading of staff throughout the Service.

This means that the Treasury's job is not to act as a censor, or as a back-seat driver, for the Departments. It must satisfy itself that every Department's management is as adequate as the resources of the Service permit; and that the techniques of management are being steadily improved and extended. Instead of being a back-seat driver, the Treasury's job is to ensure that every Department has the best possible cars and drivers and is properly equipped with maps.

The improvement of management and of financial control is a long, slow process, covering appointments, recruitment, training, O & M, staff relations, and management services of all kinds. To describe all that is happening here would take me too far afield. But I will mention one case. In the last two years we have been trying to ensure that the experience of each Department, favourable or unfavourable, in the procurement of goods and services, is made available to the others. No less than forty-two Departments are concerned with some aspect of procurement, and about half of them substantially so. It is necessary to get effective links between Departments for this purpose; less, perhaps, for the big Departments with their large professional staffs than to make sure that knowhow is available for the smaller operators when they need it.

A structure of inter-departmental committees brings together the specialists in such functions as building, land transactions, purchase of goods, accounting, and so on, with a continuous interchange of experience. In the last eighteen months, over fifty subjects of common interest have been under review in this set of committees, ranging from the improvement of engineering design to the procedures for public authority tendering and to the use of opportunities for placing contracts in development districts. One topical move, following the success of the PERT technique in the American POLARIS programme, has been the setting up of a group to exchange experience between the Departments in all techniques of this kind based upon network analysis.

There is no virtue in having committees as such. But only by coming together and by exchanging papers can the Departments learn from each other's experience. Apart from the employment of their own staffs and other public servants, the Government Departments are procuring directly about £1,750m. worth of goods and services every year. It is worth spending some resources of time and organisation to disseminate the lessons quickly throughout Whitehall.

III

This brings me to the second question which I formulated at the beginning, which is that of evaluating whether any particular expenditure proposal gives the community good value for the resources, measured in terms of money or in terms of manpower and capital, that are used in providing it. I leave on one side the question whether the nation can afford the proposed expenditure, in addition to all its other commitments. This is determined by relating the aggregates of public expenditure to the whole national economy. I am here concerned with whether the proposal itself gives an adequate social or economic return, according to the standards applied to other public expenditures.

There is an immense variety of items of expenditure, even within the field of one Department, and some common yardsticks have to be found between them. For any proposal that commends itself to a Department, the question is always whether it is worth the cost; and how it ranks alongside existing services too; for there is a tendency in a large-scale organisation to devote searching criticism to new proposals while retaining services which have lost some of their original purpose, and which could not be justified by the same criteria as the new proposals. One talks sometimes about the 'priorities', but the point at issue is not whether, say, within the health programme, building new hospitals is in general more or less important than, say, developing local welfare services; but whether an extra £5m. on the one, over and above the existing programme, is more or less worth while than an extra £5m. on the other. It is the marginal amount which is relevant to the discussion.

One criterion which can be taken into account in appraising the value of a particular expenditure is the expected effect upon the national economy; that is to say, whether the use of resources for this particular purpose has specially favourable or unfavourable consequences for the national economy, over and above the fact, common to all the expenditures, that the resources could in the normal course of events be used for something else, and that the expenditures have to be matched by taxation. One can imagine a kind of spectrum, ranged according to the impact upon economic growth. At one end of the spectrum might be expenditures, for example, which bore particularly heavily upon the balance of payments, or used particularly scarce resources of skilled manpower and industrial facilities, or hindered industrial adjustments which would increase productivity. At the other end might be expenditures which enabled industry to do its work better, which encouraged industrial mobility and flexibility, and which increased the efficiency of any part of the economy. Many would be ranged in between. Some would be purely neutral, requiring resources of average quality and without definite economic effect; others, more difficult to place, carrying long-term economic advantage but at considerable short-term cost. Such considerations could not and should not be decisive, for economic growth can be only one of the Government's desiderata. But they are an element to be taken into account.

From time immemorial, the opening move of anyone whose duty is to control expenditure or to allocate resources is to meet any proposal with the question, 'What would happen if you did not get it (or x per cent of it)?' Then the question, 'Could you not get the same result by doing y or z?' In some important parts of the public sector we may perhaps be moving towards a time when we can ask and answer these questions with a greater objectivity, and so get a surer appreciation of the relative merits of different proposals.

The success of cost/effectiveness analysis in the United States Defence Department under the Secretaryship of Mr McNamara is a straw in the wind. Its practitioners believe that by using techniques developed from the operational research of the Second World War they can appraise much better than before which is the most economical way to satisfy a defence requirement. This has in four years made a great impact upon the United States defence effort and on the defence budget. In this country proportionately comparable industrial and scientific resources are engaged in defence. In the last five years the annual cost per serviceman, at 1964 value of money, has risen from £3,325 to £5,075, i.e. by over 50 per cent; and the defence services are probably the most highly capitalised part of the economy—in the sense of having most equipment per man, on a scale not unlike oil refineries or electric-power stations. For some years the defence budget has absorbed about 7 per cent of the gross national product. The manpower employed for military purposes, in the forces and in industry, is somewhat above $1\frac{1}{2}$ million.[5] If it becomes possible by new techniques of analysis to make more effective use of this valuable block of resources, this will be highly significant. In considering the means of supporting our overseas commitments and external policy, I should also mention overseas aid, an expenditure which bears heavily on the balance of payments.

Another noteworthy development, with considerable potentialities over a long period, was the establishment by the Robbins Committee of an authoritative body of facts about higher education. This in its turn has stimulated work on the economics of education—and I should mention here the promising unit established under Professor Moser at the London School of Economics, and the work initiated by the Institute of Education. Education absorbs 5 per cent of the gross national product, having increased from 3 per cent in the last dozen years. Teaching in universities and schools and technical colleges employs 350,000 out of the 750,000 people in this country who have had full-time higher education. These are very scarce and important resources of people, and their deployment between the various levels of education, from primary to university, and between education and the rest of the national economy, may be of considerable economic significance. We do not yet know where the strengths and weaknesses of the educational system are from the point of view of the nation's economic potential; and it will be many years before there is a body of knowledge which could permit a more purposeful allocation of resources within the educational programme. But a light of one candle-power would illuminate the darkness; and we may be at a beginning.

In the field of scientific and technological research and development, of which the Government finances 60 per cent, and directly employs within its own establishments about one-quarter of the qualified manpower engaged on such work, there is need to establish criteria which could give some guidance to the question whether particular projects are likely to yield an adequate return. Here again is a deployment of men and women with critically scarce skills, very largely dominated by Government decisions, and one naturally asks the question whether we are getting the best possible contribution to the national economy.

I referred to a straw in the wind in cost/effectiveness studies in defence. There is another in the appraisal of road investment, in which considerable progress has been made in Government Departments and in academic circles. The techniques which are being developed for the comparative examination of road projects are still at an early stage; but looking ahead one can see the possibility of analysis leading to better choice and better value for money. Whether this will reach the point at which railway investment and road investment can in practical terms be examined side by side is for the future—but a very crucial element in public sector policy.

The nationalised industries themselves, which employ over 2 million workers, and dispose of net assets of nearly £8,400m., are the part of the public sector which is most important for the health and growth of the national economy. The quality of their business decisions, and particularly those determining the size and nature of investment, is fundamental; for with the scale of operation of these industries, with annual·investment of over £1,000m., the misdirection of resources of labour and capital resulting from wrong decisions can be very large, and devastating to economic growth. This is the relevance of the system of financial objectives for nationalised industries, which has been introduced in recent years. An earnings target has been fixed for each undertaking, so that a definite economic framework has been established for each industry's guidance. The details of the framework must depend upon Government policy. But to enable these industries to make their proper contribution to the national economy, it would seem essential that they should have clearly defined financial objectives which give a practical basis for energetic management and provide lucid and economically valid criteria for their investment and commercial policy decisions.

The same considerations of economic use of resources arise in the appraisal of Government action to influence private industry. The size and structure of the agricultural industry, for example, are to a considerable extent determined by the Government's support policy. In the last decade, backed by Government support, the industry's investment totalled much the same as that of the iron and steel industry; and the output per worker has risen fast. But the wage level is substantially below that of manufacturing industry; and in spite of the heavy investment the net income of the industry is hardly more than the value of the assistance received from the Government—the direct grants of around £300m. a year, and the various forms of non-Exchequer assistance.

Another kind of private investment generated by Government assistance, both directly and through discriminatory taxation reliefs, results from development district policy. This would be at the favourable end of the spectrum to which I was referring, to the extent that it was setting labour resources to work which might otherwise be idle; and thus making it possible to increase the G.N.P. and to run the economy at a higher pressure than would otherwise be possible without inflation.

The subjects which I have been discussing represent about half the total of public expenditure. The other half includes benefits and assistance, children's services, health and welfare, housing and community services, law and order. In the spectrum of public services in relation to their impact upon the national economy, most of these are perhaps more neutral than those which I have been discussing in more detail. But in many of them the problems of deciding the best course of development might be easier if it were possible to appraise more accurately the contribution that they make to social welfare in relation to the resources which are engaged in them.

I posed the question how to decide whether any particular expenditure gives an adequate social economic return. Over much of the field, no conclusive judgement can yet be made. It should become possible during the next few years to estimate the economic return on many of the expenditures which have a tangible impact upon the national economy. It should become possible in many services to determine which line of development will make the biggest contribution to defence or social welfare for the least expenditure of resources. This is in essence a problem of comparisons and choices, and within each service one would hope to see a gradual strengthening of the basis for these choices.

This leads to the question whether the present deployment of resources in the public sector makes the best contribution to the social objectives of defence, economic progress, and social welfare. It is interesting to note that this deployment changes quite fast. Even in the last four years, three out of fourteen main groups of public expenditure° have increased by over 60 per cent—they are roads and transport, overseas aid and external relations, and industrial and scientific research. Three have increased by less than 25 per cent. So the Government's direct impact upon the national economy changes.

Over the immense canvas of the public sector it is clearly impossible to envisage comprehensive or universal yardsticks—a calculus that would enable us to compare, say, defence with family allowances or agricultural subsidies with grants to the arts. In the last analysis the answer is a political one which depends upon the social considerations to which one attaches most weight. But the scope for systematic analysis is widening, and with improved appraisal of the impact of these expenditures on the economy, and improved cost/effectiveness analysis in each service, it may become possible to widen the area of objective comparison.

One may be able to see a long way ahead possible approaches to some of these problems which will rule out some choices as being expensive and inefficient means of meeting social objectives, and which will point to others as giving good value in social terms for the resources expended upon them; and which will thus present a choice between good choices for political decision and not a variety of good, indifferent, and socially extravagant choices.

IV

The third question which I posed is about the aggregates. How much can Government afford to develop the public services—the whole range of them, from defence and overseas aid to education and health and pensions and agricultural support and roads and housing and all the rest?

The Plowden Committee decided that the weakness of the traditional system of decision-making and control was the piecemeal handling of public expenditure. They said that the big issues of public expenditure should be looked at as a whole, and over a period of years, and in relation to prospective resources.

This judgement was founded upon three propositions. The first is that if all the expenditure decisions are taken independently of each other, as separate matters each to be decided, as the jargon goes, on its own merits, there is no reason to expect that the sum total of them will conform with a realistic view of what the nation can afford, or correspond to any coherent system of priorities.

The second proposition is that you cannot get any grip on expenditure by looking only at next year, for this is the wrong time-scale. Sir Winston Churchill expounded[7] the basic rule of munitions production . . . 'The first year yields nothing; the second very little; the third a lot, and the fourth a flood.' A gradual build-up is usual in most public expenditure programmes: a decision is taken today, and the consequent expenditure does not begin to flow for a year or even two or three. The Channel Tunnel report showed that even if the project had been started in 1963 the expenditure would have been quite modest until 1967 - 8. A decision today to build an aircraft carrier would involve only small expenditures before 1967 and 1968. The recent decision to build a new British Museum Library will be translated into actual expenditure running from the middle 1970s.

In many social services the growth of expenditure develops in two phases—first the capital expenditure, which in a hospital, for example, may take five years to plan and carry out, and then the continuing flow of current expenditure when the new facilities are ready for use. In some cases, there are three phases—first the capital cost of building a teacher-training college; then the cost of running the college to produce more teachers; and then the expanded cost of the schools service with the increased number of teachers: the unit of time from the decision to build the college to the flow of teachers may well be six or seven years.

So it is natural to settle some programmes far ahead; e.g. for the Ministry of Transport to announce in July 1964 a firm programme committing the level of expenditure in 1969-70; and for the Department of Education and Science to announce in September 1964 the level of university building starts up to 1968-9, in effect, determining the capital expenditure into the 1970s, and of course the recurrent expenditure long beyond that. In the hospital service, the capital programme rolls forward year by year, ten years ahead; and we are nearing the end of a four-year period with a predetermined annual rate of increase of current spending. In defence the practice of five- and ten-year costings is fully established; and in pensions the Government Actuary takes us a generation ahead.

This long-term planning is appropriate for these public services, and in terms of 'value for money' it has much to commend it. This is not because they are public services, nor because there is any special virtue in long-term planning as such; but because this is the time-scale which the technology and management needs of these services dictate. It is always unwise to commit any programme more firmly and for a longer period ahead than is strictly necessary. In a rapidly changing world, which calls above all for flexibility in the deployment of labour and capital, there is no virtue—indeed much the reverse—in taking decisions before they must be taken. Moreover, no Government can commit themselves forward over a significant part of their whole expenditure, and secure the benefits from this long-term planning, unless the aggregate prospective expenditure is within the nation's capacity; if they try to do so, they will run into crisis later when the expenditures are incurred. One cannot realistically talk about one year's planning of expenditure. The aggregate of expenditure must be reviewed over a period of years in order to get decisions that can be made to stick.

The third proposition underlying the Plowden Committee's judgement is that expenditure decisions cannot be taken realistically unless the necessary resources are considered at the same time. This seems self-evident. But there is an insuperable difficulty of timing; for one cannot avoid the fact that the time-scales of expenditure and taxation decisions are different. Expenditure decisions, as we have seen, are slow to make an impact: years may elapse after the decision is taken to go ahead before substantial spending takes place. Taxation decisions, on the other hand, become effective quickly; and can be virtually instantaneous. Thus the timing of the effect of the expenditure decisions is only rarely such that a simultaneous taxation decision is required.

In the modern Budget, moreover, taxation decisions must take much more into account than the matching of public expenditure. They are concerned at least as much with keeping in balance the level of demand in the economy as a whole. It may be desirable, as it was last year, to reduce taxes although expenditure is increasing heavily; it may be necessary to increase taxes although expenditure is falling. The taxation decisions are therefore inevitably remote from the expenditure decisions. Normally, the latter have to be matched by tax decisions not at the same moment but an unknown date in the future. So the two cannot impinge upon each other directly; and the relationship between the two sides of the operation—the expenditure decision and the taxes to match it—cannot normally be made specific and pointed at the relevant moment.

The taxation implications of the prospective course of public expenditure are important, but they are not the only thing to be considered. The prospective public expenditure must be weighed against all the other claims upon the national resources—private consumption, private investment, the balance of payments. This is what is meant by relating expenditure decisions to the prospective economic resources; and the annual review for a period four or five years ahead, which was started on a full scale in 1961, and of which certain results were published in last December's White Paper, seeks to do this.

This confrontation of prospective public expenditure against the prospective national resources is the heart of the matter. The whole concept of long-term programmes for the development of the public services depends upon the effectiveness and realism of this confrontation. The most difficult technical problem which has been encountered is the tendency to underestimate the future cost of Government policies; and if at the same time an unduly optimistic estimate is made of the prospective growth of G.N.P., expenditure decisions are likely to be reached which, when they come to fruition, will lead to the overloading of the economy.

The confrontation will show whether public expenditure is likely to rise faster or slower than G.N.P. No one can say objectively what this relationship 'ought' to be. It has changed tremendously over the years. One estimate[8] of the ratio of public expenditure to G.N.P. in the second half of the nineteenth century was 10 per cent, and in the late 1920s 25 per cent—now just over 40 per cent on a comparable definition excluding nationalised industries and including debt interest. Part of this change reflects a move from private to collective provision, such as resulted from the introduction of the National Health Service: health and welfare is about 4 per cent of G.N.P. Part reflects the expansion of social services— benefits and assistance now 7 per cent of G.N.P., education 5 per cent, housing and environmental services 4 per cent; and the State's assistance to agriculture, industry, transport, and science, which is another 3 per cent of G.N.P. Part of the increase again reflects the different kind of world in which we live—7 per cent of G.N.P. devoted to defence, which only very rarely before the Second World War absorbed more than 3½ per cent of G.N.P. in peace-time, and often less; in this item alone, there is a difference of the order of 3½ per cent of G.N.P., equivalent now to over £900m. a year.

The changes in the past have been so great that it would be imprudent to attach great significance to any absolute level, or to claim that any particular ratio of public expenditure to G.N.P., and the taxation imposed by it, would be healthy or unhealthy for the national economy. There is no consensus of opinion among economists about this; and it is difficult to draw sound conclusions either from the past experience of this country or from that of other countries. But when the ratio of public expenditure to G.N.P. is rising as fast as it has done in the last few years and is likely to do in the next few years,[9] there are more dynamic implications to be considered.

If the public sector gets a larger share of the national resources, then private consumption and private investment[10] will necessarily get a smaller share; and experience shows that the balance of trade is too easily left as a residuary legatee. The question in such circumstances is whether private consumption and investment will, so to speak, be content tacitly to accept a smaller share. Will they be sufficiently restrained to leave enough room for the growth of the public sector and for the expansion of exports which is indispensable to underpin the whole economy?

It would help greatly if people would continue to save proportionately more of their rising incomes: and if costs are kept low, the prospect of achieving the necessary export growth is strengthened. If the productivity and efficiency of the whole economy—including the public sector itself—improve, so that we get a faster growth of G.N.P., this again makes it easier.

The balance of economic resources for the future has to be weighed realistically, and not seen through rose-tinted spectacles, to answer the question 'how much in the aggregate, and how fast, can the Government afford to develop the public services?'

This approach leads to the question of the future of taxation; for taxation is the instrument which Governments must use to restrain the growth of private consumption and private investment if these are rising faster than can be accommodated. So the problem of keeping demands in balance with the supply of economic resources and the problem of taxation in relation to public expenditure come together in the long term. One may look at taxation as the means by which the Government raise the money to pay for the public expenditure. Or one may look at taxation as the instrument by which the Government restrain the growth of private consumption and private investment to the extent necessary to make room for the growth of public services on the one hand and exports on the other.

But whatever one's approach, this is the strategic point to which the long-term review of public expenditure and resources is bound to lead.

To sum up at this point, it is necessary to base expenditure decisions upon a long-term review of expenditure, because this is the time-scale of the technology and management needs of the public services. But it is impracticable in this process to match expenditure decisions with taxation decisions, because the time-scales are different: today's expenditure decisions mostly affect expenditure in years ahead; today's taxation decisions affect revenue very quickly, and have the purpose of bringing about short-term balance in the economy as well as raising the money to pay for the public expenditure. The long-term expenditure has to be considered in relation to the long-term resources and thence to the long-term claims of private consumption and private investment; and thus to the consideration of what changes of taxation will in the long-term be likely to be needed in order to enable the economy to accommodate the growing public expenditure.

It may not perhaps be unduly fanciful to see in this kind of approach the beginnings of an idea of long-term budgeting—the consideration of public sector expenditure and receipts, over a period of years, in relation to the prospective course of the national economy and the claims of private consumption, investment, and exports; with on the one hand long-term plans for the development of each of the major public services, and on the other hand corresponding long-term plans for the development of the various kinds of public sector receipts; the structure on both sides geared as far as possible to support economic growth.

This would over a period of years build up a system for the long-term balancing of the development of the economy, operating side by side with the existing system for the use of taxation measures, together with monetary and other measures, for the short-term balancing of the economy.

V

In this lecture, I have discussed three aspects of the management of the public sector; or, seen from the centre of government, three aspects of financial control. One is the size of the aggregate of public expenditure—or, put in another way, the total use of resources by the public sector. The second is the evaluation of expenditure proposals, and hence the allocation of resources, or authorisation of expenditure, to each of the public services. The third is the value that these services in the event provide for the money. Each is worth a lecture to itself; but perhaps the most relevant point is the interdependence of the three. One cannot argue the first *a priori* without a detailed knowledge of the second; or form judgements on the second without knowing what is actually happening to the third.

One single central task of government is embodied in all three—that of deciding how the Government should use the power of the purse and direct the outlay of public funds in order to further the nation's social and economic objectives. Historically, the need to carry out this task was one of the great formative influences in the development of our political and administrative institutions and machinery of government; and with the importance of the public sector growing all the time, it is most unlikely that this task will recede into the background.

NOTES

1. *Report of the Plowden Committee on Control of Public Expenditure*, Cmnd. 1432, July 1961.
2. *Public Expenditure in 1963-64 and 1967-68*, Cmnd. 2235, December 1963.
3. Statistical Note, Table iv.
4. Op. cit., para 36.
5. An estimate made for the United Nations in 1961, *Hansard*, 2 July 1964, written answer col. 282.
6. Statistical Note, Table i.
7. *The Second World War*, i, ch. 18.
8. Peacock and Wiseman, *The Growth of Public Expenditure in the United Kingdom*.
9. Statistical Note, Table i, shows a ratio of nearly 40 per cent in 1963-4, excluding debt interest and including nationalised industries investment. It has risen from 36 per cent in 1957 and 1958, which was the lowest post-war point. The White Paper estimated that the ratio might rise to 41½ per cent by 1967-8, assuming a 4 per cent per annum growth of G.N.P.
10. Except for what is generated by Exchequer payments, e. g. consumption by pensioners or investment in development districts.

STATISTICAL NOTE

I am indebted to Mr D. K. Burdett, Chief Statistician, and to others in the Treasury and Central Statistical Office for their help in collecting these figures together.

TABLE I. Public Sector Expenditure (United Kingdom)

	£ million		Increase
	1959-60	*1963-4*	%
Defence	1,573	1,898	21
External relations	159	257	62
Investment of nationalised industries, etc.	840	1,072	27
Roads and transport	293	539	84
Employment, industry, trade	52	77	48
Industrial research and research councils	79	129	63
Agriculture, fisheries, forestry	315	363	15
Housing and environmental services	772	1,149	49
Libraries, museums, arts	26	41	58
Law and order, fire services	189	293	55
Education	834	1,282	54
Health and welfare	804	1,077	34
Children's services	241	295	22
Benefits and assistance	1,281	1,829	43
Other (inc. adjustments)	436	464	7
Total (excl. debt interest)	7,894	10,765	36
Debt interest	1,095	1,325	21
Total (incl. debt interest)	8,989	12,090	35

Public sector expenditure as % of G.N.P.:

excl. debt interest	36.5	39.7
incl. debt interest	41.6	44.6

Treasury analysis of public expenditure; and Table 48, *National Income and Expenditure 1964.*

TABLE II. Nationalised Industries

	Net assets £ million	No. of workers '000	Average capital per worker £ '000
Post Office	1,204[1]	376.7	3.2
National Coal Board	900[1]	605.5[3]	1.5
Electricity Council	2,878[1]	210.4	13.7
N. Scotland Hydro-Electric Board	229[2]	3.5	65.3
S. Scotland Electricity Board	234[2]	16.0	14.6
Gas Council	765[1]	123.1	6.2
British Overseas Airways Corporation	107[1]	20.6	5.2
British European Airways	89[1]	17.1	5.2
British Railways Board	1,556[2]	464.3	3.6
London Transport Board	173[2]	74.0	2.3
British Transport Docks Board	89[2]	14.4	6.2
British Waterways Board	13[2]	3.8	3.3
Transport Holding Company	153[2]	100.0	1.5
Total	8,390	2,029.4	

[1] Accounting date 31 March 1964.
[2] Accounting date 31 December 1963.
[3] The number of workers shown relates mainly to the date 30 September 1963.

TABLE III. The Nation's Capital Assets (United Kingdom)

	Total gross capital stock at 1958 prices, new (£1,000 million)	
Agriculture	0.8	Private
Mining and quarrying	1.5	Mostly public
Manufacture and construction, excluding textiles	21.3	Nearly all private
Gas, water, electricity	8.8	Mostly public
Railways	5.5	Public
Other transport (inc. shipping)	4.4	About one-third public
Post Office, radio, etc.	2.2	Public
Distribution and other services	9.9	Mostly private
Dwellings	29.4	9.4 public
Roads	2.2	Public
Other industries and services	11.0	About three-quarters public
	97.0	

The total of 'public' on this calculation is a little below £40,000m. and about 40 per cent of the total.

National Income and Expenditure 1964, Table 68 and p. 105 for an account of the principles of valuation.

TABLE IV. Employment in the Public Sector (Great Britain)

	Thousands, mid-1963
H.M. Forces and Women's Services	427
Defence Departments[1]	311
Central Government service (civil):[1]	
Departments with nation-wide branch offices[2]	155
Other Departments	198
Education service (including universities, C.A.T.s, and other educational institutions predominantly publicly financed)	860
Health service	813
Police and fire services	117
Local government service	685
Local government construction	117
Nationalised industries[3]	2,060
Industrial and miscellaneous central and 'ocal government services	48
Total	5,791

Total in employment in Great Britain	24,533
% in public sector	23.6

[1] The total staff of public establishments provided for in the 1964–5 Estimates was as follows ('ooo):

	U.K. based	Locally engaged abroad
Non-industrial	423	35
Industrial	265	107

Estimates 1964–65. Memorandum by the Financial Secretary to the Treasury, Cmnd. 2290, March 1964, Tables XII and XIII.

[2] Ministry of Pensions and National Insurance, Ministry of Labour, National Assistance Board, Inland Revenue, Customs and Excise.

[3] The coverage is the same as for Table II, and includes General Post Office. The difference between the total for number of workers in Table II and the total here is due to the difference in date.

TABLE V. Employment of People with Higher Education
(Great Britain)

| | *Thousands, April 1961* | |
	Graduates	*People with full-time higher education*
Education	110	350
'Qualified scientists and technologists' (not in education)	120	140
Health (medicine and dentistry)	70	70
Other	150	190
	450	750

The table is from Moser and Layard, in Table 6 of *Planning the Scale of Higher Education in Britain*, Royal Statistical Society, 27 May 1964.

Over 200,000 of the graduates (about 45 per cent) and at least 450,000 who had completed full-time higher education (about 60 per cent) are engaged in public services, e.g. education (including universities but not independent schools); health (doctors, dentists); civil service, local government, armed forces, Government research establishments, BBC, nationalised industry.

These figures exclude graduates and others with full-time higher education in private industry who are engaged in publicly financed contract work in, e.g., defence, aircraft and aerospace, construction, etc.

TABLE VIA. Financing of Research and Development

| | *1961 – 2* | |
	£ million	*% of total*
Government:		
Defence Departments	246	38.7
Civil Departments	110	17.4
Research Councils	29	4.6
	385	60.7
Public corporations	23	3.6
Private industry, etc.	226	35.7
	634	100

Annual Report of Advisory Council on Scientific Policy 1961 62, Cmnd. 1920, January 1963, p. 13.

'Government' includes central and local government and Atomic Energy Authority. Research and development of £178m., or 28.1 per cent of the total, was done within Government organisations.

TABLE VIB. Employment of Qualified Scientists and
Technologists on Research and Development

	1962 Number	% of total
Total in industry and Government research establishments	46,200	
Defence R & D (Government and private industry)	about 10,000	about one-third
Civil government R & D establishments (including civil AEA)	about 5,500	
		%
Government establishments (including AEA)	11,100	24
Nationalised industry	2,200	5

Scientific and Technological Manpower in Great Britain 1962, Cmnd. 2146, October 1963, Tables
7–10, paras 22–4.

Appendix C
Excerpt from evidence given by HM Treasury to the (Robbins) Committee on Higher Education in May 1962.*

II—HIGHER-EDUCATED MANPOWER

21. In making judgments about the scale of educational facilities to be provided in 20 years' time it is necessary to look at the situation 40 years and longer ahead. Some of the estimates below therefore relate not only to the situation in 1980 when 500,000 full-time students are assumed to be undertaking higher education, but also to the situation in the year 2000 and later when these ex-students would form a large proportion of the working population.

Proportion of an age-group entering higher education
22. The proportion of the eighteen-year-old age group *entering* full-time higher education would rise from about 9 per cent now to 16 to 20 per cent in 1980. In addition substantial numbers would be receiving part-time higher education.

23. It is essential to examine the ratios for men and women separately, for the economics are different. Many more men than women receive higher education at present, and the share of places taken by men is rising. It is assumed for the purposes of these calculations that this tendency does not continue so that the proportion of men and women in the annual entry for each type of institution is the same in 1980 as for 1960. The proportions of the eighteen-year age group would then be as shown on page 192.

24. On this illustration the proportion of men entering higher education would rise from about 11 per cent of the age-group now to between 20 and 24 per cent in 1980.

* Committee on Higher Education: Evidence–Part One, Volume F (Cmnd 2154-XI), October 1963, paras 21–46 (inclusive).

		Proportion of age-group entering Higher Education		
		Men	*Women*	*Total*
1952		6.5	5.5	6.0
1960		11.2	7.3	9.3
1980	ALPHA	20 – 22	11 – 13	16 – 18 ⎱*
	BETA	20 – 24	12 – 15	16 – 20 ⎰

(* depending on length of 'academy' course)

The 'higher-educated' proportion of the working population

25. At present about 15 per cent of the entry to universities do not complete their course. For teacher training the figure is about 5 per cent. The rates are about the same for men and women. No adequate data are at present available for Colleges of Advanced Technology (C.A.T.s). The assumption has been made that for men the wastage rate in future will be 15 per cent for all forms of higher education taken together. On this basis, about 17 to 20 per cent of the 21-year-old male age-group would in the 1980's successfully complete a course of higher education, *i.e.* be 'higher-educated'.

26. With a 40-year working life this would mean that by 2020, or earlier if student numbers continued to expand after 1980, this proportion (17 to 20 per cent) of the male working population would be 'higher-educated'. The proportion rises rapidly:

'Higher Educated' Proportion of Male Working Population
Per cent.

1950	2
1960	2½
1970	4
1980	6½ – 7½
2000 – 2020 *	17 – 20

* The percentage shown would not be reached until 2020 if student numbers remained unchanged after 1980. If they continued to grow after 1980 at the rate that has been assumed for the 1970's, the percentage would be reached by 2000.

27. At the present time something over 10 per cent of the male working population have continued their education after the age of 15. On existing plans for expansion (and assuming no additions to them), about the same proportion of the male working population will be 'higher-educated' by the end of the century. If the expansion continued to 500,000 by 1980, this stage would be reached by, say, 1990.

Demand for 'higher-educated' men

28. Given the arrival of 'higher-educated' people already envisaged by existing policies, the scope for meaningful computation of 'demand' is limited. Such calculations have been of great, even decisive, importance in

carrying conviction for the expansion of scientific education and in establishing a scale for the expansion. But the 1961 report* of the Scientific Manpower Committee suggests that the plans already under way may be expected to provide a flow of scientists and technologists large enough to cover the nation's probable vocational needs for people of this training. As the Advisory Council on Scientific Policy has said on this Report, this is a healthy prospective situation, which will offer increasing availability of men with scientific training for employment in business and professions which have rarely employed such men in the past.

29. When this happens, the demand for scientists will be part of the demand for 'higher-educated' people generally. For this there is no direct form of computation, since it depends intrinsically upon what jobs, at different periods of time, are customarily manned by 'higher-educated' people; and this in its turn tends to determine the pay premium which 'higher-educated' people can command.

30. There will undoubtedly be a continuing development of the economy which will call for a steadily increasing proportion of 'higher-educated' people. The process of technological and social change will generate all kinds of new opportunities for 'higher-educated' people. But this is not the same thing as saying the needs of the economy will necessarily develop at the pace that would be implied in a growth in the 'higher-educated' proportion of the male working population from $2\frac{1}{2}$ per cent now to 17 to 20 per cent.

31. If the expansion continues to 500,000, then about 10 per cent of the male working population will be 'higher-educated' by, say 1990, and 17 20 per cent early in the new century. The first stage is a quadrupling of the present $2\frac{1}{2}$ per cent in a period of 25 - 30 years, and then perhaps a further doubling in a similar further period.

32. The speed is highly relevant. There has been a substantial expansion in the amount of qualified manpower in the 1950's — but this was only from 2 per cent to $2\frac{1}{2}$ per cent of the male working population in ten years. There is and will be a rising demand for scientists, engineers, teachers, *etc.* There is also a wide range of jobs of a professional character which are now done predominantly by men who are not 'higher-educated' in the sense in which the term is used here, but which are likely to be done by 'higher-educated' in the future—accountants, actuaries, surveyors. But the numbers here are not large in terms of a growth in the 'higher-educated' proportion of the male working population at the speed implied above.

33. Moreover, two-thirds of the 'higher-educated' at present work in fields—University and school teaching, medical service, public adminis-tration, Government research establishments (see Annex IV)—which are publicly financed. The rate of increase in jobs of this kind turns on the Government's priorities, which in turn depend upon the willingness of the

* Long-term demand for Scientific Manpower; Cmnd. 1490; HMSO, 1961.

public to be taxed to finance expansion in these services (and employment in them).

34. The quadrupling in the proportion of jobs to be held by the 'higher-educated' would therefore involve employing men who have been educated up to the age of 21 in most of the jobs now held by people who left school at 16 or 17. In the public service, this means the executive as well as the administrative grades, in local as well as central government; administrative and ancillary jobs in the health services, and so on. In the private sector, it involves a wide range of white-collared jobs throughout industry and trade. This follows inevitably from having enough 'higher-educated' men to do the top 10 per cent of jobs. In the following period, as the proportion of 'higher-educated' men rises towards 20 per cent, there could be enough 'higher-educated' men to do all the jobs now done by people with O-level or less qualification.

35. However fast the process of technological and social change proves to be it would seem likely that intense competition would develop among 'higher-educated' men for the jobs that now need them and this could lead to the replacement of women by men in those fields in which both can serve. The growing output of men with postgraduate qualifications might well tend to raise the standard of qualification for the jobs calling for high academic performance, and a postponement of the beginning of an effective career.

The return on higher education as an investment

36. These are conventional standards, and society can adjust readily enough to the idea that, for example, bank tellers or laboratory technicians or commercial travellers should all be 'higher-educated'. This is not intrinsically different from previous developments of education (though the speed would be unprecedented). In the United States this degree of 'higher-educatedness' is already widespread. But from the economic point of view (and leaving social consideration aside) it remains to consider whether, as the proportion reaches 10 per cent of the male working population and then moves up towards 20 per cent, society will get what might be called a sufficient return for the investment made in providing this education. Does the clerical worker do his job so much more effectively as a result of having an extra 5 years of full-time education that the investment can be said to have an adequate yield? Of course if he or his parents are making the investment themselves, with their own money (as it is predominantly in the United States) this is simply a form of personal consumption like any other. But if the investment is predominantly made by the community—as it is in this country—the question is whether the community gets a commensurate return in higher productivity.

37. Such considerations must affect the quantitative judgment which is required about how far, from the strictly economic point of view, it is wise for the national economy now to devote resources to higher education in

the hope of improving the rate of future economic growth. The community invests the economic cost of a higher education and the economic return is the increase in the man's earning-power or productivity over his whole working life. It is like saying that the economic cost of a higher education is covered by a loan, to be repaid by the recipient over his working life. By this standard, if the pay difference compared with what he would have earned without a higher education is more than the cost of the loan service, the investment in higher education could be said to be economically justified.

38. Neither the apparatus of economic analysis nor the statistical facts for appraising this problem have been developed adequately, and the Treasury would be very willing to participate in any attempt made or proposed by the Committee to elucidate it. The issue is so important, however, that some pointer must be attempted, though with reserve and on the understanding that research might modify it.

39. The average economic cost of a university career is now about £4,050 (see paragraph 14). If it is assumed that the bulk of the economic gain from higher education is reflected in the productivity of its recipients, a return on this investment over a man's working life of 40 years at 8 per cent (about the rate of return which the State is looking for from the nationalised industries) would require an earning differential of about £340 a year. If such a rate of return were not to be considered to take sufficient account of the elements of risk in this investment, *e.g.* of students emigrating, or of failure to complete the courses of education, the rate of return on risk capital in the private sector might be more appropriate. At 15 per cent interest the earnings differential would have to be about £630 a year. By 1980 both these differentials would have increased by half as much again. Even if the lower interest figure is taken, the question is whether even at the present time, with only 10 per cent of the age-group entering higher education, the bottom tenth of this 10 per cent have a reasonable prospect of earning an average £340 a year more over their working lives than they would have done without higher education. Or, to put it another way, would the top tenth of the 90 per cent who do not enter higher education—the skilled industrial worker, or the boy entering a City office at 16—have achieved this differential if they had received higher education?

'Higher-educated' women

40. The calculations have been done in terms of men separately because the proportions of men and women in higher education and their subsequent economic circumstances differ so widely that no economic judgments can be based on mixed figures. The non-economic considerations, of course, apply equally to women's and men's higher education.

41. The two economically relevant characteristics of 'higher-educated'

women's employment are the short average working life, and the great preponderance—even more marked than with men—of public service employment, with its greater dependence on Government priorities. The pay differential between 'higher-educated' women and other women is greater than the corresponding differential for men, and for those women who are in paid work all their lives the economic return on the investment may be greater, at the margin, than for men. But for a woman who marries early and never returns to work appropriate to her qualifications the investment is clearly uneconomic; for example, a woman who works five years after qualifying and returns in later life for, say, 15 years would need a differential of about £410 during her working years compared with the £340 given above for men. This, however, does not allow for the unpaid work that she does, which can often have a value to the community in economic as well as social terms; but this is not possible to quantify.

Use of ability

42. Another kind of consideration is the extent to which the expansion of higher education makes the most effective use of the ability of the whole community, by giving opportunity to able men and women who would otherwise work for their whole lives below their potential. The above analysis of the return on the nation's investment in higher education does not affect this question of the optimum use of ability, which would imply an increase in productivity all round, because the ablest people drawn from all classes would be enabled to fill the jobs which call for the most able people.

43. It is impossible to judge quantitatively how far maldistribution of the ablest people is damaging national productivity and economic growth. The Committee will have formed their judgment on the extent to which there are still significant numbers of able people whose contribution to the national economy is frustrated because their ability is not recognised, but would have been if they had received higher education. The fact that higher education recognises and brings out ability is, of course, a fundamental one. As Lord Macaulay observed*:

Whatever be the languages, whatever be the sciences which it is in any age or country the custom to teach, those who become the most proficient in those languages or sciences will generally be the flower of youth, the most acute, the most industrious, the most ambitious of honourable distinctions. If the Ptolemaic system were taught in Cambridge instead of the Newtonian, the Senior Wrangler would in general be a superior man to the Wooden Spoon.

If instead of learning Greek we learnt Cherokee, the man who understood the Cherokee best, who made the best and most melodious Cherokee verses, who comprehended most accurately the effect of the

* Lord Macaulay's speech on the Charter Act, 1833.

Cherokee particles, would in general be a superior man to him who lacked these accomplishments.'

44. It does not, of course, follow that there could not be a maldistribution of recognised brain-power as between private industry, publicly financed employment (which at present must absorb a majority of the men and women with good honours degrees), and the staffing of higher education. Clearly if the great majority of able men and women were concentrated on administration and teaching, the economy as a whole could not compete effectively in the modern world.

45. Higher education on the scale being discussed in this paper, or even of the order to which the Government are already committed, will call—especially given the staff standards which are customary in this country—for a great increase in the number of teachers in higher education establishments. Between now and 1980 expansion of the order being discussed would require an increase from 20,000 to 45,000 or 50,000. The university expansion programme envisaged in the current quinquennium involves an increase of the proportion of graduates going to university posts from 8 per cent to 9 - 10 per cent —and the call for high quality graduates in other fields is simultaneously very great. This is an aspect of investment in higher education which tends to be adverse to early growth in national productivity, for the economic returns from the employment of men of this ability in industry are likely to be more immediate.

46. Thus the considerations about the use of the nation's potential ability are balanced. Over the next ten years, the strain which the higher education expansion programme itself will impose upon the nation's resources of ability cannot be ignored; and the funnelling of the nation's ability through higher education carries the possibility that an undue proportion will be diverted into employments not directly concerned with production and sale of goods and services in the ordinary sense. On the other hand, the scarcest of all resources is people of high ability, and the contribution that higher education expansion makes to their discovery and most effective use is an important economic consideration.

Index

NOTE Personal names appear in the index in the style that was correct at the time of the reference.

Abbey Road Building Society, 102
Abbot, Dame Elsie, 143, 144
Academics, on NEDC, 75; writings by, xix
Accountants, 34; in Treasury unit, 134
Accounting Officer, 173; Permanent Secretary as, 34, 147, 173
Accounting specialists, 104, 174
Accounts: cash system of, 33–4; estimates and, 50; Exchequer, 33; Form of, 33; National Income and Expenditure, 33, 45, 47, 62; proper report in, 171; Public Sector, 33
Activity costing, 129
'Additional' programmes, 120, 124, 125, 130
Adjustments: of expenditure programmes, 83, 120, 185; of taxation, 120
Administration: basic test of, 171; costs of central, 44, 58; costs of local government, 77; diplomatic, 43; directly part of education, 158; directly part of health services, 158; efficiency of public services, 104; essential question in, 126; needs of, 151; of public services, 170, 171; overseas, 46; Permanent Secretary responsible for, 173
Administrative costs, 58
Advisory Council on Scientific Policy, 189, 193
Advisory services: cost-effectiveness of, 117; for agriculture, 117; for construction, 117; for manufacturing, 117
Aerospace: employment in, 189; projects, 5
Afforestation, 16

Africa, 9, 10
Aggregates of public expenditure, 42, 170, 179
Agricultural industry, 44, 99, 178
Agricultural support, 59, 68
Agriculture, capital assets, 187
Aid programme: 'basic' limits laid down, 120; forward look, 29; impact on balance of payments, 46, 176; in first PESC White Paper, 83; in Public Expenditure 'panorama', 43; means of supporting overseas commitments and external policy, 176
Aircraft projects, 33, 99, 106, 114, 172
Airey, L., 146n
Albu, Austen, 23
Aldington, Lord, 23
Allen, D. A. V., 145, 146
Allen, Sir Douglas, ix, 112, 142n, 143n, 145
Allen, Sir Philip, 134, 143n, 144
Allocation of resources: apparatus of long-term, 68; of capital, 170; of manpower, 170; of money and economic resources by Treasury, 173; regular July review and, 55
Allocations: and their control, 17–18; fixing of, 130; July 1965, 149; operations, 135
Allowances: family, 123, 131; improvement in, 78; investment (idea of replacement by investment grants), 121, 190; major structural changes in, 86; reform of, 87–8
Amory, Heathcoat, 1, 2, 21, 88
Anti-PESC: expenditure projections matched with 'target' rate of growth of resources, 31, 152–3; hope of a miraculous growth of

Anti-PESC: (*contd.*)
resources, 72–3; separation of
analytical staff from departmental
machine, 76
Appraisal: of economic investments,
134; of expenditure projects, 105;
of Government action to influence
private industry, 177
Armstrong, Sir William, xxii, 35, 49,
65, 139, 143, 145, 146n
Arts: expenditure, 43, 185; grants to,
178
Asia, 9, 10
Assistance: benefits and, 43, 44, 126,
181, 185; by Treasury to Departments, 173; programmes, 120,
123; State, 62, 98; to agricultural
industry, 83, 178, 182; to industry,
43, 68, 83, 152, 155, 182; to science, 182; to transport, 83, 182
Atomic Energy Authority, 12, 23
Attlee, Clement, 115
Aviation, Ministry of, ix, xxi, 33, 139,
143n, 160; subsidy, 155

Balance of payments: 46, 52–4, 57, 60–
3, 119, 124; affected by growth of
imports, 63; and tariff surcharge,
136n; as claim on national resources, 181; crisis, 53, 57; deficit,
85; effect on, 175–6; fast-moving
world of, xx; fears about, 53; first
PESC Report paid special regard
to, 52; grounds for vulnerability of
growth of resources, 53; hard facts
of needs of, 21; implications of PE/
GNP ratio for, 51; in 1960s and
1970s, 60n; manuscript on policy
after 1945, x; policy of concentrating on, 63; problem in 1931, 38–9;
public expenditure impact on, 46;
putting it right, 119; relieving
strain on, 112; reservations about,
62; responsibilities of Programmes
Committee for, viii; 'surplus' in
1966, 62
Baldwin, Sir Peter, xvii
Balogh, Dr Thomas, 130
Bancroft, Sir Ian, 146n

Bank of England, vii, 69, 143n; Court
of, 102
Bank rate, 61
Banker, The, 108
Barber, Anthony, 28, 50, 139
Beesley, M., 23
Benefits: all-party political undertaking
on, 98; cash benefits, 133; decision
for planning purposes on approved
annual rate of expansion, 67; earnings related unemployment benefits, 98; economic, 92; effect of
growth of, on production structure and tax structure, 92; excluded from private consumption
figures, 62; expenditure, 185; flat-
rate benefit/contribution systems,
98; in first PESC White Paper, 83;
in half-crowns, 85; increase as reflationary measure; 78; large item
in Public Expenditure 'panorama', 43–4; more money involved than in any other decision
by Ministers, 98; National Insurance and associated benefits,
113; of removal of investment allowances, 121; percentage of
GNP, 181; planned in close co-
operation between Treasury and
Department, 98; possibility of appraising relative contribution to
social welfare, 178; programmes,
120, 123, 126; related to income,
101n; sickness benefits, 98; social
security benefits, 119; universal
benefits, 133; wage-related unemployment benefits, 80; widows
benefits, 98; worst of all subjects for
peripatetic treatment, 98
Beveridge, Sir William, 2, 38, 102
Beveridge Report, ix, 38, 98
Birch, Nigel, 2
Bismarck, scheme of National Insurance (1883), 101n
Blaker, G. B., 143n, 145
Block allocations, 80, 92, 94–100, 152;
and changes of policy, 97; control
by, xvii; establishment of, 119; first
rudimentary system of, 141; for

Block allocations (*contd.*)
education, 96; for housing, 97; for miscellaneous local authority expenditure, 97–8; inclusion of investment in, 97; programmes with block allocations, 83; put into operation, 80, 92–4
Block expansion rates, 67
Blocks of expenditure: dynamic relation between capital and current expenditure in each, 93; forward-looking long-term programmes for large, 164n; growth and prospects of each, 64; notes on individual, 94–9; that need 7- or 8-year periods, 152; twelve, 82; which make political common sense, 42; which represented one Department's expenditure (or two including Scotland), 42
Bolton, Sir George, viii
Borrowing, 17–18, 46–7; by electricity industry, 169; from abroad, 149; from IMF, 56; from outside public sector, 46–7; maximum, 47; rights of local authorities, 4
Boyd-Carpenter, John A., 27, 65, 66, 71, 80, 139, 141; and 'Plowdenry', 141; Chief Secretary to Treasury (full member of Cabinet), 27, 65, 66; Parliamentary answer, 71; presentation to colleagues, 80
Bretherton, R. F., 143n, 145
Bridges, Sir Edward, xix, xx, 103, 168; and Treasury machinery, xx, 109, 132; many kindnesses, 103; Permanent Secretary of Treasury, xxii; Pollak Lecture at Harvard, xix, 109; Stamp Memorial Lecture, 103, 105, 109, 137n, 168
Britain's Blockade (pamphlet), vii
British Electrical and Allied Manufacturers Association, vii
British Museum Library, 179–80
British Railways Board: assets, workers, capital per worker, 186; deficit, 120; subsidy, 116
British Transport Commission, 11, 13
Brittan, Sam, 137n

Brook, Sir Norman, 65, 133; and longer-term thinking, 133; retirement from joint Permanent Secretary of Treasury, 65
Brooke, Henry, 27, 51, 58, 65, 66; Chief Secretary to Treasury (full member of Cabinet), 27, 58, 66; Home Secretary, 65; Minister of Housing, 51
Brown, George, 26, 110–14, 119, 125, 126, 131, 149; and fundamental review of defence, 114; and National Plan growth figures, 132; answer in Parliament, 23; firm on financial objective and target system for nationalised industries, 118; in 'ad hoc' group of nonspending Ministers, 26, 125, 126; Secretary of State for Economic Affairs, 110–12; stood firmly for PESC system, 131; stood together with Chancellor to make July 65 allocation, 119, 149
Brown, Sir Sam, 25
Buchanan, Sir Colin, Traffic in Towns (Ministry of Transport report) 1963, 16, 80, 141
Buchanan Report, 16, 18
Budget (and programme): apparatus in Departments, 134; changes, 119; concentration on short period, xv, xvi; cost of changes in, 100n; first long-term public sector expenditure budget, 118; future, 119; Gladstone's (1860), 165–7; inflationary, 91; long-term expenditure-taxation budget, 64, 65, 89, 107, 183; modern budget, 181; of 1860, 138, 165–7; of 1955, 88; of 1958, 3; of 1959, 2; of 1961, 51, 52, 82, 86, 87; of 1962, 61, 86; of 1963, 78, 81, 85–7; of 1964, 80, 84, 86, 114; of Autumn 1964, 113, 114, 118; of 1965, 120; of 1966, 122; of 1969, 88; of 1971, 50; speech, 123; taxation decision in, 181; timetable, 5
Budget Committee, 139
Budgetary control, 102
Budgeting, long-term, 107, 183

Building control, 18
Building licences, 127
Burdett, David K., 42, 185
Burnham Committees, 96
Butler, R. A., Chancellor of Exchequer, xx, 1, 7, 88; 'period', 147–8; second budget (of 1955), 88

Cabinet: appreciation of consequence of demand management policies, 84; approval for additions to 'basic' programme, 123; approval for setting up NEDC, 73; chain of command from, 31; Chancellor having his way in, xiii; Chancellor's 'batting average' in, 27; Chancellor's argument in, xvi; collective responsibility for expenditure operations, 27; decisions by, 80; decisive meeting on pensions, 101n; direct approach to by spending Ministers, xii; experiment with public expenditure Ministerial Group, 27, 28, 39n, 51, 125–6; has to find time for root issues, xii, xiii; instruction to Treasury to work out public sector plan, 51; Minister without Portfolio brought into, 69; presentation to, 38n, 39n, 57, 80; pressure on Chancellor, 115; protection of Ministers' rights with, 125; resignations after refusal of, 2, 56; risks to Chancellor in seeking agreement of, 46, 47; second Treasury Cabinet Minister, 27, 28; Secretary of, 146; specific referrals to, 94; submission of expenditure issues to, xii, 51; support, 125; time, 48; violent controversy in, 136n
Cabinet Office, economic section of, 103
Cabinet Ministers, 70, 139, 149; for social security, 98
Cairncross, Sir Alec, vii–xviii, 143n, 144, 146n
Callaghan, James, 26, 50, 81, 110–14, 119, 125, 126, 131, 149, 150
Capital allowances, 86–8

Capital assets, statistics, 187
Capital gains tax, 50, 113, 120
Car population, 16
Carter, Sir Charles, 23
Cash system of accounts, 33–4
Castle, Barbara, 126
Category A programmes, 123–7, 130
Category B programmes, 123–30
Central Economic Planning Staff, 17
Central Electricity Authority, 12
Central Electricity Generating Board, 12
Central Government: and local government, 155–6; debt interest, 44; expenditure, xx, 41; grants, 41; inclusion in public sector, 169; pressure to impose new tasks upon, 160; revenue, 47; service (employment in), 188
Central Government Departments: delegation on manpower control inadequate, 159; limits on manpower, 159
Central Statistical Office, 103, 185
Chancellor of the Exchequer: Chairman of NEDC, 70, 76; 'Chancellor's friends', 66, 68; committed to target rate of growth, 31; need for more powerful reinforcement, 163; need to strengthen position of, xii, 25–7, 59, 71, 149, 152, 160, 163; pressures on, 115; publication of expenditure plans, 31; qualities called for, 28; relations with Chief Secretary, 27; relations with Prime Minister, xii, 27–8, 150, 153, 161; responsibility after creation of DEA, 110; responsibility for long-term tax policy, 153; responsibility for public expenditure, 25–8, 47, 66, 153; responsibility of, 25, 110
Channel Tunnel project, 116, 179
Chiesman, Sir Walter, 143n, 144
China, outlook for 1960s, 9
Churchill, Lord Randolph, 6
Churchill, Sir Winston, 2, 101n, 179
Civil aircraft projects, 33, 99, 100; *see also* Concorde

Civil estimates, 33
Civil expenditure, non-economic, 117
Civil public investment, 55, 59
Civil Service: and change of Government, 100; bureaucratic tendency, 160; employment of people with higher education in, 189; grading of staff, 189; head of, ix, 143n, 154; management practice in, 34, 35, 98, 140; Ministerial pressure to reduce size of, 159; opportunities offered before First World War, 102; pay and conditions of service, 174; size of, 21; Treasury responsibility for, 35
Civil Service Department, 36, 37, 105, 159, 163; and manpower control, 159; and organisation for implementing PESC, 132, 153, 155, 163; and personnel, 95; dialogue with Departments, 37; division of central management of Government, 36, 37, 39n, 40n; help from, xxii; joint approach with Treasury to Departments, 134; separated from Treasury, 36, 105, 142n, 143n
Clarke, Sir Richard: career, vii, viii, ix, x, xx; publications, vii, viii, ix; retirement from civil service, ix; tribute to, ix–x; *see also* Stamp Memorial Lecture
Clarke's Law, 22, 137
Colvilles Ltd, 15
Commercial policy for Nationalised Industries, 117, 158, 177
Compton, Sir Edmund, 171
Comptroller and Auditor General, 104, 137n, 146n, 171, 172
Concorde project, 48, 113, 115–16
Confederation of British Industry, 70
Conservative administration, 84
Conservative Central Office, 69
Conservative Government, 98, 110, 112
Conservative opinion, 148
Conservative Party, 68
Conservative plans, 131, 132
Consolidated Fund, 165
Consolidated state, 41
Construction industry, 93, 172

Consumer subsidies, 155
Contingency allowance, 83, 125
Contracts: competitive (inability to place), 171; methods, 172; placing in development districts, 174
Control: building, xxi; by Departments over local authorities, 127; exchange, 127; in inflation, 158; investment, xxi; long-term resources, xxi; of cost of R & D, 171; of departmental manpower decisions, 159; of development, 127; of educational services, 129; of expenditure in individual departments, 132; of hire purchase, 127; of local departmental numbers, 159; of local government spending, 127, 128; of manpower, 158–60; of PESC allocations, 128; operation in PESC, 48; 'simple' control of supply expenditure, 128; sophistication of procedures, 159; Treasury statistical control of departments, 132
Corporation Tax, 50, 113, 120, 122
Cost-benefit analysis, 106, 122
Cost-effectiveness, 117, 129, 134, 176, 177, 179
Cost estimation of future policies, 181
Costing: activity, 129; 5- and 10-year (in defence), 180; of policies and programmes, 61, 68, 79, 80
Costs: and relation to Nationalised Industries' pay policy, 158; keeping them low, 182; with a meaning in the market, 158
Crick, B., ix, 39n, 69n
Crick Committee (of 1950), 34
Cripps, Sir Stafford, 74
Cromer, Lord, 69
Crossman, Richard, 123–5, 130
Crowther Report (of 1959), 16
Currency: decimalisation of, 84; world, instability and speculation, 56
Current expenditure: dynamic relation with capital expenditure in each block, 93; expansion of, 65; future (created by public service investment), 59; included in 'wide' de-

Index 203

Current expenditure: (*contd.*)
finition of public expenditure, 41;
means of moderating growth of,
55; of local authorities, 41; on
education, 55, 59; on health, 55;
on housing, 59; on social and environmental services, 59; relation
with capital expenditure, 129;
treatment of investment in relation
to, 55; viable future lend of, 59

Dalton, Hugh, 28, 115
Daniel, Sir Goronwy, 16
Dean, Sir Maurice, ix, 23
Debt interest: central government, 44;
considered as transfer payment,
30; excluded from PE/GNP ratio,
82, 104, 169, 184n, 185; included
in PE/GNP ratio, 86, 181, 185;
included in Public Expenditure
'panorama', 42; local authorities,
44; Nationalised Industries, 44;
repayment of, 44; very difficult to
handle and sometimes had to be
dropped, 42
Decimalisation, 141
Deedes, William F., 69
Defence, 'forward look' in, 48
Defence, Ministry of, xxi, 32-3, 114,
115, 132; Minister, 125; Secretary
of State, 71
Defence budget, 8; and GNP, 71, 105;
and Plowden Committee, 129;
ceiling on, 114, 119; decision-
making, 95; United States, 176
Defence construction, 93
Defence Departments, employment in,
188
Defence estimates, 33
Defence expenditure, 32, 44, 48, 55
Defence policy, 8, 95
Defence review, 114
Defence services, 105
Deflation, 148
Demand: for industrial products, 170;
for resources, 45; for university-
trained manpower, 97, 170; level
of, 181; on construction industry,
93; pressure on demand, 84

Demand management, xv, xvii, 45, 88,
155
Departments: allocations, 128; and
Treasury relationships, 34, 37,
163, 174; and Treasury/CSD re-
lationship, 154; financial control
of, 105; performance of 37; pro-
grammes, 94-5; responsibility of,
34, 173
Development districts, 78, 178
Development plans, 23
Development programmes, borrowing
for, 17-18
Diamond, John, 27, 117, 125
Diplomatic administration, 43, 56
Diplomatic representation, 9
Discounted cash flow, 33
Disposable power concept, 9
Doctors, pay of, 69, 157
Douglas-Home, Sir Alec, 85
Downing Street, rebuilding costs, 172
Du Cann, Edward, 139

Earning targets, 93, 141; for National-
ised Industries, 177
Earnings: growth of, keeping pensions
in step, 113; of manual workers,
79; of Nationalised Industries, 14,
141
'East of Suez' policy, 11, 32, 59, 114
Economic Affairs, Department of, 110,
112, 123, 124, 129, 132
Economic aid, 9, 10, 29, 56
*Economic and Financial Objectives of
Nationalised Industries* (White
Paper), 14
Economic classification, 45, 93, 100
Economic Effort of War (book), vii
Economic growth, 50, 52; *see also*
Growth rate
Economic impact of public expendi-
ture, 45
Economic Planning Board, 74, 75
'Economic strength' concept, 9
Economic Survey, viii
Education: Department of, 129; ex-
penditure, 7, 44, 54, 55, 80, 96, 97,
105-6, 172-3, 176-7
Education, higher: 191-7; and man-

Education higher: (*contd.*)
power demand, 192; and use of ability, 196; as investment, 194; cost of, 195; manpower statistics, 191; proportion of age-groups entering, 191; Robbins report, 80, 141; statistics, 189; women, 195; working population statistics, 192

Education Committee, 133

EEC, 9

Efficiency of administration and management of public services, 170, 171

Electricity investment programme, 70

Electronics industry, 172

Employment: public-sector statistics, 188; stability, 89; *see also* Unemployment

Energy needs, 13

Engineering industry, 121

Enquiry technique, 37-8

Environment, Department of, 97; Joint Treasury/CSD Committe, 155

Environmental policies, xix, 2, 62

Environmental services, 45, 55, 59, 68, 83, 131; expansion of, 148; expenditure, 185; percentage of GNP, 182

Estimates: for 1964-5, 188n; form of, 33, 39; increase, 67, 69; of cost, errors in, 172; of economic impact, 45; of future expenditure, 54, 69, 80; of future resources, 53; of programme growth, 79; reform of Form of, 33; Select Committee of Parliament on, 1, 3, 33, 164-7; supplementary, 128; supply, 56, 84; Treasury, 3, 39

Evaluation of new or existing policies, 170, 175

Exchequer, 2, 7, 12, 35; costs, 113; expenditure, 118; grants, 4; if not standing behind Nationalised Industries, 158; loans, 41, 169; local government and nationalised industries interlocked with, 169; payments, 184n; risk capital, 93; subsidies, 97

Exchequer and Audit Department Act, 1866, 147

Expansion rates, 67, 68

Expenditure, *see* Public expenditure

Expenditure Committee, 162

Exports, 21; claims on economy, 107; export orders lacking for TSR2, 136n; failure of, 62, 63, 70; favourable to, 121; fiscal incentives for, 122; growth, 182; obligation under GATT to encourage, 121; of goods and services, 62, 170; priority task, 121; provided by manufacturing industry, 149; providing stimulus to, 121; rebate, 120; resources devoted to, 170; strengthening of ability, 110, 111; tax rebate, 113; trade, 90; underpinning of whole economy, 182

Family allowances, 43, 55, 123, 131; comparison with other expenditure choices, 178

Far East: economic interests in, 115; withdrawal from, 114

Figgures, Sir Frank, xx

Financial News, vii

Financial Statement (1965), 33

'First hundred days', 112, 113, 120

Fisher, Sir Warren, 132, 147, 153, 173

Five-year programme, 47, 48, 95, 152, 156, 158

Foreign policy, 8, 10, 21, 23, 28, 29, 43, 115, 133, 176

'Forward looks' policy, 5, 29, 33, 48

Fuel policy, 13, 20

Fulton Report, 37

Gaitskell, Hugh, 11, 69

GATT, 121

General Election (1964), 72, 78, 83

Gladstone, William Ewart, founder and honorary President of PESC, 138, 142n, 165-7

Goldman, Sir Samuel, xi, 26, 32, 39, 143n, 145, 150

Gross Domestic Product (GDP), 2, 6, 39, 53, 62, 147, 149; and public expenditure ratio, 147, 152, 160;

Gross Domestic Product (*contd.*)
and public sector expenditure,
149; and resources growth ratio,
53; long-term growth, 39
Gross National Product (GNP), xiv, xv,
xix, 2, 7, 8, 10, 18, 21, 23, 45, 51,
52, 53, 55, 59, 71, 73, 79, 82, 87, 88,
89, 104, 105, 119, 124, 149, 169,
171, 176, 178, 181; and borrowing
abroad, 149; and public expenditure ratio, 8, 10, 51, 53, 55, 59, 63,
71, 79, 90–2, 170–1, 181, 182; and
tax changes, 88, 89; growth rate,
xv, 82, 119, 124, 178
Growth rate, 48, 62, 63, 81, 82, 132,
161, 166

Hankey, Lord, xix
Hardman, Sir Henry, 115
Hare, John Hugh, 51
Hartley, Sir Harold, 102
Healey, Dennis, 125
Health and Social Security, Depart-
ment of, 98, 129
Health Committee, 133
Health expenditure, 44, 54
Heath, Edward, 14, 100, 111, 122
Heclo, Hugh, and Wildavsky, A., xii,
xiv, xviii, 26, 39, 60, 125
Helsby, Sir Laurence, 35, 65, 143n, 144
Henley, Sir Douglas, 112, 146n
Hinton, Lord, 12
Holmans, Alan, 133
Home and Overseas Planning Staff
(HOPS), xx, xxi
Home Office, 98
Hopkin, Bryan, 22
Hopkins, Sir Richard, 39
Hospital service, 7, 54, 172–3
Housing and Local Government,
Ministry of, 4
Housing expenditure, 44, 97
Housing programme, 123, 124
Housing subsidies, 7, 130

Implementation problems, 132
Imports, 63; growth of, 62; of goods and
services, 62; quotas, 136n; saving
of, 110; surcharge, 113, 120, 136n

Income tax, xv, 86; as measure of
wealth of country, 165; 1919
Royal Commission on, 102; relief
for children, 131
Incomes policy, 50, 57, 58, 104, 157;
Government hostile to, 157; in
Phase IV, ix, 1, 36, 50, 57, 58, 62,
69, 71, 73, 75, 79, 85, 91, 109, 111,
164n
India, industrial expansion, 10
Industrial modernisation, 110
Industrial Reorganisation Corpor-
ation, 122
Industrial training, 79
Industry, assistance to, 68, 99
Inflation, xi, xii, 50, 60, 91, 140, 148,
158
Information, 43; Ministry of, vii, viii;
services, 56
Infrastructure, 5; 'big thing to get
right', 161–2; departmental, has
changed greatly, 161–2; pro-
grammes, 80; social, 46, 78, 80,
133; special continuing organi-
sation needed, 162
Inland Revenue, 102, 172
International Monetary Fund, 56
Investment allowances, 67, 121, 122
Investment grants, 121, 122
Investments appraisal system, 33
Iron and Steel Board, 14, 15
Iron and Steel Holding and Realisation
Agency, 14

Japan, 10
Jay, Peter, x, 37, 137n
Jellicoe, Admiral Lord, 101n
Jenkins, Roy, xiii, 128, 149
Johnston, M. E., 144
Joint committee proposal, 155

Kearton, Lord, ix
Keynes, Lord, viii, xvi, 39, 109, 173
Korea, 9, 10, 23, 67

Labour Government (1964–66), 110–
37; defence budget, 114; defence
review, 114; first hundred days,
112; fiscal incentives, 120–1;

Labour Government (*contd.*)
  Long-term Public Expenditure Programme, 118; prestige products, 115; public expenditure, 111–12; 'Statement on the Economic Situation', 112; Sterling 'Package' of July 1965, 126
Labour resources, 178; flexibility in deployment of, 180
Land: purchase and disposal, 172; tax, 165; transaction specialists, 104, 174
Lee, Sir Frank, 65, 74, 103
Lees, S. L., 144
Legislation, 4, 11; commercial, 165; fiscal incentives plan would require, 121; on National Insurance, 98; repealing of, 98
Lemon, Sir Ernest, 102
Lloyd, Selwyn, 26, 70; Chancellor of the Exchequer, 50, 51, 58, 61, 66, 86–7, 96, 126; dismissal, 65; NEDC, 73
LMS railway, 102
Local authorities, 128, 155–6, 169; and PESC, 163; education, 96, 97; expenditure, 4; grants, 7, 21; manpower control, 160
Long-term allocation, 68
Long-term appraisals, 28–9
Long-term budgeting, 107, 183
Long-term control, 68, 80, 83–4
Long-term economic assessment, xxi, 19–21, 30
Long-term expenditure-taxation budget, 64, 65
Long-term operations, 7–24
Long-term planning, 5, 20, 50, 180
Long-term programmes, 107, 118, 156, 161, 183
Long-term Resources Review, 30
Low economic priority projects, 116–17

Macaulay, Lord, 196
Machiavelli, Niccolo, 27, 28
McKean, D., 143n, 145
McLeod, Ian, 28, 51, 68
Macmillan, Harold, 1, 7, 8, 23, 26, 27, 28, 58, 60, 69, 73, 79, 85, 110, 118, 141, 147, 148
McNamara, Robert, 32, 176
Management: inadequacies of, 171; Plowden Report, 37; public sector of national economy, 168; Treasury, 140
Management Group, 134
Management services, 134
Manpower: higher-educated, 191; pay relativities of public service, 163; public services, 156–9; requirements and use, 129; scientific and engineering, 16
Manpower control, 158–60, 163
Manpower gap, 134
Marshall Aid, viii
Maude, E. W., 143n, 145
Maudling, Reginald, 31, 65, 66, 71, 78–87, 113, 125, 131, 141, 150
Methodology Handbook, 32, 39, 49, 164n
Middle East, 20, 71, 115
Middle East oil interests, 13, 115
Mills, Lord, 23
Milner-Barry, Sir Stuart, 143n, 145
Ministerial Committees, 149, 150
Ministerial decisions, 151–2
Ministerial Group, 125, 126
Modernisation theme, 78
Monnet, Georges, 110
Moser, Sir Claus, 176, 189
Motorway system, 13
Murray, Len, 74

Nasser, President Gamal Abdel, 12, 13
National Accounts, 42, 93, 94; of income and expenditure, 46
National Coal Board, assets, workers, capital per worker, 186
National Economic Development Council (NEDC), 36, 50, 70, 77, 79, 81, 111, 152; all-party acceptance of, 132; and anti-PESC, 152; and Labour Government, 75–6; and planning, 75; beginning of, 73; comparison with French Commissariat du Plan, 75; first meeting, 73; 'little Neddies' 75, 111;

National Economic Development
Council *(contd.)*
membership, 75; Neddy 4%, 152;
over-estimation of rate of growth,
160, 161; TUC participation, 70,
73
National economy, 48, 162; great importance for health and growth of
nationalised industries, 177; impact on, 178; management of public sector of, 168; running at higher
pressure without inflation, 178
National Health Service, 21, 59, 95,
127, 181
National Income Analysis, 30, 39;
could not lead to decisions, 153;
needs of, 151
National Insurance, 2, 4, 7, 41, 67, 86,
91, 92, 113, 118; benefits, 78, 113;
contributions, 46, 47, 50, 113, 121;
insurance funds, 4, 41; pensions,
78, 113; regular programme review advantageous, 98
National Plan, 76, 118, 119, 127; interaction with PESC reviews, 124;
manpower estimates, 124, 134, 157;
not rolled forward, 130; rate of
growth for, 120, 127, 132, 136;
reviews of defence and civil defence, coal, agriculture, ports etc.,
124
National Road Corporation, 4
Nationalised industries: business decisions, 106; capital expenditure,
42; division for, 13; economic
orientated investment, 45; financial objectives for, 106, 177; investment, 59, 68, 79, 177; loans, 4;
management, 141; margin recommendation, 32; planning, 120;
policy, 53, 54, 91, 157-8; price
increases, 118; problems of, 11; R
& D and design work, 117; statistics, 186; steel industry, 14-15;
White Paper, 14, 53, 92
Nationalised Industries Committee,
162
NATO, 10
Network analysis, 174

New Trends in Government, 105
Nicholson, Sir Godfrey, 1
Non-economic civil expenditure, 117
Northern Ireland, 151
Nuclear power programme, 12, 13, 15,
117

OECD, viii
OEEC, Second Report, viii
Official Secrets Act, xi
Officials (Permanent Secretaries), 30,
36-8, 41, 52, 60, 65, 66, 74-6, 89,
93, 109; ambivalence of, 100;
anodyne utterances by, 103; concepts of work of, 109; constructive
initiative of, 139; day to day business of, 139; educational background of, 143, 146; measured
discretion of, 108; need for different kind of junior, 135; not
allowed to give Ministers previous
Government papers; 100; opportunity to describe work, 108;
PESC, 138; putting in concepts,
139; rapid turnover of, 135; relationship with Chancellor, 103;
running the machine, 139; Treasury, 138-45; unable to envisage
differences of $\frac{1}{2}$%, 153
Osmond, S. P., 144
Overspending, 128
Owen, J. G., 143n, 145

Padmore, Sir Thomas, ix, 14
Panoramic expenditure table, 46
Panoramic revenue table, 46
PAR, xii, 100, 101, 154, 164
Parliamentary role, 162
'Pattern' rate, 62, 63
Pay: public service, 157, 163
Pay pause, 57, 96
Pearson, A. J., 23; 'Man of the Rail',
109
Peck, A. D., 143n, 145
Pensioners: consumption by, 184; num-
ber of, 7; political undertakings to,
98, 113
Pensions, 7, 55, 78, 79, 98; Department
of, 98

Pensions and National Insurance, Ministry of, 172

Permanent secretaries, responsibilities of, 37

Persian Gulf, withdrawal from 114

PERT technique, 174

PESC (Public Expenditure Survey Committee), x–xi, xix, xxi, 52; and inflation, 158; and Labour Government (1964–66), 110–37; and local government, 163; 'anti-PESC', 153; anti-PESC dilemma, 76; anti-PESC period, 72–3; as an instrument, 150; basic innovations, 151, 163; development of, xiii; first report (1960–61 to 1965–66), 50–60; 'forward look' arrangements, xiii; future of, 163–4; in historical and critical perspective, 147–64; in reflation (1962–63), 61–9; operation during 1963–64, 78–85; operation during 1966, 130; problem of, 132; programmes and implementation, 153; purpose of, 138; report (1961), 72; report (1962), 61; report (1963), 79, 80; report (1964), 100; results so far, 147; role of, xvii; success of, 153; technique of, 89

Petch, Sir Louis, 143n, 145

Pharmaceuticals industry, 104; public sector demand for products, 170

Plowden, Lord, xx, 1, 3, 17, 38, 74

Plowden Committee: agriculture, 99; and public expenditure, xiii, xv, assessor, xxi; basic doctrine, 59; commencement of, 25; conclusions, xii; defence budget, 129; Departments' programmes, 94; expenditure decisions, 180; growth rate, 48; 'joint working' concept, 95; long-term appraisals, 28, 179; main recommendation, 149; need to get biggest things right, 160–2, on Estimates and Accounts, 50; operating requirements, 41; PESC technique, 89; preliminaries to, 21; reflation programme, 67; Treasury responsibi-

lities, 51, 105, 173; underspend, 128

Plowden Report, xi, xix, 1–6, 25–40, 66, 99; 'Plowdenry', 140

POLARIS programme, 174

Police, 98

Policy: about local authorities, 156; advice, 31; alarums and excursions, 130; and current local government expenditure, 97; changes of, 97, 119; commercial nationalised industry, 158; current, 129; decisions (efficiency in carrying out), 170, 171; defence, 95; education, 96; evaluation of existing, 170; expansive, 148; for development districts, 178; formation and defence reorganization, 141; in Departments, 130; long-term, 120, 152, 155; longer-term thinking, 133; major issues of public, 131; medium term, 129; of departments, 173; of successive governments, 155; on rents, 97; overseas economic, 111; pensions, 98; policies behind programmes, 96; political decisions about, 161; public, 170; public sector, 106; regional, 141; social, 153; strategic, 120; subsidy, 155; tax, 152; towards industry, 155; towards private sector should have continuity, 155; very long-term, 99, 133

Politics, xix, 28, 30, 46, 51, 63–6, 68, 71, 76; dessicated out of PESC White Papers, 137n; difficult consequences of allocations, 127; earthy background necessary for critical decisions, 161; party choice of leaders, 150; PESC the real meat of, 65, 103

Population changes, 7

Population distribution, 141

Post-war credits, 67

Powell, Enoch, 2

Powell, Sir Richard, 8

Prestige projects, 115, 116

Price control, 14

Price increases, xiv; nationalised industries, 118
Price stability, 91
Prime Minister, xii, 2, 23, 24, 28, 51, 61, 66, 79, 115, 119; address to Economic Club of NY, 123; approval of necessary, 154; as inflationist, 150; as super-Chancellor, 150; as super-Foreign and Commonwealth Secretary, 150; backdoor approach to, 99; combination with Chancellor to grasp control of expenditure, 150; defence statement by, 114; set-up special Ministerial Group, 125; support of, for Chancellor, 153, 161
Prisons, 98
Private consumption, xvi, 182, 183
Private industry: assistance to, 54, 59; Government action to influence, 177-8; movement to from Civil Service, 109; publicly financed contract work, employment in, 189; relation to nationalised industries, 70, 75, 111; resistance to, 54, 59
Private investment, 19, 182, 183
Private sector, xiv, xv, xvi, 21, 36, 53, 54, 79, 90, 92, 93; attraction of educated manpower, 157; CAT, anomalously transferred to, 100n; employers, 57; Government and, 108, 177; housing, 124; industry and trade, 111; investment in manufacturing industry, 149; long-term claims of, 107; necessity for continuity of policy towards, 155; universities anomalously classified as, 100n
Productivity, 46, 110, 111; in construction industry, 172; industrial adjustments to increase, 175; of whole economy, 182
Public Accounts Committee, 137, 162
Public administration, xix, xx, xxi, 24, 37, 173; manpower requirements of, 124
Public bodies: forced to think about value for money, 159; pressure to

impose new tasks upon, 160; restraint of 'natural' growth, 159
Public expenditure: aggregate of, 42, 170, 179; and GDP, 147, 152, 160; and reflation, 67; and resources, 46, 56-8, 61, 90, 107, 160-1, 181; and supply, 4; appraisal of projects, 29-30, 105; classification, 42-4; collective responsibility for, 25, 26; control of, x, xv, 28, 31, 92, 93, 98; decisions on, 26; definition of, 41; divisions and subdivisions of, 42; economic impact of, 45; 'forward looks' at, 5, 29, 33, 48; Gladstone on, 165; growth rate, xiii, xvii, 31, 45, 51, 68, 70-3, 76, 149, 166; Labour Government (1964-66), 111-13; late 1950s, 3; long-term programme for, 107; Ministerial appraisal of, 25; Ministerial responsibility for, xii; need for new system, 4; planning, 53, 57; political attitudes towards, 26; re-shaping, 113; responsibility for, 27; stability of policy, 31; statistics, 185; time-scales in, 49; to 1966-67, 61; White Papers, 32, 64, 82-5, 131, 141, 150
Public Expenditure and Resources 1961-66, 61
Public Expenditure in 1963-64 and 1967-68, 82-5
Public Expenditure in 1966-67, 61
Public Expenditure Committee, 26, 28
Public Expenditure Panorama, 42
Public Expenditure Survey Committee, *see* PESC
Public investment, 17-19, 22, 42, 55, 57, 79
Public relations, 64
Public sector: and incomes, 57; control of, 138-46; efficiency of, 53; expenditure, 32, 53, 63, 86, 119, 149; management of, 103, 168; size and importance of, 104
Public Sector Group, 134, 135
Public sector pay problem, 58
Public service investment, 59, 66, 68, 79, 93

Public services, 54, 70, 91, 107; economic and administrative efficiency of, 104; manpower, 156–9
Public services pay, 157, 163
Public Services Pay Commission, 157
Purchase tax, 67, 78, 100, 121

Quantitative methods for public sector, 32

Railway investment, 106
Railway Modernisation Plan, 11–13
Railways: capital assets, 23, 59, 187; LMS, 102, 109; Railways Act (1921), 102
Raisman, Sir Jeremy, 25
Rampton, Sir Jack, 146
Raphael, Chaim, 143n, 145
Rawlinson, A. K., 146
Redundancy payments, 79
Reflation, 19, 50, 61–9, 72, 78, 80, 84, 140; and public expenditure, 67; first spending, 66; investment programme, 66; taxation, 67
Regional Employment Premium (REP), 121, 122
Regional policy, 15, 141; capital projects, 127; cost-effectiveness of, 106; discrimination, 121; objectives, 121; spending, 66
Relative price effect (RPE), 22
Rents/housing subsidy, 7
Research and development, 177; statistics, 189, 190
Research councils, 43, 117, 185
Resources and public expenditure, 46, 56–8, 61, 90, 107, 160–1, 181; allocation of, 170; and revenue, 46; appraisal of prospective, 72–3; deployment of, 178; growth rate, 62; prospective growth of, 53
Revenue: and resources, 46; panoramic table of, 46
Rhodes Scholars, 115
Rhodesia, 150
Richard Thomas & Baldwins, 14, 15
Road investment, 59, 80, 95, 106, 177
Robins Committee, 96–7, 176, 191–7
Robbins Report, 80, 141

Robertson, Lord, 11
Robot project, viii
Robson, Professor, W. A., ix, 39n, 69n
Roll, Sir Eric, 112
Roskill Commission, 106
Rothschild, Lord, 117
RPE, *see* Relative price effect

Sandys, Duncan, 99
Saunders, Christopher, 16
Savings ratio, 21
Schedule A taxation, 50, 165
Schedule B taxation, 165
Schedule D taxation, 165
School leaving age, 16
Scientific and engineering manpower, 16
Scientific Manpower Committee, 193
Scotland, xxii, 151
Select Committee on Estimates, 1, 3, 33, 170
Select Committee on Expenditure, 137n, 162
Select Committee on the Nationalised Industries on British Railways, 23
Select Committees, 1, 162, 170
Selective Employment Tax (SET), 121, 122
Serpell, Sir David, 8, 95
Servicemen, annual cost of, 105
Shaw, J. J. S., 144
Shipbuilding and shipping, aid for, 78
Shone, Sir Robert, 75
Short-term demand management, 45
Short-term operations, 32
Singapore, 114
Social conditions, 133
Social considerations, 169
'Social contract', 85, 157
Social economic return, 178
Social expenditure, 81
Social infrastructure, 46
Social objectives, 108, 179
Social policy, 30, 55, 62, 153
Social programmes, 113, 153
Social return, 175, 179
Social security, 30
Social Security, Ministry of: 'big thing to get right', 161; examiners, 159;

Social Security, Ministry of: (*contd.*)
first steps to in 1968, 98, 130; joint Treasury/CSD Committee, 155; pensions and benefits, 30, 119
Social services, xix, xx, 2, 7, 17, 18, 34, 38, 45, 52, 55, 64, 68, 131, 180; and value for money, 118; capital investment, 44; current expenditure, 44, 59; expansion of, 148, 181
Social structure, 92
Social value, 170
Social welfare, appraisal of contribution of public services, 178
Socialisation of Iron and Steel (book), vii
Society of Motor Manufacturers and Traders, 16
Soskice, Sir Frank, 125
Special Deposits, 61
Stamp, (Max) Arthur Maxwell, 102, 103, 108, 109
Stamp Memorial Lecture, 49, 69, 102–9, 137n, 168–90
Stamp Survey, 102
Statisticians, 62; in Treasury management unit, 134, 139
Statistics: and analysis as basis for decision-making, 129, 161; application of, 169
Steel industry de-nationalisation, 14, 15
Steel requirements, 21
Sterling crisis, 2, 18, 56, 66, 87, 116, 127
Sterling 'Package' of July, 1965, 126
Stevenson, Matthew, 13, 17
'Stop-go' policy, 64, 155
Subsidy policy, 155, 163
Supplementary estimates, 128
Supply estimates, 56–8, 84
Supply expenditure, 56
Surtax, 50
Swinton, Lord, 5

Tax consequences of expenditure policy, 47
Tax implications of expenditure programmes, 64
Tax increases, 68, 85
Tax policy, 30, 152, 181, 183
Tax rates, xvi, 86

Tax reduction, 68, 78, 81, 82, 148, 178
Tax structure, 162
Taxation, 50, 85–9, 91, 181; and expenditure, 107; future programme, 153, 182; long-term, xv; versus social services, 55
Teachers: salaries, 57; statistics, 105
Technology, Ministry of, ix, 23, 33, 117
Third London Airport, 106
Thorneycroft, Peter, 2, 18–19, 56, 148
Thornhill, W., xvii
Tomlin Commission, 132
Trade and Industry, Department of, 111
Trade unions, 70, 71, 73–5, 81
Trades Union Congress, 70; NEDC membership, 70, 73
Transport services, 16
Treasury: and Department's relationship, 34, 37; Chief Secretary to, 27; Export-Import Divison, viii; functions of, 36, 138, 168; organisation chart, 138, 143, 144–5; reorganisation, 35–6, 66, 138; responsibility of, 34–5, 105, 153, 163, 173; role of, 110; Social Services Division, ix
Trend, Sir Burke, xx
Truman, (President) Harry S., 173
TSR2 aircraft, 114, 136

Underdeveloped countries, 10
Underspending, 128
Unemployment, xii, 86–8
United States of America, 9, 10; and East-of-Suez, 114; and Mr McNamara, 115, 176; Defence Department, 176; 'disposable power', 9; Polaris programme, 174; suppliers, 117
Universities: block allocation, 96; expansion, 16
University Grants Committee, xxii, 96, 97
Uranium purchases, 12
USSR 'disposable power', 9

Vaisey, J., 23
Value-added tax (VAT), 87

Very long-term planning, 133
Vinter, Peter, 17, 20, 22, 142n, 143n, 145

Wage restraint policy, 73
Wales, 123, 151, 155
Wall, Sir John, 25
Waverley, Lord, 102
Weeks, Sir Hugh, 74, 142
Welfare expenditure, 44, 54
White Papers: annual, xiii, xv; nationalised industries, 14, 53, 92;

public expenditure, 32, 64, 82-5, 131, 141, 150; public investment, 19, 66
Wildavsky, A., *see* Heclo and Wildavsky
Wilson, Harold, 26, 110; *see also* Labour Government (1964–66)
Women, 'higher-educated', 195–6
Wood, Sir William, 102
Woolton, Lord, 147

Zuckerman, Sir Solly, 16